Routledge Revivals

Education in

First published in 1982, *Education in Africa* offers a comprehensive treatment of the development of education in Africa. Until now only scattered documents on educational growth in individual countries have been available; works devoted to Africa as a whole have tended towards the general and have, by and large, been written by outside observers. This book is a collection of illuminating syntheses of major trends in educational development in Africa, by renowned African educationists, and is the first attempt to supply the need for a comprehensive book on African education written from an African viewpoint. All but one of the chapters were written specially for the book by leading African educators each of whom has had a distinguished career and wide experience in education in his or her own country; they represent eleven nations in all. The volume is designed for African students, teachers and administrators and will also be welcomed by educational planners and by scholars working in the fields of comparative education and the history of education. It will be of special interest to departments, institutions and faculties of education in all the universities and colleges of education in Africa, and to educators and students worldwide who are concerned with comparative African education.

Education in Africa

A Comparative Survey

Edited by A. Babs Fafunwa and J. U. Aisiku

Routledge
Taylor & Francis Group

First published in 1982
by George Allen & Unwin

This edition first published in 2022 by Routledge
4 Park Square, Milton Park, Abingdon, Oxon, OX14 4RN
and by Routledge
605 Third Avenue, New York, NY 10017

Routledge is an imprint of the Taylor & Francis Group, an informa business

Publisher's Note
The publisher has gone to great lengths to ensure the quality of this reprint but points out that some imperfections in the original copies may be apparent.

Disclaimer
The publisher has made every effort to trace copyright holders and welcomes correspondence from those they have been unable to contact.

A Library of Congress record exists under ISBN: 0043701132

ISBN: 978-1-032-32661-0 (hbk)
ISBN: 978-1-003-31611-4 (ebk)
ISBN: 978-1-032-32666-5 (pbk)

Book DOI 10.4324/9781003316114

Education in Africa:
A Comparative Survey

Edited by
A. BABS FAFUNWA
J. U. AISIKU

London
GEORGE ALLEN & UNWIN
Boston   Sydney

George Allen & Unwin (Publishers) Ltd,
40 Museum Street, London WC1A 1LU, UK

George Allen & Unwin (Publishers) Ltd,
Park Lane, Hemel Hempstead, Herts HP2 4TE, UK

Allen & Unwin Inc.,
9 Winchester Terrace, Winchester, Mass 01890, USA

George Allen & Unwin Australia Pty Ltd,
8 Napier Street, North Sydney, NSW 2060, Australia

First published in 1982

British Library Cataloguing in Publication Data

   Education in Africa.
   1. Education—Africa
   I. Fafunwa, A. Babs   II. Aisiku, J. U.
   370'. 967   LA1501
   ISBN 0-04-370113-2

Library of Congress Cataloging in Publication Data

   Education in Africa.
   Includes index.
   1. Education—South Africa.   2. Comparative education.
   I. Fafunwa, A. Babs, 1923–   II. Aisiku, J. U.
   LA1501.E364   370'.968   81-19129
   ISBN 0-04-370113-2 (pbk.)   AACR2

Set in 10 on 11 point Times by Gilbert Composing Services
and printed in Great Britain
by Biddles Ltd, Guildford, Surrey

Contents

Contents

Chapter 1

African Education in Perspective

A. BABS FAFUNWA

'What is African education?' asked a sceptic. 'Is it the second-rate education imported from France, Britain, or Spain – the imperial powers that dominated the political and commercial life of the African continent for well over three hundred years?' Whatever may be the sceptic's view, educational historians know too well that even when a system is transferred in its purest form from one cultural environment to another there is bound to be a change due to certain cultural, social and/or economic imperatives. In any case no study of the history of education in Africa is complete or meaningful without adequate knowledge of the traditional or indigenous educational system prevalent in Africa prior to the introduction of Islam and Christianity.

As we have stated elsewhere, every society, whether simple or complex, has its own system for training and educating its youth, and education for the good life has been one of the most persistent concerns of men throughout history. However, the goal of education and the method of approach may differ from place to place, nation to nation, and people to people. The Greek idea of an educated man was one who was mentally and physically well balanced. The Romans, on the other hand, placed emphasis on oratorical and military training. In Old Africa the warrior, the hunter, the nobleman, the man who combined good character with a specific skill was adjudged to be a well-educated and well-integrated citizen of his community.

In Old African society the purpose of education was clear: functionalism was the main guiding principle. African society regarded education as a means to an end, not as an end in itself. Education was generally for an immediate induction into society and a preparation for adulthood. In particular, African education emphasised social responsibility, job orientation, political participation and spiritual and moral values. Children learnt by doing, that is to say, children and adolescents were engaged in participatory education through ceremonies, rituals, imitation, recitation and demonstration. They were involved in practical farming, fishing, weaving, cooking, carving, knitting, and so on. Recreational subjects included wrestling, dancing, drumming, acrobatic display and racing, while intellectual training included the study of local history, legends, the environment (local geography, plants and animals), poetry, reasoning, riddles, proverbs, story-telling and story-relays. Education in Old Africa was an integrated experience. It combined physical training with character-building, and manual activity with intellectual training. At the end of each stage, demarcated either by age-level or years of exposure, the child was given a practical test relevant to his experience and level of development and in terms of the job to be done. This was a continuous assessment which eventually culminated in a 'passing out' ceremony, or initiation into adulthood.

For the select or the elect, secret cults served as institutions of higher or further education. It was at this level that the secret of power (real or imaginary), profound African philosophy, science and religion were mastered. Irrespective of the level of education and training given during the pre-colonial days in Africa, it was functional because the curriculum was relevant to the needs of the society. Unemployment, if it existed at all, was minimal and very few young men roamed the villages and towns with nothing to do.

Education in Old Africa was not rigidly compartmentalised as is the case in the contemporary system. Today educators are beginning to talk about universities without walls, schools without classes, and subjects without grades. This is as it should be, particularly in Africa where only a handful constitutes the elite and where, if a stage is missed, all other chances may be forfeited. It is even worse if one has never seen the inside of a formal school. Certainly, one important guiding principle is that education, in the widest sense of the word, should be a continuous process, flexible enough to accommodate any mature person at any stage.

The aim, the content and the methods of traditional education are intricately interwoven; they are not divided into separate compartments as is the case with the Westernised system of education. The characteristics of traditional education in Africa are aptly summarised by Abdou Moumouni in his book *Education in Africa:*

(1) The great importance attached to it, and its collective and social nature.
(2) Its intimate tie with social life, both in a material and a spiritual sense.
(3) Its multivalent character, both in terms of its goals and the means employed.
(4) Its gradual and progressive achievements, in conformity with the successive stages of physical, emotional and mental development of the child.[1]

Because indigenous education failed to conform to the ways of the Westernised system, some less well-informed writers have considered it primitive, even savage and barbaric, but such contentions should be seen as the product of ignorance and due to a total misunderstanding of the inherent value of informal education. After all, education is the aggregate of all the processes by which a child or young adult develops the abilities, attitudes and other forms of behaviour which are of positive value to the society in which he lives; that is to say, it is a process for transmitting culture in terms of continuity and growth and for disseminating knowledge either to ensure social control or to guarantee rational direction of the society or both. All educational systems, whether traditional or Western-oriented, seek to achieve these goals irrespective of the curriculum, methods and organisation designed for the purpose.

When evaluating any educational system one must determine the extent to which it is meeting the needs of a particular society at any given time. Traditional African education must, therefore, be judged not by any extraneous consideration or some foreign yardstick but by its performance within a given social context. Many European observers tend to ignore this important factor.[2]

In this chapter, therefore, we shall discuss the three major landmarks in the history of African education prior to the era of political independence.

(1) indigenous or traditional African education before the advent of Islam and Christianity;
(2) the advent of Islam and Islamic education in Africa;
(3) the coming of the Christian Missionaries, and the colonial era.

We shall also compare and contrast how each major area operated in a number of African countries including those not represented in this volume.

I SEVEN CARDINAL GOALS OF TRADITIONAL AFRICAN EDUCATION

The objectives of traditional African education are many and varied but the ultimate goal is to produce an individual who is honest, respectful, skilled, co-operative, and who conforms to the social order of the day. Although the educational objectives cannot be neatly distinguished, seven aspects can be identified:

(1) To develop the child's latent physical skills.
(2) To develop character.

(3) To inculcate respect for elders and those in positions of authority.
(4) To develop intellectual skills.
(5) To acquire specific vocational training and to develop a healthy attitude towards honest labour.
(6) To develop a sense of belonging and to encourage active participation in family and community affairs.
(7) To understand, appreciate and promote the cultural heritage of the community at large.

Learning starts early for children in Africa as elsewhere, and more often than not begins at the mother's breast. Fed regularly, weaned when the time is ripe, the African child spends the first five years of its life in a close relationship with its mother. During this early stage the child is reared by the mother, not by the family as a whole.

In a polygamous African family there may be several 'mothers'; they all play a part in caring for the youngest generation but ultimate responsibility for each child lies with its natural mother, who carries it on her back wherever she goes, puts it to bed, looks after it when it is ill and teaches it to speak. Full of curiosity, the baby watches her every gesture, and learns to interpret her smiles, her frowns and her tears.

Little by little, this lively curiosity reaches out beyond the mother's world. Somewhere between the ages of 4 and 6 the grandparents – and sometimes uncles and aunts – begin to take part in the children's education, sending them on little errands, teaching them to be obedient and to respect their elders (this is a very important matter in African society), and to observe certain rules of behaviour. The grandparents also teach them the history of their family or of their people.

African education is 'global'. In other words, each social institution has a role in providing the moral and practical teaching that will enable young boys and girls to take their rightful place in the community.

The traditional educational system is based on age-groups, or on affinities within these groups, whose limits are defined differently by different peoples.

Age is very important to Africans. It confers economic and social privileges, particularly as far as the distribution of prey, rewards and wealth are concerned.

African children love to explore their immediate surroundings, to observe and imitate the actions of adults and to discover new horizons. In this they are no different from other children, whether in Europe, Asia, or elsewhere. What distinguishes them is their way of doing things, and above all the spontaneity with which, in societies that have retained their links with the past, they jump about, climb trees, dance, or move to a rhythm, simply because their brothers and sisters or their elders are doing so. No sooner, in fact, do they discover their limbs, than they discover how to use them.

African children perhaps differ from their European counterparts in that they have completely untrammelled access to the stimulating world of music and dance. The movements of the African dance, in their infinite variety, offer the best possible physical exercise for growing bodies. No teacher or dancing-master is needed: the children join in naturally, following the steps of adults or other children. Dancing and music are also a means of transmitting the culture of a people and of performing together as a group.

In a study of the Yoruba of West Africa, M. A. Fadipe[3] has described certain practical aspects of the education of young children.

As soon as her daughter is of age, it is the mother's duty to teach her the rules of hygienic and well-mannered behaviour observed by the group. One of the most important of these rules concerns the use of the right and the left hand.

Before the whites brought their culture to Africa, the use of forks and spoons was unknown. The right hand was traditionally used for lifting food to the mouth and – mainly for this reason – was forbidden to touch unclean objects . . .

A child caught eating before early-morning ablutions – which involved at least washing the face and mouth – would be scolded and punished by an adult member of the group . . .

The 'indirect' education received by the child in the community is almost as important as that received at school.

In certain parts of Africa character training took many forms. Parents encouraged healthy rivalry between children of the same age – sometimes as early as the age of five – by organizing wrestling matches and by setting the children competitive tasks. Fair play was also encouraged; winners and losers alike were congratulated when they played well. The main thing was not winning and losing, but playing the game. With the introduction of Islam, the Koranic schools brought additional elements of character training. Children were sent to the Mallam for three or four hours every afternoon to learn the Koran by heart, together with the principles of Islamic ethics.

Traditional education, as far as character-building was concerned, was certainly severe. But this was because of the importance which African society attaches to this aspect of education. The habit of physical exercise, apprenticeship in a trade, a religious upbringing, a respectful attitude towards one's elders and active participation in community life are indispensable coditions for any African wishing to be considered a person of consequence. The lack of more formal education can be forgiven, but a person who does not fulfil these conditions inflicts the worst possible humiliation on both his immediate family and his more distant kinsfolk.

Respect for one's elders, which is an important part of character training, includes respect for all who represent authority: village chiefs, religious leaders, soothsayers, uncles, relatives and neighbours. Styles of greeting play an essential role in the expression of respect. Salutation is a complicated affair in Africa, with different modes of addressing relatives, elders, equals, chiefs, and so on, and special greetings for morning, afternoon and evening.

There are different formulas for games, dancing, or drumming, for sitting or standing, for tilling the soil or fishing, for weaving, swimming, walking, or recovering from an illness. Anniversaries, funerals, or weddings, yam-growing ceremonies, the rituals of ancestor-worship, the Egungun festivals and other special occasions – all call for special types of greeting.

If 'intelligence' means the capacity to assimilate experience, and if 'intellectualisation' denotes abstract reasoning – as in the formation of concepts or judgements – then it can be said that traditional African education encourages intellectual development. Observation, imitation and participation are three pillars of the educational process.

African children and adolescents learn the geography and history of their community. They know their local hills and valleys like the backs of their hands; they know where the land is fertile and where it is barren. They know when to expect rain and when to expect drought. They know the right times to hunt and fish. In every family the old people are teachers of local history. The songs of praise which often commemorate great events enrich the oral tradition, creating an experience which it is difficult to forget.

Botany and zoology are the subjects of both theoretical and practical lessons, in which special attention is paid to local plants and animals. Where animals are both a source of danger and a means of livelihood their behaviour is another important subject of study.

Proverbs and riddles are exceptional wit-sharpeners, and are used to teach the child to reason and to take decisions.

Africans also have fun with their mathematics in games of skill, such as the 'Ayo' game where players must outwit their opponents in addition, subtraction, multiplication and division.

Some educators have come to believe that certain aspects of traditional African education should be integrated into the modern system, and have begun to work along these lines. This is a field which should be given priority in all developing countries.

One of the aims of education, whether modern or traditional, is to perpetuate a given culture. Traditional Africa sets great store by this aspect of human development.

As they grow up, children of traditional societies absorb and assimilate their peoples' cultural heritage, without formal teaching. They observe, imitate and mimic the actions of their elders and their siblings. They attend baptisms, religious ceremonies, weddings and funerals, the coronations of kings or chiefs, and the annual yam festival. They watch the acrobatic displays of guilds and associations, often joining in with members of their own age-group or with their families.

As we have already pointed out, responsibility for the upbringing of young Africans is traditionally shared by the entire social group. Good manners, conventions, customs, moral rules and social laws are inculcated by close relatives, by more distant members of the extended family, or by neighbours. The hallmarks of a successful traditional education in Africa are honesty, perseverance and sincerity.

Traditional Professions and Trades

Whether in the northern, eastern, western or southern African community, the aim of African education is basically the same – to produce a man or woman of *character* with the useful skill appropriate to his or her status in life.

Traditional African education is not limited to general education alone. It is also vocationally oriented:

(1)   Agricultural education – farming, fishing, animal care and animal rearing.
(2)   Trades and crafts – weaving, sculpting, drumming, smithing, soap-making, carpentry, singing, wine-tapping, pottery-making, dyeing, hair-plaiting.
(3)   Professions – priesthood, medicine, justice (police, messengers, judges), hunting, military, chieftaincy, kingship.

There are special schools in certain African countries for specific types of education; some of these institutions are known as secret societies. Some of the best known are PORO and SANDE in Liberia, Dipo Ceremony in Ghana, Fertility House in Calabar, Nigeria, and numerous initiation (graduation) ceremonies all over Africa.

Irrespective of the level of training, the method of teaching is through the time-tested apprenticeship system. The period of apprenticeship depends on the complexity of the trade or profession to be learnt. The training of a drummer or singer takes less time than that of a priest or an indigenous doctor or medicine-man.

Kanga Kalembu-Vita of Zaire describes indigenous African education in this way:

> The aim of traditional education is the preparation of the youths, their insertion and complete integration into the life of the community. This major objective implies the definition of the specific goals, among which are in particular:
>
> – ensuring education in the matrimonial, social, religious and technical domains (picking of fruits, pharmacopoeia . . .);

- ensuring training in thinking, practical wisdom, aesthetics, etc ...,
- ensuring the education of will power through asceticism, self-denial, mortification, physical endurance, self-control, etc . . .

In the African conception, education strives to make the individual pass from his status of an absolute individual to that of an integrated member of the society, to make him lose the illusion of happiness in the state of isolation so that he may accede to true happiness by being open to others, not for personal benefit but in order to create with everybody a new reality transcending individuals, namely the *community*.

In other words, education aims at making man an integral entity, indivisible in himself, a distinct entity but not separated from others, an entity in unity not only with other men but also with the whole of nature, that is the ground, water, fire, light, etc. . . . It is, finally, a question of making man pass from the situation of the individual to the social situation aimed at and finally to that of cosmic participation.

This African education centred on communal life is an education acquired for life and through life. Pululu gives its principal characteristics which he considers as a programme of the New Education: 'Sense of observation, spontaneous activities, exploitation of nature, educative games, co-education of both sexes through games and initiation rituals, learning of the art of oratory, dance, fables, and songs, these are all admirably and very naturally organized in such a way as to make complete and mentally-balanced men who are well adapted to their environment'.[4]

II   THE ISLAMIC INFLUENCE ON AFRICAN EDUCATION

The influence of the Islamic religion on African education is considerable. Most students of history are familiar with the Arab North Africa, for instance, Egypt, Algeria, Morocco, Libya and Tunisia. In this area of Africa Islam and Islamic education had established firm roots long before the Western intervention, and Islamic schools and universities flourished centuries before the arrival of Christian evangelism and colonialism. From there Islam spread to West Africa.

Thus in northern and western Africa and also in a number of eastern and central African countries Islam antedated Christianity and colonialism. Today, of about forty-five countries in Africa, over thirty-five have considerable Islamic influence; that is all of the North and West African countries, over half of the East African countries and some of those in Central Africa. Indeed, Islam has played a major role in the shaping of culture and education in most countries of Africa.

Islamic Education

Wherever Islam has spread rudimentary knowledge of the Qur'an, the Hadith (traditions of the Prophet) and the Shari'a (canon law of Islam) are still taught to its followers.

One Islamic tradition states: the best man among you is one who learns the Qur'an and then cares to teach it.' Islamic learning began on this prophetic advice,[5] with the result that teaching religion to others was considered a duty for which a person should expect no reward. This noble principle, which was successfully applied at the early stage of the development of Islamic education, reduced the status of a teacher (*mallam*) to that of a beggar: he came to occupy socially a rather low status. He had to wander from place to place looking for charitable Muslims to patronise him and give him food and shelter. Whenever his efforts were not sufficient to procure the bare necessities of life, he had to send his pupils from door to door asking for charity. They were considered to be *muhajirun* (emigrants) who had left their homes in search of knowledge. Even today a pupil in the traditional way of education is called Al-Muhajir, meaning an emigrant. But the higher grade of teachers, the *'ulama,* who were deeply learned in the science of the Qur'an and the Hadith, Islamic theology and etymology, were highly respected right from the time that Islam was first established.

The Qur'anic School System

The system described below is typical of the one most frequently encountered in Black Africa.[7]

A Qur'anic school is usually found in or outside the mosque itself. Indeed, the oldest Muslim university, Al-Azhar in Cairo, was established in a mosque. Today thousands of these schools are located in mosques, private houses, or specially built premises.

As early as the third year of life Muslim children are expected to start the first stage of Qur'anic education. At this stage the pupils learn the shorter chapter of the Qur'an by rote. The only pleasure they can derive from the system at this stage lies in the choral recitations, which often follow a sing-song pattern. The pupils seem to enjoy reciting these verses to themselves in their homes and at play. The method of instruction is as follows, the teacher recites to his pupils the verse to be learnt and they repeat it after him. He does this several times until he is satisfied that they have mastered the correct pronunciation. Then the pupil (or group) is left on his own to continue repeating the verse until he has thoroughly memorised it. The verse is then linked with the previously memorised verses and in this way the pupil gradually learns by heart whole chapters of the Qur'an.

The Qur'an is divided into sixty parts (or *esus*), each of which contains a number of chapters (although very long chapters or parts thereof form certain *esus*). A pupil at what we may call the 'primary' level of the system is expected to memorise one or two of these sixty *esus*, often beginning with the short chapters. These chapters are usually those he would most require for his daily prayers.

From here the pupil moves on to the next stage at which he learns the alphabet of the Arabic language. The Arabic alphabet is composed of twenty-six letters, all of which are consonants. Some teachers divide these letters into three, often in the ratio 5:5:3, and teach the pupil to recognise the letters by writing some of them on his slate and making him repeat the sounds several times over. This stage lasts between six and thirty-six weeks, depending on the rate at which the pupil learns to recognise the individual letters. When the teacher is satisfied that the pupil has attained the standard required for reading Arabic characters, he introduces him to the formation of syllables with 'vowels'. There are only four vowels which are simply four different notations (or signs) written above or below a consonant to indicate what vowel sound should go with it. When he is able to do this competently, the pupil then employs his newly acquired skills in the reading of the first two parts of the Qur'an all over again.

This stage is affected by the linguistic background of the teacher since variation in the pupil's pattern of articulation could be due to the teacher's accent. It lasts for six to eighteen months, depending, again, on the capabilities of the individual pupil. The spelling pattern, once correctly grasped, enables the pupil to read at sight any texts written in the Arabic language. This is usually the final stage in the acquisition of reading skills.

The teaching of writing starts at different times in different schools. Some pupils start learning how to write Arabic characters as early as the first stage of the system. Others do not start until much later, for example, when they are learning the alphabet. This is generally a very slow, painstaking and rather tedious process during which the teacher writes out the model of the verse on the writing board and the pupil copies it out below several times.

Many people think that Qur'anic education ends here, but this is only the end of what may be regarded as the primary level of the system. Although the pupil has committed the first two *esus* to memory and is now able to read and write in Arabic, he still generally does not know the meaning of the verses of the Qur'an, except for a few translations which he picks up unconsciously either at sermons or during other ceremonies. This is the level every Muslim must pass through if he is to be able to pray and perform other religious duties since the prayers, birth, death, marriage and other religious ceremonies are usually performed in Arabic.

What we may regard as the 'secondary' level of the system has a much broader and deeper curriculum. The pupil begins by learning the meaning of the verses he has committed to memory. The teacher does his best to explain the Arabic texts. But this is usually far too difficult for young minds and, in many cases, for the teacher as well. Besides knowing the meaning of the verses of the Qur'an the pupil is also introduced to other writings, such as the Hadith. The translation method is largely used and repetition is still fully exploited.

In the traditional system this level merges imperceptibly into the higher level (which in current usage may be termed the 'post-secondary' level). It is at this stage that the pupil begins to learn grammar. The method used capitalises greatly on the mechanical rote-learning of grammatical rules. This, as the linguists often point out, is not the most effective way to each a language meant for communication.

The course of study at this level includes grammatical inflections, syntax, logic, arithmetic, algebra, rhetoric and versification, jurisprudence, scholastic theology, commentaries on the Qur'an, treatises on exegesis and the principles and rules of interpretation of the laws of Islam, and the traditions of the Prophet and commentaries thereon. These are regarded as different branches of learning and it is not often that a teacher attains perfection in all of them. A scholar who is good at jurisprudence may be relatively weak at arithmetic. That is why, at this stage, the student of the Qur'anic system is often instructed by more than one mallam.

It is also at this stage that the student decides in which area he wishes to specialise. This marks the beginning of the university level. Having chosen his specialist subject, he proceeds to a university (usually one of the celebrated universities at Fez, Sankore, Timbuktu, or Al-Azhar) or continues at home learning from local specialists. By this time the student has acquired some proficiency in the Arabic language and is able to read, understand and interpret many of the works of earlier scholars in his field. At the end of his studies he receives a 'licence' empowering him to practise as a teacher, an *imam,* or an *alkali,* depending on his area of specialisation.

In Qur'anic schools, unlike formal schools, there are no rigidly codified rules, but there are a few conventionalised ways of behaviour which guide the pupils – and the teachers. The teacher regards himself as the custodian of his pupils, his duty being primarily to train them to be good citizens. The school week starts on Saturday and ends on Wednesday. There is no bell to summon the pupils to school; nor is there a fixed dress.

Fees are paid in cash and kind. There is no fixed amount, as this varies from teacher to teacher. The teacher collects the 'fees' from his pupils. These do not usually amount to more than a few pennies. The teacher may also receive gifts, such as grain, meat, cooked foodstuffs, a piece of cloth, or a prayer mat (almost invariably a goat's skin), particularly during one of the Muslim festivals.

Helping with onerous chores is considered part of a pupil's duties to his teacher. During the month of Ramadhan the older pupils accompany their teacher to his preaching ground – usually a busy and conspicuous part of the street. There it is their duty to get the place lit and the chairs arranged and to treat the audience to melodius songs and poems in praise of the Prophet.

On ceremonial occasions – such as the Eid-el-Fitr, Eid-el-Kabir, Maulud Nabiyi (the Prophet's birthday) and the Lailatul Qadr ('The Night of Greatness', a night in the month of Ramadhan) – the pupils present 'plays' based on the life of the Prophet. These are very similar to the Roman liturgical plays and the medieval miracle plays that succeeded them.

Qur'anic School Teachers

The qualifications of Qur'anic schoolteachers differ from person to person and from place to place. Sometimes they are highly learned *ulama,* well versed in Islamic studies, but this is rare. Then there are those whose only qualification is that they can recite the Qur'an and write Arabic characters. Such people usually start up a class with their own children, and neighbours are encouraged to send their children along.

Some Qur'anic school proprietors do not insist on a set fee to be paid by the pupil. But recently some Arabic schools have introduced various fees for admission, award of certificates and monthly or annual tuition fees.

Most of the Qur'anic schools are run according to the discretion of their individual proprietors, who are invariably Qur'anic schoolteachers themselves. As a result, instruction differs from school to school, and there is no uniform curriculum, nor are there prescribed qualifications for teachers. In most schools former pupils are appointed as teachers at extremely low wages. Considerable reform is being carried out in many of these schools today.

It should be noted, however, that Muslim institutions of higher learning and universities are organised and administered along modern lines like other universities in the world, for example, the universities of Algiers, Libya, Cairo and Rabat.

III   THE COLONIAL PERIOD

The vast exploration of Africa in the early nineteenth century and the evangelistic and trading activities that followed led to the 'scramble for Africa' in the 1880s, and the eventual establishment of colonial rule over large portions of the continent. Among the principal 'winners' in the scramble were Britain and France. Thus, all the countries covered in this work, except Liberia and Ethiopia, were at different periods in their history under the colonial rule of these two countries – Britain and France.

Although Liberia was never a colony, nevertheless, its history as a nation is usually traced to the activities of the 'American Society for Colonizing the Free People of Colour of the United States of America'. Similarly Ethiopia, though never colonised, also had some experience of foreign incursion through the Italian occupation of 1935–41. Cameroon represents a country with a dual colonial experience, while Egypt stands as an exemplar of a country which had a diluted experience of multiple foreign interventions, having been occupied at different points by the French, the Osmani Empire and then the British.

Thus, either by way of occupation, direct colonial rule, or through massive migration (as was the case of Liberia), all the countries covered in this work shared a common history of foreign intervention. The impact of such influences on the educational development in Africa is the subject of this part of the chapter.

The first general remark on the history of education in colonial Africa is that foreign missions (Christian or Islamic) with interests in Africa pioneered and dominated the educational sector for many years. This pioneering work in education should be judged in the context of the missions' early recognition of the supreme importance of education in the successful prosecution of their evangelistic assignments. Therefore, education for the propagation of the gospel – to win African souls for Christ – was made a central objective of mission education in colonial Africa. In the later years of colonisation, when the colonial governments began to show interest in education, the general goal of education did not seem to have changed. What seemed to have changed was the shift in emphasis – a shift from a purely religious education to a diluted semi-secular education which emphasised the role of the school in the continued furtherance of colonial interests in Africa. All the countries covered in this work shared this common characteristic in the development of their educational systems.

A third general observation common to Africa's colonial system of education is that there were conscious and obvious attempts, first by the foreign missions and later by the colonial governments, to educate the African away from his culture. This feature was more pronounced in the French colonies where education meant 'frenchifying' the African. This is not to play down Britain's guilt in this attempt. For example, indigenous schools, usually referred to as the bush schools, were reinstituted into 'catechetical' schools (as in Kenya, for instance) and the first village elementary schools. The highly sophisticated PORO school system in Liberia and Sierra Leone was almost completely eradicated in the colonial period.

A fourth common characteristic of the colonial system of education in Africa was the lack of co-ordination, particularly in the early years of colonisation when the missions, to the near exclusion of the governments, dominated the provision of education to the people. Indeed, each mission or voluntary agency concentrated on its respective area of operation without much regard for developments outside it.

Thus far, we have noted the missionary dominance of educational objectives which, in turn, limited the curriculum of the mission schools to the essentials of the Christian or Muslim life. In addition to religion, reading, writing and arithmetic were made the pillars of every school curriculum. The narrowness of the school curriculum remained relatively unchanged even after the increased government involvement in education. Religious education still dominated the curriculum while the entire school system grew increasingly bookish and examination-oriented. This development was common to both the British and French colonies where schools were used basically for preparing the African for the semi-skilled job market. In fact, the volume and quantity of education the colonial administrators were willing to give to the Africans were the barest minimum necessary for such auxiliary positions as clerks, interpreters, preachers, pupil-teachers, and so on.

Over this issue of the volume and quantity of education Britain, France and others showed remarkable differences. Britain, under the policy of 'imperial trusteeship' which, according to Allison Smith, meant a 'limited liability and a reluctance to undertake large-scale projects because of the risks involved',[6] pursued an educational policy which guaranteed a steady flow of African manpower. Britain, unlike France, recognised that the colonised countries might eventually revert to self-rule. Consequently, facilities were expanded in British colonies to provide secondary and higher education much earlier than in the French.

Britain's recognition of its colonies' possible return to self-rule, a possibility unrecognised by France, accounted largely for the differences in both countries' colonial policies including their colonial education policies. For example, while Britain embarked on a policy of partnership soon after the Second World War in 1945, France intensified its policy of assimilation and association intended to ensure continued and perpetual consolidation of French colonial influence and authority in Africa. In fact, the French saw their colonies as overseas units of European France. Therefore, rather than develop an educational system which upheld African values, culture and ideals, determined efforts were made to make colonial education a close replica of the educational system in France. And as far back as 1924 all mission schools in the French colonies were required to conform to a state model – that of the schools of metropolitan France.

In terms of quality, structure, curriculum, examinations and certificates, the French colonial schools were almost exactly like their counterparts in France. The curricula were decided by officials in the

Ministry of Colonies in Paris. The African schoolchild had to recite French poems, sing French hymns and learn French literature, and was taught French geography and the history of France. He had to contend with French teachers, particularly at the secondary schools (lycées) and, of course, grapple with a foreign language as the medium of instruction. By the time the child qualified for the Baccalauréat he was, in the words of Mumford and Orde-Brown, 'French in all but the colour of his skin'.[8] According to an on-the-spot assessment of the quality of French colonial schools, with the Bamako schools at Mali as reference, Mumford and Orde-Brown wrote:

> the general impression gained from a visit to the Bamako School was that the institutions were equal in standing and equipment to the best that Europe can produce. Using the term in its biological sense, these schools are the 'growing points' of French civilization in Africa.[9]

In general, French colonial education was essentially a means of producing a nucleus of native aristocracy who would eventually propagate French ideals and uphold French ways of life.

Britain, on its part, showed some concern for the adaptation of education to the African situation. In fact, the policy statement issued by the British government in 1925 as a result of the Phelps-Stokes Commission on African Education noted: 'Education should be adapted to the mentality, aptitudes, occupations and traditions of the various peoples, conserving as far as possible all sound and healthy elements in the fabric of their social life . . .'[10] Consequently Britain suggested vocational education in place of the prevalent concentration on academic education. But this preference was not sufficiently backed up in practice since there was no corresponding growth in industry, agriculture and commerce to guarantee recipients of vocational education a place in the job market. Hence, for example, the insistence on the primacy of industrial and manual education in Sierra Leone as far back as 1926 failed to change the people's preference for classics and literary academic work.

While Britain made efforts, though somewhat superficial and insincere, at adapting colonial education to African situations, France's colonial duty in the field of education was, according to Governor Roume, to produce native trained staff who must be auxiliaries in every field and assume the status of a carefully chosen elite. The other task of education, Governor Roume added, was to bring the masses through schools nearer to France and to transform the 'native' system of living. Thus, in place of British partnership and adaptation, the French stood for association and assimilation: and the French colonial school system consequently remained wholly French in character, structure, content and methodology.

Another feature of British colonial education was the principle of racial segregation perpetuated in Kenya and Tanzania. There was also the 'indirect rule system' in northern Nigeria with its consequence of an imbalance of educational development between the northern and southern areas of that country.

In Kenya and Tanzania different schools were established for the different racial groups: Europeans, Asians, Arabs and Africans. In Nigeria the Qur'anic schools were allowed to flourish in the Muslim north while Christian education flourished in the Christian south. One of the effects of this segregational feature of British colonial education was the lack of uniformity in standards and in facilities amongst the African schools. This became in the later years of colonisation the target of attack by a few educated Africans in those countries. Another effect of this development was the growth of community involvement in education in British colonies.

Apparently in recognition of the need to promote local participation in education, Britain decentralised the control of education and the Advisory Committee on Education in the Colonies, instituted in 1923, gradually shed its controlling powers, first to territorial departments of education and later to regional and local bodies.

Closely associated with this decentralised control of education was the introduction of a new system of administration and supervision of educational development in the whole of British tropical Africa. This new system also became necessary for the implementation of a new financing system introduced in response to the demand of missionary and other voluntary bodies for government financial assistance. The financial assistance system known as grants-in-aid, which was meant to supplement the efforts of the missions and other voluntary agencies, soon developed to permit government's supervision and inspection of non-government schools to determine qualification for recipients and to ensure some uniformity in standards. Schools which did not qualify for government grants were privately run, drawing their finances exclusively from contributions of the missionary bodies, private individuals, local authority and community organisations. In some countries non-government schools began to earn such grants-in-aid as early as 1870, and by 1925 grants-in-aid rules were already laid down in countries such as Kenya, Ghana and Nigeria.

The introduction of the system of grants-in-aid, and the resultant classification of schools into aided and unaided schools in British colonies, intensified the Africans' demand for more government involvement in the provision of more and better education for the people. In Tanzania political parties were used to press the agitation for more schools; the Tanganyika African National Union (TANU), as it was then called, opened primary schools and turned them over to parents' associations. The role of such political parties, local communities and unions in the development of education during the colonial era is an important landmark in the history of education in British Africa, whereas in French Africa during the same period such laudable development was comparatively non-existent. The French policy of association and assimilation seemed to have drowned the few nationalist voices in French Africa in this direction. For example, rather than expand higher education facilities in the French colonies, the French Colonial Office in Paris preferred to give scholarships to Africans for higher studies in Paris. Mali had no higher institution of university status but, in the 1959–60 school year, for example, there were 158 Malians receiving higher education on government scholarships.[10]

The school systems varied between the British and French colonies partly because the French were obliged to follow the metropolitan pattern. Nevertheless, in spite of differences of nomenclature and organisation, the conventional division into primary, secondary and higher levels can be discerned in the respective chapters of this book.

While higher education in the British colonies was largely the development of academic intellectualism, some measure of professionalisation and vocational education was introduced by the French. Mali, as an example of the French system, had separate specialised institutions to cater for the different professions and vocational trades. In contrast, Britain established single institutions to offer specialisation in a number of professions and trades. In Nigeria, for example, trade centres were opened at the secondary level while at the higher education level the Yaba Higher College offered specialisation in medicine, agriculture, engineering, surveying and teacher training.

In all the countries covered in this work all educational institutions, including primary schools, were fee-paying under the colonial system. Furthermore, primary education expanded disproportionately to secondary education while higher education was pathetically inadequate. Although primary education was expanded, illiteracy was very pronounced in the colonial era. Primary schools were few and scattered; pupils had to walk long distances to schools. It was to avoid the necessity of schoolchildren having to walk long distances and because of the missionaries' belief in the negative influence of the pupils' homes on their Christianising efforts that some schools were made into boarding schools. The boarding system, predominant at the secondary school level, limited its growth, thereby intensifying the bottleneck at this level of education. That was the system inherited by British colonies upon the attainment of independence, and when independent African countries embarked upon free and, in some countries, such as Tanzania, Kenya and Nigeria, compulsory primary education, they had to grapple with this bottleneck situation at the secondary education level. Kenya and Tanzania have since abandoned the boarding system.

We now come to the years immediately preceding independence. As noted earlier, British Africa led the French in the agitation for increased quantity and improved quality of education. As early as 1929 the Kikuyu Independent Schools Association was formed in Kenya and that movement was very active and vocal between 1929 and 1936, expressing strong dissatisfaction with the quantity and quality of education provided by the missions. In that same country Tom Mboya launched the famous Airlift of 1959 in which the young Kenyans of African descent were flown to the United States of America and later to other parts of the world, especially London, for education. There was also the pioneering contribution of the TANU party in Tanzania and President Julius Nyerere's personal leadership in the advancement of an educational system founded on African values and ideals.

The United Gold Coast Convention and later Kwame Nkrumah's Convention People's Party (CPP) also championed the call for more and better education for the people of Ghana. And in Nigeria ethnic groups formed unions like the Ibo Union and the Egbe Omo Oduduwa to add support and voice to the agitation of the newly emergent nationalist movements. In these countries community-sponsored schools – primary and secondary – were established; and in addition the various unions offered scholarships to deserving sons and daughters of their members for overseas education. The Harambee school in Kenya exemplifies Africa's voluntary and community endeavour in the context of African-directed Western education.

That was the picture in the closing years of colonial education in Africa. Young educated Africans, political parties, ethnic groups, and so on, began to ask for more education and for a redefinition of the goals and purposes of education. There was general discontent expressed against the colonial education, especially in British Africa. This is not to claim that all was calm in French Africa. Guinea, though not represented in this book, championed the call for self-government and the demand for an educational system that reflected African conditions. Mali, soon after independence in 1960, embarked on a thorough educational reform meant to give it a truly Malian system of education.

On the whole, whatever the differences and similarities between the British and French colonial systems of education, the essential and common concern of the colonial schools was the provision of a modicum of education necessary for the African to fit into colonial expectations. It was in the post-independence period that the respective governments began to transform education to promote national awareness, economic productivity and political consciousness. How each country carried out this business of transformation of education along national ideals will be seen in the contributions on individual countries.

NOTES: CHAPTER 1

1 Abdou Moumouni, *Education in Africa,* trans. N. Phyllis (London: Deutsch, 1968) p. 15.
2 A. B. Fafunwa, *History of Education in Nigeria* (London: Allen & Unwin, 1974), p. 17.
3 N. A. Fadipe, *The Sociology of the Yoruba* (Ibadan: Ibadan University Press, 1970), pp. 111–13.
4 Kanga Kèlemba-Vita and others, 'Black civilization and education', paper presented at Second World Black Festival of Arts and Culture in Lagos, 1977, p. 3.
5 A. R. I. Doi, *Introduction to the Hadith* (Lagos: Islamic Publications Bureau, 1970), pp. 90–5.
6 A. Smith 'Trusteeship and partnership in British Africa', *The Year Book of World Affairs, 1953* (London: Stephens, 1953), p. 170.
7 S. A. Jimoh, 'A critical appraisal of Islamic education in Nigeria', mimeographed M. Ed. term paper, Faculty of Education: University of Ye, 1971, pp. 10–15.
8 W. Bryant Mumford and G. St J. Orde-Brown, *Africans Learn to be French: A Review of Educational Activities in the Seven Federated Colonies of French West Africa based on a tour of French West Africa and Algiers undertaken in 1935.* (London: Evans, 1936), p. 47.
9 ibid, p. 44.
10 Advisory Committee on Native Education in the British Tropical African Dependencies, *Education Policy in British Tropical Africa* (London: HMSO, 1925), p. 4. (See also note 2 of Chapter 5.)
11 H. Kitchen, *The Educated African* (New York: Praeger, 1962), p. 498.

Chapter 2

Education in Cameroon

SOLOMON SHU

I BRIEF HISTORICAL OUTLINE

Inherited Diversity

The story of Western education in Cameroon is often synchronised with the chequered political history of the country, whose seventy-seven years of colonial rule, from 1884 to 1960, under the three Great Powers, Germany, France and Britain, with their considerable differences in colonial policies, administrative tactics, social behaviour and educational philosophies, have left behind systems of education so extremely rich in diversity that harmonisation into a single system is not an easy task. Cameroon combines a diverse indigenous culture with a diverse heritage from history. The noteworthy elements of that rich diversity which exert varying influences upon the practice of education in Cameroon today are:

(1) the two official languages, English and French, which are the media of instruction at all levels of education;
(2) the multiplicity of vernacular languages and dialects, with none of them emerging, as yet, as a *lingua franca*;
(3) the heterogeneity of Cameroon religious communities with Catholics, Protestants, Muslims, Franco-Arabs, atheists and animists all living side by side and all taking part in the education enterprise (there are government schools as well as private schools and schools without any religious affiliation);
(4) the diverse ethnological groupings – their varying degrees of faith in education have given rise to imbalances in regional development of education, especially in the education of girls. There are regions with as much as 90 per cent of school-age population in school as well as others with only 20 per cent.

All these factors render the Cameroon system of education inherently complex from the synchronic as well as from the diachronic perspective; and such diversity within one and the same system makes the Cameroon system a unique situation for students of comparative education.

Education and Political Milestones

The development of Western education in Cameroon from its inception to the present day may conveniently be divided into seven periods.

(1) Pre-annexation: forty years of missionary pioneership in education, from 1844 when the first missionary, Alfred Saker, arrived in Cameroon, 'to spread the Gospel of Christ to heathens through the medium of school' until 1884 when Nachtingal annexed Cameroon for imperial Germany.

(2) Thirty years of German rule and German education from 1884 to 1914.

(3) Education in the dark years from 1914 to 1922.

(4) Twenty-five years of education in British Cameroon and in French Cameroon under the League of Nations from 1922 to 1946.

(5) Fifteen years of education in British Cameroon and in French Cameroon during the United Nations trusteeship period from 1946 to 1960/61.

(6) Twelve years of post-independence education in the Federal Republic of Cameroon from 1961 to 1972.

(7) Education in the United Republic of Cameroon from 1972 to present day.

The Three Levels of Education

The introduction and development of the three levels of education in Cameroon could be oversimplified as follows.

(1) The years 1844–1922 saw the implantation and development of primary education in Cameroon, predominantly in the hands of missionary bodies.

(2) The period 1922–46 witnessed a very timid introduction of the second level of education, i.e. teacher training, secondary schools and vocational/technical education.

(3) The period 1946–60 under the United Nations trusteeship brought in external aid for the development of secondary education.

(4) The development of the third level of education in Cameroon started after independence with the inauguration of the University of Yaoundé in 1962.

Responsibility for Education

For sixty-seven years, from 1844 to 1910, responsibility for education and the education policy to be applied in the mission field of Cameroon was often entirely determined by the mother house or home board of the missionary societies which sent out missionaries to Cameroon.

The period 1910–61 saw an era of fifty-one years of collaboration as and when German, French and British colonial governments in varying degrees espoused the cause of mission education. Educational policy was often the result of interaction between popular opinion in mission circles on the one hand and government ideals for native education on the other.

Finally, a third period, starting with independence in 1960, saw an independent national government assuming full and direct responsibility for education, evolving an educational policy to deal with the realities of the Cameroon situation, and making every conscious effort to shape the destiny of an independent Cameroon. The tempo of educational development in this post-independence period is remarkably fast.

Some Noteworthy Facts about Cameroon

(1) Before the coming cf the white man, Cameroonians lived together in ethnic groups under natural rulers but in the colonial era artificial boundaries split some groups and even some families.

(2) Reunification into the Federal Republic of Cameroon took place on 1 October 1961, the French-speaking Cameroon having attained independence in 1960 and the English-speaking Cameroon in 1961. On 20 May 1972 the Federal Republic of Cameroon became the United Republic of Cameroon.

(3) The population of Cameroon in 1976 was 7·5 million and the growth rate is 2·2 per cent per annum.

(4) The area of present-day Cameroon is 475 square kilometres and the density of population is 15·8 inhabitants per square kilometre.

(5) The per capita income of Cameroon in 1976/7 was 600 francs CFA or 250 United States dollars.

(6) In so far as territorial administration is concerned, the whole republic is divided into seven provinces (Central-South, Littoral, West, North, East, South-West and North-West) with a governor in charge of each province. Each province is subdivided into divisions which in turn are sometimes subdivided into subdivisions and districts.

(7) Two of the provinces, North-West and South-West, are English-speaking, while the remaining five provinces are French-speaking. Bilingualism is fast reducing this distinction.

II ORGANISATION

Nursery Education

Primary eduction is subdivided into nursery education and primary education. Nursery education, which is optional, is available only in the main towns (for example, Yaoundé, Doula, Victoria and Buea) for children between the ages of 3 and 6. Only about 5 per cent of the children of this age-group attend the nursery schools. In the school year

1976/7 there were altogether 34, 069 pupils in attendance in 512 nursery schools under 996 teachers. Compared with the previous school year (1975/6), when enrolment was 30,686, there was an increase in enrolment of about 12 per cent in one year. Nursery education is highly developed in Central South Province which in the school year 1976/7 had an enrolment of 15,045, constituting over 40 per cent of the figure for the whole republic. For historical reasons nursery education is least developed in the two English-speaking provinces where the enrolments in the 1976/7 school year were 921 for South-West Province and 252 for North-West Province. In the same year there were 16,990 pupils in government or public nursery schools as against 17,079 in private nursery schools. This shows a fifty–fifty relationship between public and private nursery schools.

Primary Education

The duration of the primary school course is historically six years in the five French-speaking provinces and seven years in the two English-speaking provinces. At the second national seminar on education held at Yaoundé in February 1976 it was agreed that the primary school cycle should last for seven years. Formal primary education is provided in both government schools and private schools for children between the ages of 6 and 14 years. This age-group accounts for one-fifth of the total population of Cameroon (which is 7·5 million according to the 1976 census). In the school year 1976/7 there were 1,156,199 pupils in all the primary schools, representing about 65 per cent of the 6–14-year-olds. With 22,763 teachers looking after 1,156,199 pupils, the average number of pupils per teacher was 51. Compared with the enrolments of the previous year, 1975/6, when there were 1,107,545 pupils in the schools, primary education showed an increase in enrolment of 3·2 per cent in one year and during the ten years from 1967/8 to 1976/7 enrolment increased from 816,861 in 1967/8 to 1,156,199 in 1976/7, giving an average growth rate of 4·1 per cent per year. In the two English-speaking provinces, which prior to September 1971 had no government schools, there were in the school year 1976/7 a total of 91,342 pupils in government schools as against 133,304 in private schools. The corresponding figures for the previous school year 1975/6 were 80,981 pupils in government schools and 160,317 in private schools. This shows an increase of over 10 per cent in one year in the fast-growing government schools, and a decrease of about 17 per cent in the enrolment of the private schools. Although coeducation is the practice throughout the primary school system, the boys almost always outnumber the girls; in the 1973/4 school year there was in the schools a total of 568,455 boys as against 445,680 girls. Thus for every four girls in the primary school, there are at least five boys. Primary education has spread to every small village and in the 1976/7 school year there was a total of 4,634 primary schools in the whole republic, giving instruction in 23,573 classrooms under 22,763 teachers.

Secondary Education

In so far as secondary grammar school education is concerned, the school year 1976/7 saw a total of 120,207 studying in 188 first-cycle schools and 82 second-cycle schools, run by both government and private authorities. Whereas the location of private secondary schools is determined by the convenience of the proprietor, government secondary schools are distributed by a policy of attaching a school to each government administrative centre such as the provincial, divisional, district and local council headquarters.

By passing a competitive entrance exmination 15–20 per cent of Cameroon primary school children enter secondary schools at the age of 11-plus and do a seven-year secondary school course ending in either the GCE (General Certificate of Education) Advanced Level or the baccalauréat, normally taken at the age of 18-plus. Although Francophones are free to do the GCE just as Anglophones are free to do the baccalauréat if they so wish, it is noteworthy that there are structural differences in that the first cycle of the Anglophone system lasts five years and leads to GCE Ordinary Level while the first cycle of the Francophone system lasts four years and leads to the BEPC (Brevet Elémentaire du Premier Cycle). Consequently the second cycle of the Anglophone system is two years while that of the Francophone system is three years. It is remarkable that in the purely bilingual establishments such as the bilingual grammar school in Buea the same candidates present themselves for the examinations of both systems.

Enrolments for the school year 1976/7 show that government secondary schools had 57,429 students which is 48 per cent of overall total enrolment in secondary schools, while private secondary schools had 62,778 students which is 52 per cent.

Compared with the situation ten years ago (in the school year 1967/8) when the enrolment in all the secondary schools was 37,369, the 1976/7 enrolment of 120,207 shows an average annual growth rate of over 30 per cent.

Secondary Technical Education

Secondary technical education is provided in three main types of institution:

(1) The SAR (section artisanale rurale) and the SM (section ménagère) as well as in the EM (école ménagère) where primary school leavers do artisan courses and domestic science courses respectively for a period of two or three years. (These courses are

often regarded as post-primary vocational education rather than as technical education.)

(2) The CET (collège d'enseignement technique) where primary school leavers who pass a competitive entrance examination undergo a five-year programme in various technical courses ending in the City and Guilds examination for the Anglophones and in the CAP (certificat d'aptitude professionelle) for the Francophones. The CETs have such variations as CETIC (collège d'enseignement technique industriel et commerciel) and CETIF (collège d'énseignement technique industriel féminin).

(3) The lycée technique, like the ordinary lycée (grammar school), provides a seven-year course, and is made up of a first cycle of four years ending in the CAR (certificat d'aptitude rurale) and a second cycle of three years ending in the 'Bac Technique'.

In the school year 1976/7 a total of 33,999 students were studying in 128 secondary technical schools with 973 classrooms, some of them specially equipped. In the same school year the SAR, SM and EM had a total enrolment of 5,653 of which 5,486 students were in government institutions and only 167 in private institutions. The total number of institutions giving these vocational courses was 94 of which 87 were government and 7 private. There were in all 106 ordinary classrooms as against 74 specially equipped classrooms.

Compared with the enrolment figures ten years ago in 1967/8 when there were 11,054 students in all the secondary technical colleges, the 1976/7 enrolment figures of 33,999 show an average yearly increase of about 31 per cent.

Teacher Education

With the reorganisation of teacher education in 1974/5 there are two main categories of teacher training colleges in the United Republic of Cameroon. First, there is the ENIA (école normale d'instituteurs adjoints) which produces instituteurs adjoints or grade II teachers. Entry into ENIA is by a competitive entrance examination open to holders of GCE Ordinary Level or the Brevet Elémentaire du Premier Cycle (BEPC) and the Probatoire. Then there is the ENI (école normale d'instituteurs) which produces instituteurs or grade I teachers. Entry into ENI is open to holders of the grade II Certificate and GCE Advanced Level or holders of the Baccalauréat. Both the ENIA and the ENI courses are of one year's duration. Another small category of teacher training exists as the ENEMC (école normale d'énseignement ménager et couture) for training domestic science teachers.

The government policy for the distribution of teacher training colleges ensures that each province is self-contained, having its own ENIA and ENI which are the official government teacher training colleges for the province, quite apart from any other teacher education offered by private bodies.

There were during the 1976/7 school year 11 ENIAs with 664 students on roll, and 7 ENIs (some of them with ENEMCs) with 646 students on roll. The corresponding enrolment figures for the previous school year (1975/6) were 652 for ENIAs and 513 for ENIs. This shows an overall increase in one year of 12 per cent for ENIAs and ENIs taken together.

Higher Education

Higher education in Cameroon centres on the University of Yaoundé and its schools, institutes and annexes. Founded in 1962, the University of Yaoundé started off with three faculties (Arts and Human Sciences, Law and Economic Sciences and Science) and the Ecole Normale Supérieure. But since the transitional period ending in 1967 the university has expanded into ten diversified establishments of higher education grouped around the university and growing rapidly to cope with the many-sided manpower needs of a country that is determined to produce locally its own technical, scientific, commercial and professional staff. The ten establishments of the university, which are all in Yaoundé (except the Institut d'Administration des Entreprises which is in Douala and two annexes of the Ecole Normale Supérieure which are in Bambili and Douala) are:

(1) the Faculty of Law and Economic Sciences
(2) the Faculty of Arts and Human Sciences
(3) the Faculty of Science
(4) Ecole Normale Supérieure (ENS) i.e. the Institute of Education
(5) Centre Universitaire des Sciences de la Santé (CUSS) i.e. the Medical School
(6) Ecole Nationale Supérieure Agronomique (ENSA) i.e. the Agricultural School
(7) Ecole Nationale Supérieure Polytechnique (ENSP) i.e. the Engineering School
(8) Ecole Supérieure Internationale de Journalisme de Yaoundé (ESIJY), i.e. the School of Journalism
(9) Institut d'Administration des Entreprises (IAE) i.e. the Business Administration School
(10) Institut des Relations Internationales du Cameroon (IRIC), i.e. the Institute of International Relations.

Admission to the faculties is automatic for holders of GCE Advanced Level or Baccalauréat. It takes four years of full-time study to obtain a first degree. Admission to the specialised schools and institutes is usually through a competitive entrance examination in addition to satisfying prescribed minimum entry requirements. The Medical School admits about forty students a year, who hold the Baccalauréat or the GCE Advanced Level with passes in at least biology, chemistry and physics. They take six years to qualify. The Ecole Normale Supérieure admits holders of the Baccalauréat or of GCE Advanced Level and gives th 'm three years of theoretical and practical training to enable them to work as secondary school teachers, secondary technical teachers, inspectors of primary and nursery education and teachers in teacher training colleges. The National Agricultural School admits holders of the Diploma of General Scientific Studies awarded by the Faculty of Science of the University of Yaoundé, and other science students who qualify at the entrance examination. The Engineering School admits candidates with Baccalauréat or GCE Advanced Level with passes in mathematics, physics and chemistry; they train for three or five years according to specialisation. The International Institute of Journalism serves Cameroon, Gabon, the Republic of Central Africa, Rwanda, Tchad and Togo. Holders of Baccalauréat or GCE Advanced Level as well as practising journalists are offered admission to study for three years. The Institute of International Relations offers postgraduate courses in international relations and admits eligible candidates from any African country.

It is noteworthy that the School of Administration and Law, the National Institute of Sports and the Inter-Services Military School are strictly speaking institutions of higher education but do not fall under the University of Yaoundé.

In the school year of 1976/7 the University of Yaoundé (together with all its schools) had 8,221 students on roll and an academic staff of 395 lecturers. This represents about twenty students to one lecturer. During the last ten years the number of students in higher education in Cameroon has increased almost fourfold, from 2,025 in the 1967/8 academic year to 8,221 in 1976/7. This represents an average yearly increase of about 30 per cent.

Since 1967 the yearly percentage of university students pursuing general education (as opposed to technological and professional education) has been diminishing– from 87·65 per cent in 1967/8 to 79·16 per cent in 1973/4. On the other hand the yearly percentage of university students pursuing scientific, technological and professional studies has been increasing as follows: 10·2 per cent in 1967, 14·46 per cent in 1968, 17·68 per cent in 1969 and 25·49 per cent in 1973/4. This increase is a result of the professionalisation policy described below.

In the 1975/6 school year, out of a total of 7,169 students in the University of Yaoundé, there were 6,125 boys as against 1,004 girls. In other words, girls obtained only 15 per cent of the places in higher education.

In 1974 the Council for Higher Education and Scientific and

Technological Research introduced reforms in Cameroon higher education which laid down that higher education must henceforth be geared to economic production and the transformation of Cameroon society through the training of high-level and intermediate manpower. This was to be effected by the professionalisation of academic degrees in the University of Yaoundé. Consequently each degree now has a professional tag attached to it, for example, BA History for Teaching. A university of technology was envisaged in addition to the present University of Yaoundé.

By a recent presidential decree a university campus has been established in each of the following four provinces with the necessary facilities to meet specific needs of Cameroon: at Nchang in Western Province for agriculture; at Ngaoundéré in Northern Province for animal husbandry; at Douala (the commercial headquarters of the republic) in Littoral Province for commerce; and at Buea in South-West Province for languages.

Generous scholarships are available for higher education within Cameroon, and a limited number for studies abroad in fields not available locally.

No discussion of higher education in Cameroon can be complete without mention of the scientific research which is vigorously in progress, not only in the University of Yaoundé, but elsewhere in the following places and organisations:

(1) the National Office of Scientific and Technical Research (ONAREST) which accommodates the National Centre of Education (CNE)
(2) the Office of Scientific and Technical Research Overseas (ORSTOM)
(3) the National Institute of Geography
(4) the Bureau of Geological Research
(5) the Pasteur Institute
(6) the Institute of Demographic Research (IFORD).

All these research projects strive to discover the best means of adapting education and other services to the realities of Cameroon.

Non-Formal Education

Non-formal education is understood to include informal education, continuing education and popular education as well as all 'post-scolaire' and extra-curricular educational activities taking place outside the normal school system described above. Though often lacking in statistical data, non-formal education in Cameroon is quite extensive. There are adult education centres or adult literacy classes organised and run by the Ministry of Youth and Sports whose popular education services also run various mass education programmes over the radio network. Evening classes are organised by private entrepreneurs under the direction of the Department of Private Education of the Ministry of National Education. Refresher courses and in-service training as well as initial training courses for new recruits of each technical or professional service are organised by the department concerned, such as the nursing schools of the Medical Department; the P & T schools of the Posts and Telegraph Department; the warders' training courses for the prisons services of the Ministry of Territorial Administration; the police training colleges and military training centres of the Ministry of Armed Forces; the agricultural schools of the Ministry of Agriculture; the clerical school courses of the Ministry of Public Service; accounting courses and store clerks' courses of the Ministry of Finance; the National School of Administration and Magistracy (ENAM) of the Ministry of Public Service; the Survey School of the Lands and Survey Department; the Institute of Sports of the Ministry of Youths and Sports; the medical technicians' courses for the medical services; the Co-operative School of the Ministry of Agriculture. There are also various forms of group and individual apprenticeships giving vocational training outside the normal school system, for example, driving schools.

III ADMINISTRATION

Outline Organisation of the Ministry of National Education
The Ministry of National Education, one of nineteen ministries in the government of the United Republic of Cameroon, is responsible for all education services except those which come under the Ministry of Youths and Sports and some of those designated non-formal education.

It is headed by a minister assisted by a vice-minister, each of whom has his own secretariat. The civil service head of the ministry is the secretary-general who is responsible to the two ministers.

The general secretariat runs the central services of the ministry, the central administration of the professional departments and the provincial offices of the ministry.

The central services are as follows:

Inspectorate-General of Pedagogy
Educational Planning and Development and School Equipment
School Building
Scholarships
Extra-Mural Activities
Documentation
University and School Health Services
Translation.

The central administration is organised in seven departments each under a director, as follows:

(1) The Department of General Administration, dealing with personnel, finance and other administrative matters;

(2) The Department of Higher Education, dealing with the teaching and research activities of institutions of higher education and planning new institutions; it also provides a service for the evaluation of qualifications;

(3) the Department of Secondary Education, responsible for the establishment and administration of government schools (lycées) and other government secondary schools which offer a general education, colleges d'enseignement secondaire (CESs) and colleges d'enseignement général (CEGs); it also provides professional services for teachers and deals with personnel matters;

(4) the Department of Secondary Technical Education, responsible for the establishment and administration of government technical schools which include lycées techniques, collèges d'enseignement technique, sections artisanales rurales and écoles et sections ménagères; it also provides professional services for teachers and deals with personnel matters;

(5) the Department of Primary and Nursery Education, responsible for the establishment and administration of government primary and nursery schools; it provides correspondence courses and other professional services for teachers and deals with personnel matters;

(6) the Department of Examinations, responsible for all examinations, qualifying and competitive, in the republic;

(7) the Department of Private Education, responsible for the control of private education in all its aspects, finance, administration, inspection, opening and closure of private institutions and provision of the appropriate services.

The Work of the Ministry in the Provinces

In the headquarters of each province (Yaoundé, Douala, Buea, Bafoussam, Bamenda, Garona and Bertona) the ministry is represented by a provincial delegate who is supported by an assistant delegate and sub-delegates. His duties are to administer and co-ordinate all educational activities and to keep the minister fully informed on every aspect of education in the province. The Provincial Delegation has four main sections:

General Administration and Finance
Planning, Statistics and Development

Examinations
Professional Matters.

In provinces with difficult communications or extensive areas, sub-delegations have been created to serve groups of divisions or districts within a provincial delegation.

In each of the forty administrative divisions of the republic there is an inspectorate of primary and nursery education under a divisional inspector. In order to deal on the spot with the problems of difficult or large divisions a total of forty-eight sub-inspectorates of primary education have been established throughout the republic.

The Administration of Educational Establishments

Administration within a primary or nursery school is entrusted to a headmaster or headmistress appointed by the Minister of National Education. The headmaster or headmistress supervises the staff of the school to ensure that everybody does his duty, that the children are learning in a suitable environment and that school property is safe.

At the second level of education (secondary grammar school, secondary technical school, secondary commercial school and teacher training college) the administrative responsibility is entrusted to a principal (proviseur in the case of a lycée and directeur in the case of other colleges) assisted by a vice-principal (censeur), a bursar (intendant), a discipline master (surveillant-général) and a stores accountant.

At the level of higher education each faculty of the university is under a dean of the faculty (doyen) assisted by a vice-dean and a secretary-general of the faculty. In the case of the other establishments of the university each school or institute is administered by a director assisted by a director of studies (directeur des études) and a secretary-general. The central administration of the university rests with the Chancellor, the Vice-Chancellor and the Secretary-General who are *ex officio* members of the Administrative Council. Its members include the deans of the faculties, the directors of schools and institutes of the university and heads of departments. The Administrative Council of the university in turn constitutes part of the Council of Higher Education and Scientific Research.

IV CONTROL

Pedagogical Control

In so far as nursery, primary and secondary education are concerned, the Inspector-General of Pedagogy in the Ministry of National Education, assisted by national inspectors of each discipline and level (for example, national inspectors for English and for mathematics, national inspectors of nursery education), inspects the schools and colleges regularly, advises the teachers, writes reports and re-inspects to ensure that the right subject-matter is being taught in the right manner. In this way both content and method are kept under control. Syllabuses and schemes of work are sometimes so detailed that the same lesson takes place at the same time everywhere.

The Inspectorate-General of Pedagogy is charged with drawing up syllabuses and teaching methods for the various subjects, and the Inspector-General of Pedagogy has a duty to co-ordinate the work of all the national inspectors and render accounts thereof to the Secretary-General, the Vice-Minister and the Minister of National Education.

In addition, there are in each provincial delegation of education advisers (conseillers pédagogiques provinciaux) and divisional inspectors who assist the national inspectors and through whom they pass their instructions and directives to the schools and colleges. The head of each establishment also has a duty to control content and method in his school or college.

As far as the University of Yaoundé and its schools and institutes are concerned, there is a system of internal control operated by its deans and heads of departments and some of the examinations are supervised by external examiners.

Control of Private Education
The Directorate of Private Education in the Ministry of National Education is specifically charged with the control of private education, and only those teachers specifically authorised by the minister may teach. It controls the opening, the running and the closure of schools and colleges. It sends out inspection teams to schools and colleges in order to keep content and method under control as well as to ensure their proper running. It controls the distribution and utilisation of government subventions paid to private education. There is also a National Commission for Private Education which classifies private educational establishments for purposes of government subventions, fixes the rates of school fees chargeable in private schools and colleges and advises the minister on various aspects of private education.

Control of the Meagre Resources Available for Education
Education is an important social service but also such a consuming service that, if left unchecked, it could easily consume all the national resources at the expense of all other services. So the budgetary provision available in the annual government estimates sets limits to what can be spent on education.

Besides the finance offices in the General Administration Department of the Ministry of Education, the Ministry of Finance has installed within the Ministry of National Education an office of the Controller of Finance whose staff vigilantly keep every aspect of educational spending under control.

Control of Rights, Functions and Powers

Authority to act in educational matters has been conferred on certain officials by various legal instruments and administrative instructions. Thus since the constitution has provision for education the President of the Republic appoints the Minister of National Education by a presidential decree which confers on the person so appointed certain rights, functions and powers as far as policy, organisation, administration and control of education are concerned. Another presidential decree may remove the Minister of National Education at any time the head of state considers it necessary in the interest of the nation to do so. Senior officials of the ministry are appointed by the President or by the Prime Minister on the recommendation of the minister. These too can be relieved of their posts at any time as long as the same legal procedure which was used to appoint them is employed. By ministerial arrêtés, the Minister of National Education appoints principals of colleges and headmasters of primary schools, and by the same instrument can change them at any time, thereby keeping things constantly under his control. The control at every stage is therefore two-dimensional, for one must be legally invested with the authority for action in a given capacity, and one's hierarchical superiors must be satisfied with output, performance and conduct.

Control of Various Educational Activities

From time to time the Ministry of National Education issues circulars, arrêtés and decisions to control various aspects of public and private education, such as the hours of attendance, school terms, minimum staff requirement, mode of supervision, discipline, movements of staff, manual labour and new syllabuses.

V CURRICULUM

Bi-Culturalism and the Curriculum in Cameroon

By reason of its bi-cultural situation, the first priority of Cameroon in the field of education is inescapably the harmonisation of its inherited English and French systems of education into a distinctly Cameroonian national system of education. Until harmonisation is accomplished the two systems will remain, and it will not be possible to talk about a 'Cameroon system of education'.

The Traditional Curriculum

The traditional curriculum from the nursery school right up to the university can be summed up as follows:

(1) In the nursery schools the curriculum consisted of musical education and physical education.
(2) At the level of the primary school the curriculum consisted of the three Rs, preparing the pupils for a white-collar job and not for a blue-collar job.
(3) The secondary school curriculum was bookish, offering a classical education or literary studies in arts and science subjects in preparation for such examinations as the GCE and the Baccalauréat, the Probatoire and the Brevet.
(4) At the level of higher education the university offered purely academic studies, predominantly in letters and law, with little attention to sciences, and no room at all for technology.

The Tyranny of Examinations

The traditional curriculum from primary school to university was inspired and sustained by the various bookish examinations leading to the coveted certificates, which counted more than anything else in the employment market and determined the economic and social status of their possessors. This state of affairs could not last for ever since the economy of the country increasingly proved incapable of absorbing the products of the educational system. Ways and means had to be found to mitigate the tyranny of the examinations and gradually replace the unprofitable aspects of the classical or bookish type of education with practical education adapted to the needs of Cameroon.

The Cameroon Curriculum Centres

Three separate curriculum research centres working together in close liaison, with each carrying out a clearly defined curriculum research assignment, exist in Cameroon to evolve new curricula geared to the goals of the new reforms in Cameroon education. IPAR Yaoundé (Institut de Pédagogie Appliquée à Vocation Rurale), established in 1967, is devoted to primary education reforms in the Francophone zone of Cameroon, while IPAR Buea, created in 1973, is concerned with reforms in primary education in the Anglophone zone. CNE Yaoundé (Centre National de l'Education), created in 1973 as Institut National de l'Education, is concerned with the reform of secondary and higher education, the co-ordination of the work of the two IPAR establishments and harmonisation.

IPAR Yaoundé has since its inception been training new rural teachers, retraining existing teachers, working out new syllabuses, producing school textbooks, introducing various teaching aids and running some 290 experimental classes where research findings relating to content and method of teaching are tried out. IPAR Buea has just completed the first phase of its research on the Anglophone system of education and new syllabuses are now being drawn up to introduce desirable changes in the primary schools and training colleges. CNE Yaoundé (formerly INE Yaoundé) is now preoccupied with research for reforming the whole national system of education, from nursery to university.

The Seminars on the Reform of Education in Cameroon

Apart from the work of the three curriculum centres on reform of education in Cameroon, there have been three important seminars which have established the national objectives for the curriculum innovations. The first of these seminars, sponsored by UNESCO and other multilateral and bilateral funding agencies, took place in Cameroon in March 1973 and concentrated on primary education. The second took place in December 1974 and it involved an intensive one-week working session of the Council for Higher Education and Scientific and Technical Research, in which far-reaching decisions were taken on the reform of higher education in Cameroon. The third seminar, sponsored by the Cameroon government, took place in April 1977. Thus the national objectives, the learning experience and the operational processes called for by the proposed reforms have already been established, ready for application.

Main Features of the New Curriculum for Cameroon

The reforms aim at applying the notions of 'functionalism' and 'practicality' to the whole educational system, thus adapting the educational system to the economic or production system of the country. The three-dimensional reform aims to achieve the following:

(1) to harmonise the two inherited systems of education;
(2) to replace the unprofitable aspects of the classical or bookish type of education with practical education adapted to the Cameroon milieu;
(3) to evolve an educational system which puts into the hands of its products the practical know-how for earning an independent livelihood without recourse to, or expectation of, white-collar jobs.

Thus the new primary curriculum now being evolved emphasises functional literacy in the lower classes and rudimentary vocationalisation in the higher classes. The natural learning process is and must be one of experimenting, doing things, discovering new knowledge and learning from real life rather than memorising encyclopaedic facts. At the secondary level the emphasis is on vocationalisation in order to attain self-reliance as well as produce intermediary manpower. Primary and secondary school leavers who do not go further with their education should at least be agents of production capable of transforming their environment to give themselves a better life. At the level of higher education the reform emphasises the professionalisation of university degrees, the extensive expansion of scientific studies, the establishment of technological and commercial studies and the creation of a university of technology in Cameroon.

Problems of the Cameroon Curriculum

Of the many problems besetting the Cameroon curriculum development projects the following three call for special mention.

(1)   Cameroon's bi-cultural situation at once raises the problems of bilingualism, and the situation becomes more disconcerting in a pluralistic society where a *lingua franca* or local language of instruction cannot easily be chosen from among the two hundred vernacular languages, dialects not included. Cameroon is, therefore, forced to use as its medium of instruction two foreign languages imposed by the country's historical and political past. What are the possibilities of future curriculum development overcoming this problem?

(2)   There is a scarcity of suitable books to cope with the innovative curriculum; those textbooks which are available rapidly become obsolescent; and there is a lack of competent textbook writers to reflect the true spirit of the reform.

(3)   There is a need for constant formative and summative evaluation of the curriculum in terms of objectives, learning experiences, operational processes and outcomes. What machinery must now be built into the system to make systematic curriculum development and evaluation an ongoing process?

VI FINANCE

The Finances of Education in General

In the school year 1976/7 the government recurrent expenditure on education, excluding the university which has an autonomous budget, amounted to 11·6 milliard francs CFA which represents about one-eighth of the national budget amounting to 90·9 milliard francs CFA. The budget of the university for the same period amounted to 3,699,300,000 francs CFA. The total government recurrent expenditure (excluding capital expenditure of 2,658,300,000 francs) for the education service from nursery to university for the year 1976/7 was therefore 15,356,672,000 francs CFA, which constitutes 4 per cent of the GNP.

Whereas it is extremely difficult to ascertain per student costs borne by parents, guardians and students themselves for various items such as transport to school, feeding, lodging, pocket money, clothing, private coaching, books and other school equipment, it is possible to establish the per student costs paid from public funds in government establishments. In the school year 1976/7 the per student costs per annum to government, in government establishments, were around 8,000 francs CFA per primary and nursery school pupil; 80,000 francs per secondary school student; 95,000 francs per secondary technical school student; 488,000 francs per student in teacher training colleges; and 500,000 francs per university student. In private education the per student costs paid for by government subventions amounted to 3,500 francs per primary school pupil and 14,500 francs per secondary school pupil.

Educational Spending by Departments and by Levels of Education
Almost 80 per cent of the budget for education is spent on personal emoluments, about 10 per cent of it goes for running expenses, while the remaining 10 per cent goes for scholarships, maintenance of buildings and miscellaneous expenses (see Table 2.1).

Table 2.1   *Education Budget Distribution for the School Year 1976/7*

Department	Thousand Francs CFA
Primary and nursery education	357,614
Secondary education	34,825
Secondary technical education	62,457
Higher education	24,013
Examinations	105,440
General administration	276,993
Private education	29,715
Provincial delegations including teachers' salaries	8,863,764
General secretariat of the ministry	1,184,647
Ministers' secretariats	42,167
BIRD project office	4,130
Scholarship and sundry expenses	600,000

Although an attempt has been made to show how much expenditure goes into primary education, technical education, secondary education and higher education, there is a great deal of overlapping since there are many common services. The Department of General Administration handles the running expenses in respect of all the other departments; the Inspectorate-General of Pedagogy serves all levels of education; the same provincial delegate of national education and his colleagues may invigilate the university entrance examination in the province, inspect secondary schools and hold conferences with primary and nursery schoolteachers on the same day. In the circumstances the expenditure figures for each level are unrealistic, even though they serve to indicate the general trends of educational spending.

For the school year 1976/7 scholarships for Cameroon students studying abroad amounted to 284,600,000 francs CFA, while local scholarships for government secondary schools, government technical colleges, private secondary schools and teacher training colleges amounted to 469,912,000 francs CFA.

Educational Spending on Higher Education in Cameroon

In the school year 1976/7 about a quarter of overall spending on education went into higher education where a total sum of 3,699,300,000 francs CFA was spent, of which common central services cost 660,139,000 francs CFA, the three faculties (of letters, law and sciences) cost 748,892,000 francs CFA, the six professional schools and institutes cost 885,842,000 francs CFA, scholarships within the University of Yaoundé amounted to 1,344,427,000 francs CFA, while a sum of 59,765,000 francs CFA was devoted to research within the university. By comparison with the university's expenditure for the preceding academic year 1975/6 there was an increase of over 12 per cent in the 1976/7 academic year.

Government Subventions to Private Education

Apart from school fees and any other means by which private education may raise funds to pay its way, government subventions to private education for the running of primary and nursery education amounted to 1,625,461,050 francs CFA in 1976/7 while a further sum of 368,132,000 francs CFA was paid to the 125 private secondary schools in the republic. Total government spending on private secondary education was thus 22·7 per cent of government spending on private primary education.

It is noteworthy that of the government subventions to primary education, the two Anglophone provinces got 48·9 per cent of the total subvention while the five Francophone provinces got 51·1 per cent (830,481,431 francs) and of the secondary schools subventions the two Anglophone provinces got 39·2 per cent (144,325,000 francs) while the five Francophone provinces got 60·8 per cent (223,807,000 francs). The

Table 2.2   *Percentage Enrolments, 1976/7*

Level	Government	Private
Nursery	49·9	50·1
Primary	59·3	40·7
Secondary	47·8	52·2
Secondary technical	33·9	66·1

historical reason for this apparent disproportionate allocation of the subvention is that the former grants-in-aid system of the two Anglophone provinces has been taken into consideration.

School fees are not charged in government schools, nor in government colleges and the university. From Table 2.2 it can be seen that by combining school fees with government subventions private schools and colleges have the financial resources to make a substantial contribution to enrolments at all levels of education except at the higher education level.

APPENDIX: ANNUAL STATISTICS OF PUPILS AND TEACHERS IN SCHOOLS, 1969/70 TO 1978/9

(a) Primary

School Year	No. of Pupils	No. of Teachers
1969/70	889,060	—
1970/1	923,234	13,914[1]
1971/2	930,131	14,703[1]
1972/3	967,561	19,813
1973/4	1,014,135	19,719
1974/5	1,074,021	20,803
1975/6	1,122,900	22,209
1976/7	1,146.582	23,029
1977/8	1,202,841	24,046
1978/9	1,246,127[2]	24,923[2]

Notes:
1 These figures do not include North-West and South-West Provinces.
2 Projected figures for the 1978/9 school year.
Source: Annuaire Statistique for the corresponding school years.

(b) Secondary General

School Year	No. of Students	No. of Teachers
1969/70	48,131	1,724[1]
1970/1	56,031	1,922[1]
1971/2	65,360	2,719
1972/3	72,540	2,988
1973/4	82,205	3,322
1974/5	93,934	3,699
1975/6	106,266	3,309
1976/7	121,054	4,318
1977/8	135,518	4,728
1978/9	145,930[2]	—

Notes:
1 These figures do not include the North-West and South-West Provinces.
2 Projected figures for the 1978/9 school year.
Source: Annuaire Statistique for the corresponding school years.

(c) Secondary Technical

School Year	No. of Students	No. of Teachers
1969/70	15,782	673[1]
1970/1	17,400	770[1]
1971/2	19,244	950
1972/3	22,771	1,017
1973/4	24,352	1,038
1974/5	27,524	1,240
1975/6	31,135	1,395
1976/7	35,601	1,545
1977/8	40,376	1,681
1978/9	48,470[2]	—

Notes:
1 These figures do not include the North-West and South-West Provinces.
2 Projected figures for the 1978/9 school year.
Source: Annuaire Statistique for the corresponding school years.

(d) Teacher Training

School Year	No. of Students	No. of Teachers
1972/3	2,021	201
1973/4	1,452	158
1974/5	1,115	130
1975/6	1,284	110
1976/7	1,572	162
1977/8	1,712	144
1978/9	—	—

Source: Annuaire Statistique for the corresponding school years.

(e) Higher Education

School Year	No. of Students	No. of Teachers
1969/70	1,909	210
1970/1	2,575	220
1971/2	3,334	284
1972/3	4,484	328
1973/4	5,533	356
1974/5	6,171	—
1975/6	7,187	376
1976/7	8,207	367
1977/8	10,001	—
1978/9	—	—

Source: Annuaire Statistique for the corresponding school years.

Chapter 3

Education in Egypt

ABDELAZIZ SOLIMAN

I HISTORICAL BACKGROUND

Historical reviews of education in Egypt usually start with the pioneering work of Mohamed Aly, who came to Egypt first as a leader of the Osmani Empire troops to expel the French who were occupying Egypt at that time.

Mohamed proved a great success and was appointed governor of Egypt in 1805. As governor of a country just liberated from foreign rule, Mohamed realised the need for a very strong army including engineers, physicians and technical specialists to back up the infantry. He also realised the need for a sound educational system to prepare the professionals and specialists needed in the army. Consequently, Mohamed opened primary schools, high schools and various institutes. Educational committees were also set up and in 1836 one of these committees decided that the aim of primary education in Egypt was to disseminate the essentials of science among the people. In other words, right from the very beginning science education was highly valued and encouraged in the Egyptian educational system.

In pursuance of this emphasis on science education experimental centres were set up in different parts of the country. In 1843 Rifaa El-Tahtawy, a scientist of Al-Azhar, a religious university, began to implement the idea of popular education of the Western type. Governor Abbas, who succeeded Mohamed Aly in 1849, was opposed to Western education and he closed all the educational centres opened by his predecessor. This anti-education policy of Governor Abbas was also followed by the next governor, Said (1854–63). During this period the whole educational system was destroyed.

In 1882 came the Orabi National Revolution and Egypt was occupied by the British. This occupation awakened national interest in education and as a result the idea of popular education, abandoned in 1849, re-emerged in 1886. Henceforth literacy was made a requirement for any person aspiring to be a member of the parliament. The parliament issued some decrees which spelt out the true meaning of popular education. Some of the issues highlighted in the decrees included:

(1) The goal of primary education is not to prepare officers but to educate and enlighten people.

(2)   Primary education is a national obligation and the government
       should be the sole organisation responsible for its supervision and
       carrying its financial obligation.

Ali Mobarak (the so-called father of education in Egypt) issued the
'Ragab' regulations which ensured the necessity of spreading education
among the people. Ali encouraged the founding of public schools under
the supervision of the government. Many societies, including some
political ones, founded national schools to spread education among the
people (for example, the Society of Arts in 1871). Schools established by
foreign organisations (European or American) totalling 160 and
enrolling 5,591 pupils were put under the supervision of the government.

In 1880 education laws were issued on the suggestion of Aly Ibrahim,
chief of the Education Commission. Also in 1880 the certificate system
was introduced for the first time to ensure promotion and improvement
of education. The Certificate for General Education, introduced in
1887, was awarded upon the completion of secondary school.

During the British occupation of Egypt (1882–1922) the European or
Western system of education was introduced into the country – a system
which aimed at spreading the English culture. English was used as the
medium of instruction. All subjects except Arabic language and religion
were taught in English. Consequently, schools employed a great number
of English teachers.

During the same period very little expansion of education took place.
Despite the increase in the population of the country – from 7 million in
1882 to 11 million in 1907 – very few new schools were founded. The
British administration at the time of the occupation also cancelled free
education and tuition fees were charged at all levels. This prevented
poor people from going to school. Furthermore, jobs were limited to
certificate holders. In general, the administration of education became
very strict, whereas England during the same period had an open and
liberal educational policy.

Great changes in the educational system began to occur in 1906 with
the appointment of Saad Zaghloul as Minister of Education.
Improvement in the provision of educational facilities was achieved by
increasing government spending on education. For example, the
education share of the budget rose from 0·7 per cent in 1890 to 3 per cent
in 1910. Arabic replaced English as the medium of instruction and
partial free education was introduced. Completely free primary
education was implemented in 1944 and secondary education became
free as from 1950. With the independence of Egypt in 1922 great
developments in education took place. Compulsory education was
implemented in 1925/26 and 762 schools were opened during that
period. By 1947 primary school enrolment had risen to 750,000.
However, it should be pointed out that popular education which was

made free and compulsory proved in the long run unsatisfactory, as quality suffered adversely.

Experts in education, for example, Klabaried, a Swiss, and Mena in 1928, presented recommendations for improving education in Egypt. In 1940/1 attempts were made to unify the different types of primary schools and by 1951 all such schools had been unified. Two schools of thought about the education of the country emerged. One was in favour of free primary and secondary education. Dr Naguib El Hilaly, Minister of Education 1942-4, and his consultant Dr Taha Hussein, were proponents of this free education policy. Against free education was Ismail El-Kabany, Minister of Education, who thought that secondary education should be limited to the elites. In 1952 a kind of nationalist educational revolution started and educational goals began to reflect more and more the needs and aspirations of the country. The entire system became geared towards economic growth and public enlightenment. Education became public under the direct control of the government. All types of schools (except the American schools) were put under the direct supervision of the government and nine years later, in 1961, the American schools, like the others, came under direct government supervision. Henceforth, the provision of education became entirely the responsibility of the national government.

II ORGANISATION AND CONTROL

The first constitution enacted upon the country's attainment of independence in 1923 made specific references to education. Some of the provisions in the 1923 constitution included:

(1) Education should be encouraged as long as it is consistent with the national way of life.
(2) Education should be organised and regulated by law.
(3) Primary education should be compulsory and free.

In 1956 a new charter specifically for education was issued which made it the responsibility of the government to regulate and supervise the entire educational system. The government was also charged with the responsibility of ensuring that academic freedom was maintained in all educational institutions.

In 1964 another charter, meant to be tentative, was promulgated. The charter among other provisions, emphasised that equal chances should be given to everybody throughout the entire educational system including university education which from that date was made free. When a new charter was promulgated in 1971 most of the provisions in the 1964 charter were ratified. Additionally the independence of the universities and research centres was established. The drive towards literacy was made a national obligation.

The year 1957 saw the establishment of a National Planning Organisation to study the needs of the country, to delineate the responsibilities of the different ministries and to be responsible for the five-year national development plans that were issued later. The first of such plans was issued in 1960, providing for:

(1)   enrolment of all children aged 6–12 in the country's primary schools;
(2)   differentiation in secondary education to meet students' capacities;
(3)   expansion in technical education to meet the manpower requirements of the nation;
(4)   improvement of standards and quality of education.

All educational matters were to be controlled by law and the national government was vested with the sole responsibility for organising and controlling education.

III   ADMINISTRATION

The administration of education, including supervision, is the responsibility of the national government through appropriate agencies headed by the Ministry of Education.

The ministerial system was instituted as far back as 1837 and it has existed ever since under different names. Over the years the Ministry of Education has undergone several changes designed to make it more efficient.

In 1962 the functions and authority of the ministry were properly defined and it was made responsible for all types of pre-university education. Specifically, the ministry

(1)   ensures that every child reaching the age of 6 enrols in a primary school, and
(2)   reviews the educational system in order to satisfy the requirements of the Economic Development Plan, particularly in the area of manpower supply.

The Ministry of Education now delegates some of its administrative responsibilities to the provincial councils.

Departments exist to take charge of specific aspects of education as follows:

(1) primary education and teachers' colleges
(2) preparatory and secondary education
(3) technical education
(4) central services and foreign relations
(5) administration and finance.

For each of these areas the department is responsible for planning and organisation as well as for school building, curricula, books, various pupil activities and examinations.

The Ministry of Education is headed by a minister appointed by the President. The minister as the legislative head of the ministry is responsible for all high-level appointments within it, including the administrative and professional staff. He represents the ministry in the Parliament. He is assisted in the day-to-day running of the ministry by highly qualified consultants. His immediate subordinate is the under-secretary of state appointed by the President himself on the recommendation of the minister.

Almost all administrative matters are dealt with by the under-secretary. However, endorsement of their decisions by the minister is essential for such decisions to have effect and government backing.

Directors-general rank third after the under-secretaries and the minister. A director heads each of the departments of the ministry – primary, preparatory and secondary. Directors are appointed by the minister on the recommendation of the under-secretary of state for the particular section or department concerned. They are chosen from among the highly qualified supervisors who show evidence of exemplary efficiency. They are responsible for planning and supervising all educational matters in their department. Decisions of the directors have to be endorsed by the under-secretary of state concerned for such decisions to be effective.

Supervisors responsible for specific areas of education come next to the directors. The position of supervisor has existed since 1868 and their functions were redefined in the 1883 decree. The entire supervisory system was thoroughly overhauled in 1943 when fresh thought was directed to its role which was changed to that of a guide – to direct and lead in addition to supervising.

The supervisory section of the ministry has undergone remarkable changes over the years, especially since the introduction of the local government system in 1962. Since 1969 senior supervisors have been appointed as professional and subject-matter consultants. They have become the essential planners, responsible for developing curricula, teaching techniques, teachers' preparation and training and for books and examinations. These consultants constitute the highest professional group of the Education Ministry. Their responsibilities were outlined in the 1969 ministerial decree as follows:

(1) setting up committees to study curricula and books;
(2) initiating and strengthening relations with organisations responsible for developing instructional materials and methods of teaching within universities and research centres;
(3) suggesting studies and applied experiments needed for the purpose of developing and modifying curricula;
(4) solving educational problems in their field of concern.

Various experiments have been made with administrative procedures to include the involvement of local government bodies, educational research centres, colleges and institutions for the purpose of improving administration.

At the grassroots level every school has its own administrative body headed by the headmaster and composed of senior members of staff. Selected people from among the pupils' parents form an advisory body. The school administration determines needs, controls school finances, chooses areas of innovation in the school curriculum and buildings and maintains positive teacher–parent and school–home relationships. In carrying out these functions the school enjoys government approval and obtains sanction through the provincial education offices.

IV FINANCE

The role education plays, or the role education should play, in national development is well recognised in Egypt. This recognition is reflected in the country's annual budget of which education takes the greatest proportion. The huge educational expenditure is understandable because the provision of educational facilities such as buildings, equipment and teachers' salaries costs a considerable amount of money. On average, education consumes between 4 and 5 per cent of the national annual income. Teachers' salaries take the largest share – between 60 and 80 per cent of the total budget for education. Of the various educational levels, primary education takes the greatest share of the budget. The educational budget in Egypt has been increasing yearly

Table 3.1   *Increase in Education Budget in Egypt, 1968–73*

Academic Year	Educational Budget in £E.	Total Country Budget in £E.
1967/8	89,379,000	—
1968/9	96,254,000	—
1969/70	104,780,700	706,742,100
1970/1	107,215,000	760,298,600
1971/2	111,937,400	838,334,000
1972/3	126,577,678	—

since 1968. This increase in the annual education budget is shown in Table 3.1.

An examination of the government's expenditure on education reveals a considerable loss in the process of financing education. This loss takes different forms, the most prominent being the high drop-out rate of pupils at different stages of education, particularly during the primary stage. Drop-outs are more obvious in the rural areas than in the cities due to environmental circumstances.

The decrease in the productivity level of the school, that is, lower standards, is also generally considered an educational loss. This is because the performances of school graduates in terms of efficiency and scholarship do not justify the expense of their education.

V PRIMARY EDUCATION

One of the provisions in the First Five-Year Development Plan (1960–4) was for the expansion of primary education facilities to ensure places for all children of school age, which was fixed at 6 years, for a course of six years. Thus children aged 6–12 were expected in the primary schools.

The Development Plan also expected all school-age children to be in schools by 1970. This plan for 100 per cent enrolment by 1970 was to be pursued in stages: 69 per cent enrolment in 1960/1, 87·3 per cent in 1965 and 100 per cent in 1970. The enrolment plan was based on an estimated yearly population increase of 2·1 per cent. Unfortunately, this estimate was lower than the actual increase of 2·4 per cent in the 1960s. School-age children in 1970 numbered 103,800 more than the projected estimate for the same year. Consequently, the expected 100% primary school enrolment could not be realised in 1970.

In the Second Five-Year Development Plan (1965–70) the emphasis was not only on quantity, that is, expansion of education. The concern was to set up an educational system best suited for rapid economic development, particularly for meeting the country's high-level manpower needs. The Second Five-Year Plan also paid attention to primary education in the rural areas where there was hitherto very little

Table 3.2   *Enrolment in the Provinces, 1975*

Province	Actual Enrolment (%)	Shortfall (%)
Matrough	56·6	43·4
Souhag	59·1	40·9
Kenna	60·2	39·8
Behaira	60·5	39·5
Assint	66·0	34·0
Minyia	66·1	33·9

appreciation of education in general. None of the provinces achieved the expected enrolment target (see figures in Table 3.2).

The 1967 war against Israel greatly affected the execution of the Second Five-Year Plan. School enrolment fell to 71·9 per cent in 1967/8. This percentage increased gradually at the rate of 2 per cent annually in the years following.

VI CURRICULUM

Primary school education is under the direct control and supervision of the Ministry of Education which through its appropriate departments decides curriculum issues. Primary education is free except in the private schools which charge fees. These are mostly the ones that teach foreign languages – English or French.

The primary school curriculum is very broad, consisting of a good number of subjects in the Arts and Science. Language, that is, the national language, Arabic, is the most prominent. Mathematics, arts and drawing come next in that order of importance. Science and public health receive less attention, while history and geography occupy the least time. However, all the subjects mentioned above are taught throughout the primary school years.

Foreign languages are not taught in the government schools. This is because of the emphasis placed on the national language, Arabic. However, private schools have permission to teach any foreign language in addition to the national language.

Criticisms of primary education have always centred on the noticeable fall in standards. Others have criticised primary education for not keeping pace with the country's socioeconomic development and life outside the school. The schools, it has been alleged, alienate the pupils from their homes. The level of education in general is far below the expected standard and this fall in standards is usually attributed to the increase in the number of pupils enrolled in schools. It has been observed that the numbers of pupils enrolled are far beyond the capacity of the schools, thereby sacrificing standards for the sake of numbers. Furthermore, the pupil teacher ratio has been increasing annually as shown in Table 3.3.

Table 3.3   *Pupil/Teacher Ratio, 1953–5, 1966–9*

Academic Year	Pupil/Teacher Ratio
1953/4	30·3
1954/5	36·6
1966/7	39·6
1967/8	39·7
1968/9	40·9

Poor school facilities inappropriate textbooks and the curriculum content are other causes of low standards in the primary school. The poor quality of the teaching force is another factor generally identified as the cause of lower standards in the country's primary schools.

VII THE PREPARATORY SCHOOLS

The preparatory stage of three years was introduced in 1953 as an intermediate stage between primary and secondary education. Pupils enter preparatory schools, which have an age-range of 12–15 years, after successful completion of primary education. The Third Five-Year Development Plan (1970–5) extended the period of compulsory education to include the preparatory stage. Consequently there was a sharp increase in the enrolment of these schools, which were unable to expand sufficiently to accept all those who completed primary education. Many pupils were forced to terminate schooling upon the completion of primary education. In fact, until recently, only a quarter of the pupils finishing primary education found places in the preparatory schools.

As with the primary schools, there are a few private preparatory schools which charge fees but the majority are government-owned and do not charge fees.

The curriculum is narrow and theoretical. However, it is encouraging to note the large proportion of time devoted to the following subjects:

Science	11·1%
Mathematics	13·8%
Foreign language	16·7%.

The pupil-teacher ratio is very high – it rose to 37·1 in the 1968/9 school year. The optimum pupil teacher ratio recommended for this level is 25·1 or 30·1 at the highest.

The major problems facing the preparatory schools can be summarised as follows:

(1) The inadequacy of the number of schools results in many primary school graduates not finding places.
(2) The curriculum is narrow.
(3) There is lack of provision for choice of subjects–all pupils study the same subjects.
(4) Most of the subjects taught in the schools are not related to actual life in the society.
(5) The preparatory schools are poorly equipped. For example, pupils cannot carry out any of the experiments in science lessons because

of inadequate laboratory facilities. Consequently, most of the experiments are done on a demonstration basis by the teacher.

VIII   SECONDARY EDUCATION

Secondary education was of six years duration prior to 1953, when the preparatory stage of three years duration was introduced and secondary education was reduced to three years. It is free.

Admission of students into the secondary schools is very competitive as only about 8 per cent of qualified primary school leavers are accepted. There has been a longstanding debate whether to expand secondary school facilities to permit more entrants, or whether to keep the facilities as they are, thereby restricting entrants and perpetuating an elite system.

Dr. Taha Hussein, for example, suggested secondary school expansion to take in all pupils who complete the preparatory school. On the other hand, Ismael El-Kabany, the under-secretary of state (and later Minister of Education), and Dr Abdel-Aziz El-Kousy, consultant to the Ministry of Education, opted for a controlled system in secondary school enrolment. They were against any move to increase secondary school intake without concern, first of all, for standards and facilities. Quality before quantity was their educational slogan.

Proponents of controlled enrolment got their chance when Ismael El-Kabany became Minister of Education. The concept of popular education gave way to a competitive and selective system. During this period of El-Kabany's ministerial authority only the very few pupils considered intellectually capable of academic study up to university level were accepted into the secondary schools.

Requirements for entry included success at the preparatory school certificate examination, and an age not exceeding 18 years at the beginning of the academic year in which admission was sought.

Subjects studied in the secondary school include:

religion
two foreign languages
mathematics
sciences
social sciences
philosophy
sociology
home economics
military training
arabic society and socialism
political and applied technical and cultural subjects
    which vary according to local environment.

All the subjects are offered in the first year of secondary education but in the second and third years the sciences are separated from the arts, with students specialising according to their choice, capacity and potential. The grouping of subjects into arts and sciences affects only the general academic secondary schools, not the technical secondary schools which offer practical and applied subjects. Usually science enrolments exceed those in the arts section.

Language teaching in the secondary schools is emphasised. In the first year only English is taught. In the second and third years the science pupils continue to study English as a single foreign language while pupils in the arts section study one other foreign language in addition to English. Usually the second foreign language for the arts pupils is French, introduced in the second year and continued in the third year. However, there is an option of German or Italian, though these are very seldom chosen by the pupils.

Language teaching occupies 30 per cent of the timetable in the second year while it extends to about 33·3 per cent in the third year in the arts section. In the science section it is only 12 per cent in the second year and 16·6 per cent in the third year.

Problems facing secondary education are:

(1) Limited openings for new intakes: there are not sufficient places for all those who complete preparatory education.
(2) A kind of academic discrimination perpetuated by the technical general secondary school differentiation: ample provision and encouragement is given to general secondary school pupils to enter universities while the technical secondary school students are not supposed to enter them.
(3) The curricula do not adequately reflect life in the society at large.
(4) There is lack of guidance for students in terms of subjects and job openings.
(5) The poor academic performance of the students results in a good number of them being unable to gain admission to the universities. This failure to gain admission is responsible for the high drop-out rate – a major problem in the country's educational system.

IX TEACHER EDUCATION

Teachers for primary schools are recruited from those who have completed the preparatory stage of education, but some who have completed general secondary education are also admitted for a three-year as opposed to a five-year course. The first three years of the course provide a common-core curriculum after which students specialise for two years in one of the following:

(1) Arabic language and social studies
(2) science, mathematics and either home economics for girls or agriculture for boys
(3) physical education
(4) art education
(5) musical education
(6) nursery and kindergarten teaching.

The Azhar teachers' institutes aim to prepare primary school teachers who, in addition to being able to teach religious education, will have the necessary professional and cultural background to deal with children of present-day society. The qualification for admission is the completion of two years in an Azhar secondary school.

Teachers for preparatory and secondary schools are trained at higher institutes which are dealt with below. The course is of four years' duration and includes general education, professional studies and practical teaching.

X   HIGHER EDUCATION

Although higher education in Egypt follows a pattern not dissimilar to many other countries, the religious (or Azhar) institutions form a distinctive element in it. University enrolments have increased greatly of recent years. Between 1968 and 1972 there was a 50 per cent increase. About 25 per cent of the students are women.

Al-Azhar, founded in AD 970, is renowned as one of the most ancient universities of the world. Its classical, theological curriculum continued with little change until 1961 when a great modernisation programme began. It is now a remarkable combination of ancient and modern, while remaining true to the ideals of its foundation. It includes within its constitution higher institutes and colleges which provide different specialisations, for example, theology, law, science and literary studies. However, all these institutions require the study of religion in addition to specialisation and all pay primary attention to Islamic culture and the evolution of Arab civilisation.

The first modern university, now, after a number of changes of name, called Cairo University, was founded in 1908 by private initiative and funds after the British protectorate government had refused to provide financial assistance. There are now nine state universities of which five, including one technical university, were established in the early 1970s. There is one private university, the American, founded in 1919.

Admission to universities is based on the results of the national examination for the General Secondary Certificate. Students with the best results are given priority in the fields of medicine, pharmacy, dentistry, veterinary medicine, science, engineering and economics.

The first (bachelor's) degree is awarded after four years' study for most disciplines but pharmacy, dentistry, veterinary medicine and engineering require five and medicine six years. The master's degree requires two or three years' study after the first degree, the first year being spent in classwork and the second in writing a thesis. The doctorate requires two or three years' further study.

The higher institutes offer courses which also lead to first degrees equivalent to those of the universities. There are four-year courses in teaching, art, music, liberal arts and commerce and five-year courses in agriculture and scientific subjects.

Finance for higher education is provided by the government. There are not tuition fees. Grants are paid to certain classes of students.

Control is vested in the Ministry of Higher Education which is responsible for establishing policies in the light of national development goals and for drawing up and implementing plans which will lead to these goals. Its general administrative oversight of universities and higher institutes, however, excludes certain departmental (for example the Ministry of Health) training establishments and some faculties of Al-Azhar which come under the Ministry of Religious Endowments and Al-Azhar. The Supreme Council of Universities is responsible for planning and co-ordinating university education and defining education and research policies in relation to national goals. It is the co-ordinating body in matters relating to academic studies, conditions for the award of degrees, relations between academic departments and faculties and staffing questions. The council is also responsible for the distribution of funds between the universities, and for determing admission policy.

Chapter 4

Education in Ethiopia

GERMA AMARE

I INTRODUCTION

Despite its long recorded history, dating back without a break to the first century AD, Ethiopia remained isolated from the rest of the world for centuries due to its mountainous terrain which made it almost inaccessible. Only since the end of the Second World War did it effectively overcome its isolation and become an integral and effective member of the international community.

The Ethiopian population which, according to one estimate, is about 28 million, is composed of diverse groups of peoples with different languages, dialects, religions and customs. Difficulties of communication posed a formidable obstacle to contact among these groups and prevented the creation of a strong national sentiment of unity and common goal. Nevertheless trade and inter-regional wars went on through the centuries thus providing some opportunities for settlements of peoples in different regions and inter-marriages. The church laid down the basis for national culture by spreading an indigenised Christian faith which was originally introduced to Axum in AD 329. It also propagated the Amharic language via its schools. One of the important responsibilities with which the Ethiopian monarchs were charged was the preservation of the existing social order and of the national integrity and unity. On the day of their coronation they took an oath to 'maintain the orthodox religion, the land of the Empire, the integrity of the country and to support the family, the religious schools and institutions'.[1]

Centuries of isolated existence contributed to the excessive conservatism of the people and to the country's economic backwardness. The tangible as well as the intangible aspects of the Ethiopian culture remained unchallenged. Ethiopia best fits Toynbee's description of 'an arrested civilization'. Today, as in the past, agriculture is the most important industry and engages over 90 per cent of the population. It contributes significantly to the total Gross Domestic Product (GDP). In 1969, for example, agriculture's share of the total national GDP of Eth. $3,301·7 million was 56·4 per cent. The remaining 19·2 per cent and 24·4 per cent were contributed by industry and the service sectors respectively. What is more, 90 per cent of the country's export consists of agricultural products and 86 per cent of the employed labour force is engaged in agriculture.[2]

Despite the importance of agriculture, the life of those who are engaged in it is a perpetual struggle for existence at a mere subsistence level. By contrast urban dwellers enjoy a much higher per capita income than their counterparts in the agricultural sector. For example, in 1969 the per capita income of urban dwellers was over Eth. $1,509 while that of the farmer was a little over Eth. $90·00. The gap is even greater when measured in terms of cash earned by the two groups. Again for the year 1969 the monetary GDP per capita of the rural sector was only Eth. $35·3 while that of the urban sector was Eth. $479·8.[3] These figures indicate the state of abject poverty in which the overwhelming majority of the Ethiopian population lives.

II BRIEF HISTORY OF MODERN EDUCATION

The gradual emergence of the country from its state of isolation and the increasing diplomatic and military contact with Europe revealed the inadequacy of church education to meet its new demands and challenges. Ethiopia's military victory over Italy at the Battle of Adowa in 1896 taught the people that the future survival of the country depended on its readiness to accept innovations, particularly in the scientific and technological fields. Among the first to realise this was Emperor Minilik who, despite fierce opposition from the conservative forces of his court and grave financial constraints, succeeded in establishing the first state-supported modern school in 1906 which was named after him. A year later he issued a proclamation urging parents of children over 6 years of age to send them to school. Minilik's success at overcoming almost insurmountable opposition to his innovative efforts was due to his tactful approaches to them. In accordance with the wishes of the clergy he hired Coptic Christians from Egypt and Middle Eastern countries to teach in the modern schools and consented not to interfere in the church's traditional educational activities. To attract students he offered financial rewards to those who attended school. At the time of the emperor's death in 1913 four schools were in operation, in Addis Ababa, Ankober, Dessie and Harar. A department of education called the Directorate-General of Public Instruction had also been created.

Minilik's immediate successor, Emperor Eyasu (1913–16), did not show as much concern for education as his grandfather. He was too much engrossed in domestic political disputes to give sufficient attention to education and other constructive undertakings. It was only with the ascent of Tafari (later Emperor Haile Selassie I) to political prominence that modern education found its most ardent supporter. As regent he was far in advance of his time in many respects. He himself was educated by European missionaries and was among the first group of students to attend Minilik's modern school. He was also one of the few noblemen to visit Europe very early in his long political carer. These experiences no doubt made him one of the few enlightened and progressive members of the ruling nobility of his time. In his effort to carry on with Minilik's plan to spread modern education he was assisted by a small group of well-educated young Ethiopians. He reiterated Minilik's proclamation that all children should become literate and appealed to parents to send their children to school.

The opportunity for modern education was quickly seized by the poor people as a means for social betterment. They responded to the emperor's call favourably while the members of the wealthy families who were already in privileged positions disregarded it. As John Markakis rightly observes: 'The nobility of that time had little interest in education. Consequently, the majority of the first generation of educated Ethiopians have humble origins and owe their subsequent rise to their own efforts and royal favour.'[4] Within a short period many individuals from the low socioeconomic strata acquired important positions in the government and assumed growing influence in the state. The emperor, who was aware of the potential power of the new group of educated Ethiopians, succeeded in 'establishing a growing parental bond between himself and the first generation of modern educated Ethiopians'[5] in order to win for himself their loyalty and, with their support, balance the influence of the powerful traditional elite.

At the beginning of the Second Italo-Ethiopian War in 1935 some thirty government-supported modern schools were opened all over the country and had an approximate enrolment of 5,000 pupils. Most of these schools were established in the provincial capitals. As might be expected, these schools were mere copies of the European schools on which they were modelled. The books, the course of studies, the teachers and even the style of the school buildings were imported from abroad. The Coptic teachers who were brought from Egypt and Syria were no less European in their educational orientation, as they themselves had been educated in Europe and the educational systems in their own countries were also copies of European educational systems.

Much of what has been accomplished during the prewar period was destroyed by the Italians. Most of the educated were killed, the government schools were converted to Italian schools, the missionaries who were assisting the Ethiopian government in education were expelled and churches and their schools were turned into ammunition stores.

The war reinforced a lesson learnt previously by Ethiopia at the Battle of Adowa that modern education was the only guarantee of survival in a modern technological world. As a result, educational reconstruction proceeded at a relatively fast pace immediately after the end of the war in 1941 with generous assistance from Britain, the United States and other friendly countries. Within a decade it was possible to create a complete system of education from the kindergarten up to university. By 1953–4 about 412 government primary schools had been established with a total enrolment of about 62,387 students and a teaching force of 1,541 persons. In addition, eleven secondary schools and programmes (academic, commercial, technical and teacher training) were fully operational. At this time a sufficient number of high school graduates was being produced to warrant the establishment of fully fledged degree granting colleges in the country. Between 1950 and 1955 six degree-granting, autonomous colleges were established. These were the University College of Addis Ababa, the College of Engineering, the Building College, the Imperial Ethiopian College of Agriculture and Mechanical Arts, the Theological College and the College of Public Health. In 1961 all these colleges were integrated to form the Haile Selassie I University, now changed to Addis Ababa University.

From this brief historical sketch we can now proceed to examine more fully the system of education, the curricula, the teacher training programmes, financing and other related aspects of modern education in Ethiopia.

III   THE SYSTEM OF EDUCATION

The present system of education is the culmination of changes and modifications that have been introduced since 1941 in response to the changing needs and conditions of the country. From 1941 to 1948 elementary education consisted of six grades followed by four years of secondary education. A slight modification was introduced in 1948 by extending the elementary school programme from six to eight years. The addition of two years was intended to alleviate, at least momentarily, the strong public pressure the government was facing to provide secondary school places for an ever-growing number of sixth grade graduates. Pedagogical considerations also favoured the addition, for it was believed that the two extra years would give time for the further intellectual maturity that children required to cope with the demands of high school work. There was also the underlying belief, mainly held by American advisers, that every Ethiopian was entitled to eight years of elementary education as a matter of right and that the government shoud aim at providing the minimum education for all Ethiopian youth in the future.

In the later part of the 1950s a 6–2–4–4 system was adopted, which is the present system of education in Ethiopia. This consists of six years of primary education, two years of junior secondary education, four years of senior secondary education and four years of university education. Except for the primary level all instruction is given in the English language.

Although there is no fixed age of admission to school the average age for entering primary school is about 7. The medium of instruction at this level is Amharic and the textbooks and reading materials are locally produced and specially adapted to the background and experiences of the Ethiopian child by the Educational Material Production Department of the Ministry of Education.

Promotion from one grade to the next is not automatic, but is based on highly competitive examinations during and at the end of the year. For this and other reasons, such as family pressure, student unrest and unfavourable study conditions at home, the drop-out rate among primary school children is considerable. Over one-third of the students who enter grade I drop out before completing their primary education. Since a minimum of four years of formal education is required to achieve permanent literacy the majority of the drop-outs revert to illiteracy shortly after they have left school.

The Sixth Grade National Examination is the final qualifying examination administered to those who have successfully completed their primary grades. The examination constitutes the first formidable bottleneck in the educational system. Only a few students pass the examination. In the 1963 examination, for example, out of a total number of 68,164 children who sat the examination only 35,645 or 52 per cent passed. It is interesting to note that the highest number of passes were from a few educationally privileged provinces such as Shoa (16·7 per cent), Addis Ababa (21·1 per cent) and Eritrea (15·1 per cent). By contrast the underprivileged regions such as Bale and Gemu Gofa had only 1·1 per cent and 1·6 per cent of the national passes respectively. This glaring discrepancy in educational opportunity between the regions was one of the major causes of dissatisfaction with the previous regime.

No further educational opportunities are open to children who fail their examinations at this stage. Most of them are within the age-range 13–15 and come from the rural areas to which they are reluctant to return. Instead they remain in the urban centres to become shoeshiners, car cleaners, vendors or mere vagabonds. The number of such youngsters has grown considerably in the last decade and they have become one of the major threats to social stability in these areas.

Those who pass the examination enter the two-year junior high school. The Eighth Grade Leaving Certificate Examination is administered to students who have successfully completed their junior high school. As in the case with the sixth grade examination the casualty rate is very high. The failures join the low-paid labour force as office boys and junior clerks, while many enter the police and military forces as privates. Successful candidates may choose from among many alternative programmes. They may join either the general secondary schools which directly lead to the university via the Ethiopian School Leaving Certificate or one of the three vocational-technical schools: the Commercial School, the Technical School, both in Addis Ababa, and the Vocational Trade School in Asmara. The Bulgarian-supported Yared Music School and the Art School also admit talented students to their four-year courses from junior high schools.

Both the junior and senior secondary schools have, since 1961, been converted to comprehensive or multilateral schools which offer technical and vocational programmes in addition to academic studies. However, the overwhelming majority of the students enter the academic streams with the intention of going on to the university. Class promotion in the senior secondary school is decided on the term and yearly examination performances of students plus their total classwork assessment. Some students leave for other courses of study after grade XI and only a fraction complete the four-year course.

The Ethiopian School Leaving Certificate Examination is given at the end of every academic year in July to students who have successfully completed their senior high school. As indicated in Table 4.1 this examination, like the other two national examinations, is the third major bottleneck in the educational system in which a large number of students fail. Out of 5,263 students who sat for the examination in 1971 only 944 (or 17·9 per cent) passed while the pass figure in the previous year (1970) was only 827 (or 17·4 per cent) out of 4,751 students. The passes for 1969 and 1963 were 724 (or 22·2 per cent) out of 3,255 and 711 (or 24·7 per cent) out of 2,869 respectively. The great discrepancy in the pass figures for the different provinces should also be noted. In 1971, for example, 49·6 per cent of the students who passed were from Addis Ababa while only 0·2 per cent were from Gemu Gofa province. This again reflects the great variation in educational opportunities among the different provinces of the country, about which the Ethiopian government has been reminded on a number of occasions.

Up to 1965 students who passed the Ethiopian School Leaving Certificate in five subjects – Amharic, English, mathematics, science and geography or history – with 'C' average or grade point average of 2·00 were automatically admitted to the university. However, even with the high rate of failure in the ESLC the university was unable to accommodate all the passes and as a result had to raise its admission requirement to a grade point average of 2·2. This meant that a pass in the Ethiopian School Leaving Certificate Examination is no longer a qualification for automatic admission to the university. Furthermore, since the ESLC papers are prepared by the university staff and are marked by them, the level of difficulty of the papers and the standard of marking varies from year to year depending on the availability of space in the university. In order to redress the great discrepancy in the

Table 4.1 *Ethiopian School Leaving Certificate*

Province	1963 Sat	1963 Passed	1969 Sat	1969 Passed	1970 Sat	1970 Passed	1971 Sat	1971 Passed	% pass 1971
(1) Arussi	19	8	17	6	60	15	55	14	1·6
(2) Bale	—	—	20	1	25	2	21	4	0·5
(3) Begemidir	115	8	132	9	170	27	183	17	2·0
(4) Eritrea	369	96	510	137	648	59	823	123	14·2
(5) Gemu Gofa	20	1	9	2	33	2	36	2	0·2
(6) Gojjam	109	5	52	4	112	10	135	17	2·0
(7) Harar	208	33	313	29	361	35	324	60	6·9
(8) Illubabor	14	0	5	0	28	2	11	1	0·1
(9) Kaffa	34	2	49	4	86	4	73	10	1·2
(10) Shoa	261	45	272	35	450	70	509	62	7·1
(11) Addis Ababa	1,099	401	1,069	337	1,525	437	1,830	469	53·9
(12) Sidamo	56	4	55	1	87	4	91	10	1·2
(13) Tigre	146	23	172	41	231	18	254	38	4·3
(14) Wellega	28	1	30	9	52	11	86	24	2·8
(15) Wollo	49	3	49	4	207	21	246	18	2·1
Govt total	2,527	634	2,754	622	4,075	719	4,677	869	100·0
Private total	342	77	501	102	676	117	586	125	
Grand total	2,869	711	3,255	724	4,751	827	5,263	944	

Source: S. Inqui *et al.*, 'Educational opportunities', *Education Sector Review*, 8 July 1972, p. 44.

educational opportunities among the various provinces, the university has also made special provisions to accept more students from the educationally underprivileged areas by introducing a quota system.

A number of post-secondary short-term diploma and certificate programmes provide opportunities for further education to students who fail to gain admission to the university. Many students join these programmes and some even achieve admission to the university as a result of their outstanding performance. The most important post-secondary programmes include: the two-year Junior Teacher Training College in Addis Ababa, the one-year teacher training course, the two-year diploma course of the Baher-Dar Polytechnic Institute, the three-year statistics certificate and diploma courses. The university also runs a number of diploma and certificate programmes for students who fail to gain admission to the degree programmes. The Department of Technical Education offers a two-year diploma course for students who have only three passes in the Ethiopian School Leaving Certificate. Similarly, the School of Social Work, the Faculty of Business Administration, the Department of Libary Science and the College of Agriculture offer various diploma courses. The university's extension division has a variety of programmes in various areas leading to diplomas and certificates.

The degree programme of the university ranges from four to seven years. The Faculties of Arts, Education, Science, Law, Agriculture, Business, Public Health, Social Work and Theology offer four-year courses leading to bachelor's degrees. The Faculties of Architecture and Engineering offer five-year courses for the first degrees while the Faculty of Medicine offers a seven-year course for the MD degree. Student enrolment in these faculties for the academic year 1977/78 is shown in Table. 4.2.

None of the faculties offers postgraduate courses leading to masters' or doctors' degrees. This is due less to shortage of qualified staff or inadequacy of facilities than to the committment of the university to put all its resources to the production of large numbers of university-trained personnel with strong first degrees rather than disperse its energies and resources in postgraduate programmes for a few students. A large number of foreign aid programmes and government scholarships are available for outstanding students who wish to pursue postgraduate work abroad.

The university has so far produced 14,327 graduates with certificates, diplomas and degrees, including 881 graduates from the five colleges which formed Haile Selassie I University in 1962. The breakdown of this figure for the different years is shown in Table 4.3.

Many of the university graduates went abroad for higher studies and on their return some joined the teaching staff of the university with the result that within a short period the profile of the university staff which

Table 4.2   *Addis Ababa University Student Enrolment, 1977/78*

Faculty/College	i	ii	iii	iv	v	vi	Total
				Year			
Arts	—	153	84	6	—	–	243
Business		76	51	53	—	—	180
Planning and Development	—						
Administration	—	—	—	66	—	—	66
Education	111	155	78	94	—	—	438
Elementary		(13)	(11)	(15)			
Secondary		(91)	(63)	(76)			
Psychology		(5)	(4)	(3)			
Technical Teacher Education	(111)	(46)					
Law	—	47	34	15	43	—	139
Day		(47)	(19)	(15)	(23)		
Evening			(15)		(20)		
Medicine	—	11	53	27	38	5	134
Medical			(39)	(25)	(29)	(5)	
Pharmacy		(11)	(14)	(2)	(9)		
Science	—	161	86	50	—	—	297
Science		(95)	(86)	(50)			
Pre-Med.		(66)					
Social Work	—	36	19	—	—	—	55
Technology	50	82	106	51	35	—	324
Engineering		(68)	(79)	(47)	(31)		
Architecture	(17)		(6)	(4)	(4)		
Building	(33)	(14)	(8)				
Survey			(13)				
Freshman	3,216	—	—	—	—	—	3,216
Arts	(1,206)						
Life Science	(1,136)						
Physical Science	(874)						
Alemaya	—	41	111	64	—	—	216
Debre Zeit	200	—	—	—	—	—	200
Awassa Jr. Agric. College	197	231	—	—	—	—	428
Agriculture	(179)	(212)					
Home economics	(18)	(19)					
Bahir Dar Science Teacher Training	168	—	—	—	—	—	168
Public Health	—	88	113	39	—	—	240
Health Officers			(32)	(39)			
Community Nurses		(40)	(42)				
Sanitarians		(32)	(27)				
Lab. Technicians		(16)	(12)				
Total (Other Campus)	565	660	224	103	—	—	1,252
Grand Total	3,942	1,031	735	465	116	5	6,344

Source: Higher Education in Ethiopia: Facts and Figures, Commission for Higher Education, (Addis Ababa), September 1978, pp. 29–31.

Table 4.3   *University Graduates, 1952/77*

		Degree	Dip. and Cert.	Total
1952–1962	Pre-HSIU	557	324	881
1963–1973	HSIU	3,695	5,822	9,517
1973–1974	HSIU	111	943	1,054
July 1974	HSIU	4	2	6
Oct. 1974	HSIU	7	162	169
July 1975	HSIU	27	819	846
Oct. 1975	HSIU	18	120	138
July 1976	HSIU	68	256	324
Oct. 1976	HSIU	360	180	540
Sept. 1977	HSIU	574	288	862
Total Graduates		5,421	8,916	14,337

Source: Commission for Higher Education, *Voice of Higher Education,* (Addis Ababa), no. 1 (1078), p. 26.

had been predominately expatriate became Ethiopian. As shown in Table 4.4, 85 per cent of the university staff in 1976/7 was Ethiopian with some faculties like Business and Social Work having no foreign staff at all.

Various para-statal agencies, business establishments and private organisations and missions operate in-service programmes and evening classes of various levels and duration in order to upgrade the level of skills of their employees.

Table 4.4   *Total staff members, Addis Ababa University, 1976/7*

Faculty	Number of Staff		
	Ethiopean	Expatriate	On Study Leave
Medicine	22	8	6
Technology	21	7	5
Building College	12	3	—
Science	56	22	20
College of Business Admin.	11	—	5
Education	26	2	13
Arts	51	16	21
Law	6	1	2
School of Social Work	6	—	1
College of Agriculture (Alemaya)	16	6	27
Public Health College	28	3	—
Theology	5	5	—
Total[1]	260	73	100

Note:
(1) Awassa Junior Agricultural College not included.
Source: As Table 4.3.

Privately owned evening schools offer a variety of courses in commercial and secretarial fields for office employees and for those who seek employment. The schools also prepare students who either cannot attend day school or have failed in any one of the national exminations. While evening schools have become lucrative businesses, and have increased in number as a result, they have helped in raising the level of public education quite significantly. And with an effective control by the Ministry of Education of standards of education and cleanliness of the school, the overall quality (curriculum and physical outlook) of these schools has been greatly enhanced. It is estimated that it would cost the government 8 million dollars to take over and administer these schools.

The most important evening institution is the Extension Division of Addis Ababa University which provides a variety of diploma, certificate and degree courses for office employees. The courses are controlled by the various colleges and faculties of the university to ensure uniformity of standards.

The enrolment of the division has grown considerably over the last few years and at the present rate of growth it may shortly become self-supporting. The division has opened two branches, in Asmara and Harar, and others are envisaged in other provincial towns. Extension

Table 4.5 *Extension Programme: First Semester Enrolment by Programme, 1977/8*

Main Campus			
Degree		*Engineering Extension*	
Arts	84	Pre-engineering (degree)	185
Business	300	Civil engineering (diploma)	86
Education	54	Mechanical engineering	
Government affairs	627	(diploma)	57
LLB	34	Statistics (diploma)	218
Public administration	58		
		Total	546
Total	1,157		
		Grand Total = 1,225 + 546 = 1,771	
Diploma			
Accountancy	30		
Executive secretarial			
science	6		
Public administration	29		
Social work	3		
Total	68		
Total degree and diploma	1,225		

Source: As Table 4.3, p. 28.

student enrolment at the Addis Ababa campus of the university reached 1,845 students in 1977/8 of whom the majority were government employees or members of business organisations. They pursued courses related to their occupation which contributed to their professional growth and occupational advancement. Table 4.5 shows the distribution of these students in the various programmes available in the division.

IV   TEACHER EDUCATION

Teaching is the least attractive of the professions for many reasons, among which are the meagre pay of teachers, their low status in society, the hardship suffered particularly in the rural areas where health and recreational facilities do not exist, and the limited possibilities for professional growth. Not only are young people not attracted to it but also those who are in the profession tend to leave for other jobs, as Dr Aklilu Hapte's[6] survey of 1968 has indicated. The situation has not changed much since that time.

According to the 1971 census of the Ministry of Education there were 8,992 primary schoolteachers in charge of some 654,824 students. this gives a teacher pupil ratio of 1:73 in the primary schools. The teacher pupil ratios at the junior and senior high schools were 1:32 and 1:22 respectively. Practically all the teachers in the primary schools and a large majority of the teachers in the junior and senior high schools are Ethiopians. Expatriate teachers mainly of Asian origin are found in the higher levels of the educational system and in the vocational-technical schools and teacher training institutes. Almost half of the teachers in the institutions of higher learning are expatriates.

The qualifications of teachers at both primary and secondary levels are below the required standard. Many of the primary shoolteachers are priests with no more than four years of formal education. Others are drop-outs from grade VI or VIII who joined the profession after a crash programme in teaching methods. In the junior high school in 1971 only 615 teachers out of 1,931 had the minimum qualification required to teach at this level. Similarly only 853 out of 2,120 senior high schoolteachers were graduates of institutions of higher learning.

The teacher training programmes may be divided into five categories. These include programmes for the preparation of:

(1) primary school teachers,
(2) junior secondary schoolteachers,
(3) senior secondary schoolteachers,
(4) technical-vocational schoolteachers,
(5) teachers for teacher training institutes.

Teacher Training Institutes

The first teacher training college for primary schools was opened in 1944 in Addis Ababa and was later transferred to its present site in the provincial town of Harar. It is now the major institution for the preparation of primary schoolteachers. The other four are located in the provincial towns of Debre Berhan, Asmara, Jimma and Addis Ababa. Except for the institute in Addis Ababa which operates a one-year emergency training programme for grade XII graduates, the other four offer a two-year training course for grade X graduates. The five institutes have a total capacity of little more than 3,000 trainees.

Those who join these institutions do so not so much because of their interest in becoming teachers as for other more practical considerations such has having board and lodging facilities and security of jobs after graduation. Most of the graduates are known to leave for other jobs as soon as they get the opportunity to do so. The attrition rate among primary schoolteachers is high.

Three other training institutes are operated by missionaries in the provincial towns of Adwa, Yirgalem and Dembidolo. They follow the same curriculum as the others and maintain the same standards. Though most of the graduates are absorbed by the mission schools some are employed in government schools.

The College of Teacher Education

There is only one government-operated teacher training college for the training of junior high schoolteachers. It is located in Addis Ababa and admits students who have three passes in the Ethiopian School Leaving Certificate. There is also one mission college in Debre Zeit which is accredited by Addis Ababa University, and another at Kuira. The total capacity of all these colleges does not exceed 500 students a year. The limited supply of qualified teachers has made the junior high schools dependent upon unqualified teachers and expatriates. The Ministry of Education has a plan to open another college at the provincial town of Nazreth.

The Faculty of Education, University of Addis Ababa

Senior secondary schoolteachers are trained by the Faculty of Education which started as a very small department of the Faculty of Arts but is now one of the largest units of the university with a total enrolment of over 800 students. It is largely staffed by Ethiopians and has four major departments: Elementary Education, Secondary Education, Technical Education and Library Science. The Elementary Education Department trains teachers for the teacher training institutes and its work is now supplemented by the Pedagogical Institute at Baher-Dar. The Secondary Education Department trains teachers for the senior high schools while the Library Science Department prepares librarians and teachers in library science. The Technical Education Department trains teachers to teach technical-vocational subjects. The faculty also has a Psychology Department, a Research Unit and an Audio-Visual Centre.

The Faculty of Education offers only the professional courses while the academic courses are given by the Faculties of Arts and Science. Constant clashes in timetable and misunderstandings with these faculties led at one point to a serious consideration of transforming the Faculty of Education into an autonomous college. However, financial constraints and other considerations forced the continuation of the status quo. Students who join the Faculty of Education are recruited from three main sources. The first and most important is the Laboratory School which itself recruits its students from among eleventh grade graduates of all the schools in the country who join after one year of preparatory programme. In this way the faculty admits the best students in the empire. Students accepted in this way are under an obligation to remain in the faculty and teach after graduation or to reimburse the university the sum of Eth. $500 if they wish to transfer to another faculty. This amount represents what the university spends on the food and lodging of these students during their one-year stay in the Laboratory School. The faculty also admits students who have entered the university through the normal channel of the Ethiopian School Leaving Certificate and have opted to become teachers. A third group of students are those whose performance has been outstanding in the summer in-service programme.

Even though the Faculty of Education is the largest unit of the university in terms of numbers of students, it has not been able to cope with the growing demand for secondary school teachers. A high attrition rate of students is among the major problems of the faculty. Out of an approximate yearly intake of 300 students in the freshman year not more than 200 graduate after five years. Academic failures, student unrest, deferred graduation practices and voluntary withdrawals contribute to this. The senior high schools still depend heavily on the services of expatriate teachers. In 1968 about 47 per cent of the teaching force at this level was foreign.

Efforts at expanding the faculty's programme to meet the growing demand for teachers led to the launching in 1973 of the three-year graduate science programme at the Agricultural College at Alemaya. Students were drawn from among the best students of the laboratory school and were given a two-year course (including summer vacation courses) leading to a diploma. After two years of compulsory teaching (including one year of national service) those who wished to get their degrees would return for an additional one-year period. Finally, the preparation of French teachers for senior high schools is carried out by the Ecole Normale Supérieure of the Lycée Gabremariam, which is run by the Ministry of Education with technical assistance from the French government.

Teachers for Vocational-Technical Subjects

A recent survey indicates an acute shortage of up to 40 per cent of industrial arts teachers and 26 per cent of teachers in agriculture and home economics. The Department of Labour of the Ministry of National Community Development and Social Affairs reported in 1968 that:[7]

> One of the bottlenecks in expanding vocational training is the shortage of teachers . . . There is need to consider the adequacy of the number and quality of instructors in the light of the need to train the large number of personnel who are required in connection with economic development during the next few years.

There are at present six post-primary vocational-technical schools that give specialised training in one of the following areas: agriculture, economics, business and industrial arts. Training in industrial arts is given in two technical schools in Addis Ababa and at the Polytechnic Institute in Baher-Dar at a higher level. Two agricultural schools – one at Ambo and the other at Jimma – give training in agriculture. The commercial school in Addis Ababa gives training in commercial and secretarial fields. In addition, all comprehensive high schools have two or more vocational-technical streams which offer a variety of courses in these areas.

None of the above institutions trains teachers of vocational-technical subjects. the only institution that does this is the Technical Teacher Education Department of the Faculty of Education. It prepares 'para-professional techers in commercial training, industrial arts and home economics for the junior and senior comprehensive schools and conducts in-service programmes for practical and vocational teachers without previous pedagogical preparations'.[8] It offers a two-year diploma course in business education, industrial education and home economics which is designed to give students not only sufficient preparation in technical and vocational fields but also an adequate foundation in general and professional education. Graduates from the department teach in the junior and senior secondary schools.

Those presently teaching vocational-technical subjects in the schools are drawn from various institutions. About 16 per cent of the teachers come from the comprehensive secondary schools while 65 per cent come from technical-vocational institutions such as the technical schools in Addis Ababa and Asmara, the agricultural schools in Ambo and Jimma, the Polytechnic Institute in Baher-Dar and the Technical Education Department of the university. As much as 12·1 per cent of the teachers are university students doing their national service. The remaining 7 per cent of the teachers are expatriate teachers and graduates from foreign universities.[9]

In-Service Teacher Education

The overwhelming majority of the teachers in primary levels and many in junior and secondary schools have inadequate qualifications. Many of them teach in rural areas where opportunities for professional improvement are not available. The most effective means of upgrading the professional standard of these teachers and keeping them abreast of new educational ideas and techniques is through in-service programmes.

For many years the Ministry of Education and the university have co-operated in organising in-service courses for teachers. The divisions of Teacher Education and Curriculum Development of the Ministry of Education have been organising periodic summer programmes and workshops for primary schoolteachers during the holidays. The Faculty of Education has also been running regular training programmes for over twenty years during summers for primary schoolteachers, school administrators an supervisors. It awarded diplomas to successful students and accepted to its regular degree programme those with outstanding performance in these courses.

Unfortunately, these programmes have benefited only a small percentage of the teachers. The Educational Sector Review suggested in 1971 expanding the programme by involving other agencies through the creation of a central organ for supervising and running in-service programmes and by making fuller use of existing facilities in the teacher training institutions.

V VOCATIONAL AND TECHNICAL EDUCATION

Despite the fact that agriculture is the basis of the Ethiopian economy, agricultural development has been largely neglected up to now. In 1971/2, for example, only 2 per cent of government expenditure was earmarked for agriculture while 31 per cent went to defence. Similarly the entire educational orientation has remained essentially academic and elitist while other forms of education such as commercial and technical education, and notably agriculture, received little attention. At present there are only three agricultural institutes located in the provincial towns of Ambo, Jimma and Nazereth. The first two were established in the early years of the 1950s as vocational secondary schools and offered a four-year course in vocational agriculture to eighth grade graduates. Since 1966 a two-year diploma programme for secondary school graduates has replaced the former programme with the aim of preparing agricultural technicians, modern farmers, teachers in agricultural subjects and managers and technicians for commercial farms and national agricultural organisations. The Animal Health Institute at Debre Zeit laid greater emphasis on animal husbandry.

Like agriculture, technical and commercial fields were also neglected. Up to recent times skills in such vocations as pottery, blacksmithing, metalwork and weaving were transmitted by traditional artisans to their sons who served as apprentices to them. It was only after the Italo-Ethiopian War ended that technicians, mechanics and engineers came to be regarded as indispensable in a modern society. The first technical school was established in Addis Ababa in 1941 and another was opened at Asmara twelve years later. Both institutions offer a four-year course to eighth grade graduates and concentrate on such activities as automobile driving, carpentry, welding and forging, electrical installation, bricklaying, masonry and plumbing.

In 1963 the Polytechnic Institute at Baher-Dar was established and started by offering a four-year programme to eighth grade graduates to prepare them to be skilled technicians. In 1969 the four-year programme was phased out in favour of a two-year post-secondary programme for high school graduates who passed the entrance examination of the institute with the aim of preparing 'highly skilled technicians in the fields of science and technology to meet the trained manpower needs of the country'.

Finally, the need to create a modern economy not only required skilled agriculturalists and technicians but also businessmen, office workers, accountants, and the like. In response to this need a commercial school was established in Addis Ababa in 1942 to offer a one-year course in clerical subjects. The programme was later expanded to a four-year programme with the aim of training 'skilled and commercial and office personnel'. It offered two types of programmes of different durations and standards: a four-year course for eighth grade graduates and a two-year postgraduate programme for secondary school graduates. The first of these was phased out in 1971/2.

VI   CURRICULUM

The curriculum in all educational institutions has undergone a number of revisions since 1941 in order to make it as relevant as possible to the needs of the country. One of the most important aspects of the revision is the transference of emphasis from academic in favour of practical and vocational subjects. Since the declaration of socialism in the country in 1976 further changes have been introduced. However, these changes have not yet taken final form and we shall therefore consider the curricula as they were prior to the declaration.

Primary and Secondary School Curricula

During the prewar period the schools placed heavy emphasis upon the teaching of foreign languages such as French, English, Italian and Arabic. This was due to the urgent need for nationals who would serve as translators, ambassadors and emissaries to foreign countries with which Ethiopia established contact. Other courses included in the curriculum were history and geography, science and mathematics and Amharic. Courses such as dressmaking and house management were given to the few girls in attendance.

The first step to educational reform took place in 1948 with the extension of the six years of primary education to eight years and the inclusion of a few practical courses in the curriculum. These minor reforms were followed by more significant changes in the second half of the 1950s. At the General Education Conference[10] held in February 1957 it was decided, among other things, to restructure the 8-4 system to 6-2-3 (shortly afterwards changed to 6-2-4), to replace English by Amharic as a medium of instruction in the primary grades, to include more practical subjects in the curricula of the junior high schools, to train Ethiopian teachers to teach in Amharic, and to prepare textbooks and other teaching materials in the national language. These recommendations provided the impetus for major curricular reforms that soon followed. Not only was Amharic adopted as a medium of instruction in the primary grades, but also a large number of practical subjects such as agriculture, health, education, culture and handicraft, physical training and economics were introduced in the curriculum. The adoption of Amharic as a medium of instruction encouraged the production of textbooks and reading materials for schools by Ethiopian authors. The two-year junior high school has served as a very useful transition period between primary school, where all subjects are taught in Amharic, and senior high school where the medium of instruction is English. A concentrated course in English is given to make up for possible deficiencies in the teaching of the subject a the primary level. An extensive guidance and vocational programme was introduced to assist the less academically inclined students, and thus reduce the number of drop-outs in the secondary schools.

A further milestone in de-emphasising the predominantly academic character of the curriculum was passed during the 1960s; all junior and senior high schools were transformed into comprehensive institutions. The high drop-out rate, the growing demand for skilled manpower and

the increasing difficulties of access to the university made the change
necessary. The aims of comprehensive education were also consistent
with the recommendation and deliberations of the 1961 Addis Ababa
Conference of African States on the Development of Education in
Africa that the purpose of education in the continent should be 'to
provide a full and balanced educational programme' which would
enable 'every individual male and female to make maximum
contribution to the society which his mental endowments and physical
conditions will permit'.[11] The courses offered in the comprehensive
junior and senior high schools are indicated in Tables 4.6 and 4.7.

It should be noted, however, that despite these fundamental
departures from the traditional highly academically oriented
curriculum the overwhelming majority of the students entering high
schools continue to pursue their studies within the academic stream in
preparation for university studies. For example, in 1968/9 some 91 per

Table 4.6   *Comprehensive Secondary School Curriculum I for Junior
Secondary Level*

Subject Areas Prescribed by Ministry of Education	Grade VII	Grade VIII
Area I: General Education		
History	3	3
Geography	3	3
Mathematics	5	5
Science and Health	5	5
Amharic	3	3
Sub-Total	19	19
Area II: English Language Concentration	9	9
Area III: Fine and Practical Arts		
Physical Training	1	1
All students will spend 3 periods per week on each of any 3 of these fields[1] Music	3	3
Arts and Crafts	3	3
General Shop	3	3
Agriculture	3	3
Commercial Training	3	3
Sub-Total	10	10
Area IV: Guidance, Supervised Study, etc.	2	2
Grand Total	40	40

Note:
[1]A period is 40 minutes long; a week has 5 school days; a regular year has 36 instructional
weeks.
Source: Ministry of Education, *Secondary School Curriculum Book I, 1968/9.*

EDUCATION IN ETHIOPIA 81

Table 4.7 *Comprehensive Secondary School Curriculum II for Senior Secondary Level*

Area	Subjects	Grade	IX	X	XI	XII
I	Mathematics		6	6		
	Science		6	6		
	History		4	4		
	Geography		4	4		
	Amharic		5	5	4	4
	English		6	6	8	8
	Physical Education		1	1	1	1
		Sub-Total	32	32	13	13
II	Domestic Science or Industrial Arts, or Agriculture, or Commerce		4	4	12–14	12–14
	or					
	Domestic Science or Industrial Arts, or Agriculture, or Commerce *and* Any subject field from Area III		4	4	6	6
	or					
	Fine Arts or Music		4	4	12–14	12–14
	or					
	French and any subject field from Area III		4	4	4	4
		Sub-Total	4	4	4–14	4–14
III	Mathematics				6	6
	Science				6	6
	History				6	6
	Geography				4	4
		Sub-Total			8–20	8–20
IV	Educational, Vocational and Moral Guidance and Study		4	4	3–5	3–5
		Grand-Total	40	40	40	40

Source: Abdullahi, B. et al., 'Vocational technical education' *Education Sector Review,* 8 July 1972, p. 8.

cent of the students were in the academic stream while only 7 per cent were in the technical-vocational stream and only 2 per cent were in the primary teacher training programmes.

Vocational-Technical School Curriculum

In addition to the comprehensive schools, the technical-vocational institutes offer practical subjects. The two technical schools, one in Addis Ababa and the other in Asmara, offer a four-year course in technical subjects to students who have completed junior high school. Eight areas of specialisation are offered in each of these two institutions: automechanics, building, trade, drafting, electricity, general mechanics, machine shop, radio electronics and surveying. Some of the graduates of these schools join the two-year diploma programme of the Technical Education Department of the university upon satisfying an entrance examination.

The Polytechnic Institute at Baher-Dar offers a two year post-secondary programme to students who have completed their secondary education and has as its objective the training of highly skilled technicians in one of six areas of specialisation: agromechanic, electrical technology, textile technology, metal technology, wood technology and industrial chemistry. Students are required to pursue a core of common subjects which comprises mathematics, technical English, engineering mechanics and industrial electricity.

The two agricultural schools – one at Ambo and the other at Jimma – offer a two-year diploma course to high schools graduates. The courses offered include English, agronomy, horticulture, animal husbandry, agriculture extension, farm management and farm machinery. The Animal Health Institute at Debre Zeit specialises in animal husbandry.

The Commercial School offers two areas of specialisation; accounting and administration. All students pursue the same courses but the time they spend on them depends on their specialisation. The courses offered are divided into three broad areas:

(1) general education consisting of physical training and moral education;
(2) general related education consisting of Amharic, English, French (optional), commercial arithmetic and social science;
(3) specialised training consisting of Amharic typing, English typing, shorthand, book-keeping and business training.

By the time the students graduate from the school they will have had 5,472 periods of instruction, and will have spent 55 per cent of their time on general related education and about 40 per cent on skill training.

Health and medical personnel are trained by the Ministry of Public Health as well as by private mission hospitals. The Ministry of Public Health offers a three-and-a-half-year course to tenth grade graduates in science, public community hygiene, nursing arts, communicable and tropical diseases, operating-room techniques, professional adjustment and ward management and supervision. The general course offered in these schools includes general and related education in English, mathematics, science, nutrition, cookery and human behaviour. Most of the nursing schools are attached to hospitals. At the completion of the programme students sit for the National Registration Nurse Examination.

Finally, there are many para-statal and private organisations which offer pre-employment and on-the-job training in technical-vocational areas. In 1969/70 there were about 160 such programmes in which some 1,176 students were participating.

Teacher Training Curriculum

The curriculum of the teacher training institutes which prepare teachers for primary grades include academic, professional and practical courses with heavy emphasis upon the academic. Out of forty contact hours as many as twenty-five periods are set aside for academic subjects consisting of Amharic, English, mathematics, science and social studies. The remaining fourteen periods a week are divided between professional subjects such as child development, general methods and educational organisations, and practical courses such as home economics, rural science, arts and crafts, music and physical education. Not more than five periods a week are spent on professional subjects, while the practical arts receive about ten.

The rationale for attaching so much importance to the academic subjects is to raise the level of academic competence of the trainees who have had only ten years of formal education. However, educational critics consider this a major weakness in the preparation of teachers and suggest that more time should be spent on practical and professional subjects instead. They further point out that since the trainees would be teaching in Amharic, their own training should be conducted in the same language. This poses the formidable difficulty of providing teaching material in Amharic and teachers who have themselves been trained in Amharic and can teach in it.

The Department of Teacher Education is the only institution that prepares teachers for technical-vocational subjects. It has three major areas of specialisation: business education, industrial education and home economics. A common core of subjects in general and professional areas is given to all students which consists of English, Amharic, psychology and methodology, development of instructional materials, workshop organisation and management. The department admits students who have three passes in the Ethiopian School Leaving Certificate. Upon graduation they teach in the junior and senior high schools.

VII   SCHOOL POPULATION

In 1971 the population of Ethiopia was estimated to be 28 million, growing at an annual rate of 2·2 per cent. The distribution of the population according to age was estimated to be as follows:

below 15 years	45·0%
15–59 years	50·4%
above 60 years	4·6%

The primary school age-group (5-14 years) numbered more than 7 million of which 6 million were estimated to be in rural areas. The secondary school age-group (14–18 years) was estimated at 3 million.[17]

Out of the 7 million primary school-age children only 700,000 or 10 per cent attended primary schools. There were 14,229 primary schools of which 5,237 were non-government and a total number of 201,300 children or 25·3 per cent of the school population attended these schools. Of the 3 million secondary school-age population only 11,712 or 3·4 per cent attended school. Of these 73,000 attended junior secondary schools and 53,000 senior secondary schools. There were in addition 72 vocational-technical and 9 teacher training institutes with enrolments of 60,000 and 2,800 respectively. About 7,000 students attended post-secondary institutions of which 1,000 were enrolled in technical and teacher training institutions while the remaining 6,000 were at the university. Hence, 82·3 per cent of the total enrolment was in the first level, 17 per cent in the second level and 0·3 per cent in the third level.

Table 4.8 indicates the growth of the school-going population over a nine-year period (between 1963 and 1972). It will be observed that the primary school enrolment rose by 130 per cent over the nine years while the increases in the junior and senior high school enrolment were 293 per cent and 409 per cent respectively. The average yearly growth for the three levels was 10·5 per cent for primary, 18·7 per cent junior secondary, 23·2 per cent senior secondary, and 6·9 per cent special secondary schools.

These increases are unimpressive when examined against the background of the total number of children still out of school and in relation to the rapid rate of growth of this group. It will be noted that 86 per cent of the primary school-age population and 96·3 per cent of the secondary school-age population were still out of school. At the present annual increase in primary school enrolment it will take about twenty-five years to accommodate all 7 million children in school. By the time this is realised, however, the primary school-age population will have grown to 9 million. It will be remembered that the Conference of African States on the Development of Education in Africa in 1961

Table 4.8 *Enrolment in All Schools, 1963/72*

Year	Primary 1–6	Increase %	Junior Secondary 7–8	Increase %	Secondary 9–12	Increase %	Secondary Special School	Increase %
1963/4	313,240	—	21,121	—	11,927	—	5,497	—
1964/5	347,770	11·02	24,697	16·9	15,637	31·1	7,337	33·4
1965/6	378,750	8·9	28,812	16·6	21,623	38·2	5,150	29·9
1966/7	409,710	8·1	36,480	26·6	23,832	10·2	6,674	29·5
1967/8	452,457	10·4	44,777	22·7	26.690	11·9	8,067	20·8
1968/9	513,981	13·5	56,918	27·1	31,943	19·6	9,559	18·4
1969/70	590,445	14·9	63,215	11·1	42,487	33·5	8,968	6·1
1970/1	655,427	11·0	73,121	15·6	53,236	25·2	9,389	4·6
1971/2	721,500	10·0	83,000	13·5	61,900	16·2	8,600	8·4
Average	—	10·5	—	18·7	—	23·2	—	7·8

Primary School Population Increase   130·3%
Junior High School Population Increase   293·0%
Senior High School Population Increase   419·0%
Secondary Special Population Increase   56·4%

Sources: ECA Summaries of Economic Data; Ministry of Education Report on the Organisation of Education in Ethiopia 1971–2 and 1972–3, Addis Ababa, June 1973.

Table 4.9   *1971 Primary School Enrolment and Participation*
Rate in Provinces, 1971

Province	No. of School-Age Children	Enrolment in Govt. School	% Participation Rate in Govt School
Arussi	134,600	22,956	17·0
Bale	164,000	10,833	6·6
Begemidir	213,400	28,294	13·3
Eritrea	303,400	51,523	17·0
Gemu Gofa	110,400	11,305	10·2
Gojjam	275,200	27,362	9·9
Harar	529,100	29,890	5·6
Illubabor	109,400	19,938	18·2
Kafa	203,000	17,961	8·8
Shoa	702,200	79,525	11·3
Sidamo	391,000	30,908	7·9
Tigre	288,300	24,480	8·5
Wellega	900,400	40,838	4·5
Wollo	388,800	28,686	7·4
Addis Ababa	132,800	46,579	35·1
Total	4,146,000	471,077	

Source: Inqui *et al.,* op. cit., pp. 33–6.

recommended universal primary education in all African countries in
1980. At the present rate of growth Ethiopia cannot hope to have more
than 50 per cent of the elementary school-age population in school in
1990.

Another point to note is the obvious disparity in the distribution of
educational opportunities among the fifteen provinces. Table 4.9 shows
the enrolment figures in the government primary schools for the fifteen
provinces in 1971. As will be seen from the table, the participation rate
varied from 5·6 per cent for Harar province to 35·1 per cent for
Addis Ababa. The national average of participation rate was 12 per cent
and out of the fifteen provinces ten had a participation rate less than
the national average. Yet another form of disparity in educational
opportunities is that which exists between the male and female
population of the country. The illiteracy rate of the country is 93 per cent:
88 per cent of males and 98 per cent of females. In the schools girls
constitute only 31 per cent of the total student population at the primary
school level, 23 per cent at the secondary school level and 8 per cent at
the university level. Table 4.10 shows the percentage of girl students in
the different levels of the educational system over a three-year period.
The percentage growth of the female school population during these
three years is almost insignificant. Girls are still the victims of tradition
which maintains that their place is in the home and that education is
unnecessary for them.

Table 4.10   *Girls as a Percentage of Students, 1968/70*

Educational Level	1968	1969	1970
Primary	30·5	30·6	31·4
Junior secondary	27·1	27·1	26·4
Senior secondary	19·1	20·5	20·8
Teacher training	12·1	16·4	17·3
Vocational-technical	7·4	7·6	8·0
University	7·4	7·6	8·0
ALL LEVELS	29·2	29·5	30·2

Source: Gulilet, T. *et al.*, 'Education for development', *Education Sector Review*,
          8 July 1972, p. 16.

VIII   EDUCATIONAL FINANCE

Educational institutions in Ethiopia are operated by three important agencies, government, para-statal and private, which share the cost of education. The government, as the main agency responsible for education, spends the largest amount of money while the remainder is borne by the two other agencies. An examination of the budgetary figures for the year 1970/1 (Table 4.11) shows that of the total amount of Eth. $141,116 million spent on education, the government agencies spent Eth. $123,325,000 (87 per cent) while the private and para-statal agencies spent Eth. $16,588,000 (12 per cent) and Eth. $1,200,000 (1 per cent) respectively.

A large portion of educational funds is acquired from internal sources, but some comes from external sources. It will be noted from the table that for the year 1970/1 out of the total expenditure of Eth. $141,116 million the amount of Eth. $102,121 million was acquired from within the country, notably from taxes, fees and household and business contributions. The remaining Eth. $38,995 million was contributed from external sources.

Table 4.12 indicates the relationship of educational expenditure to the GDP and the government domestic revenue for the period 1967–75. It will be noted that 15·8 per cent of the domestic revenue was spent on education in 1966/7. This figure rose to 20 per cent in 1975, representing 2·3 per cent of the GDP. These amounts include the recurrent and capital expenditures of the Ministry of Eduction, appropriations for the Universities of Addis Ababa and Asmara, the Antiquities Administration and other activities of the ministry. In terms of government priorities as reflected by its budget education occupies second or third place (Table 4.13).

Local communities also contribute funds, labour and materials towards the construction and maintenance of schools in their areas. In

Table 4.11 Summary Estimates of Educational Funds spent by Government, Para-Statal and Private Agencies on Formal and Non-Formal Education by Sources, 1970/1 (1971 Eth. $thousands)

Agency	Internal Resources							External Resources		
	Total Resources	Ministry of Finance (taxes, etc.)	Other than Ministry of Finance				Total Internal Resources	External Loans	External Assistance	Total External Resources
			Household Resources	Business Resources	Miscellaneous Resources	Total				
Grand Total	141,116	92,068	9,510	189	354	10,053	102,121	3,963	35,032	38,995
Total Govt. Agencies	123,325	91,155	1,210	—	4	1,214	92,370	3,963	26,992	30,955
Total Para-statal Agencies	1,203	512	120	189	20	329	841	—	362	362
Total Private Agencies	16,588	400	8,180	—	330	8,510	8,910	—	7,678	7,678

Source: F. G. Kiros et al., 'Financing education', Education Sector Review, 8 July 1972, p. 33.

Table 4.12   *Gross Domestic Produce, Central Government Revenue and Government Total Expenditure on Education, 1967–75 (Eth. $ millions)*

Period	GDP	Govt. Domestic Revenue (Fiscal Year)	Govt. Total Expenditure on Education		
			Amount (Fiscal Year)	As % of Govt. Revenue	GDP
1967	3,558	360·2	56·9	15·8	1·6
1968	3,690	362·8	59·6	16·9	1·6
1969	3,861	394·6	75·6	19·2	2·0
1970	4,020	406·1	81·1	20·0	2·1
1971	4,188	439·3	84·6	19·3	2·1
1972	4,364	465·8	90·1	19·3	2·1
1973	4,554	497·0	95·9	19·3	2·2
1974	4,758	526·7	103·8	19·7	2·3
1975	4,969	559·3	111·9	20·0	2·3

Source: As Table 4.11, p. 68.

Table 4.13   *Ordinary Expenditure: Comparative Figures from Three Budgets (Eth. $)*

Ministries	1957/8	1965/6	1970/1
Civil List[1]	3,968,055	5,755,628	9,669,102
War/Defence	39,000,000	102,548,275	87,380,275
Interior	23,270,511	78,994,548	74,111,984
Justice	4,140,161	7,131,147	7,153,147
Information	1,256,519	6,050,268	7,171,383
Education	14,554,736	63,882,386	76,978,983
Health	4,605,797	25,355,342	23,399,615
Agriculture	1,656,803	10,251,589	11,545,676[2]
Community Development	2,856,593	3,327,170	4,373,267
Commerce and Industry	634,805	1,374,890	2,332,399
Ordinary expenditure total	158,535,978	403,213,234	507,097,969
Capital expenditure	67,706,350	104,372,349	124,278,718

Notes:
[1] Includes the Imperial Court, the Ministry of Pen and Haile Selassie's Private Cabinet.
[2] Includes the Ministry of Land Reform, the Awash Valley authority and the Wild Life Conservation Department.
Sources: Adapted from M. Perham, *Government of Ethiopia,* 2nd edn (London: Faber, 1969), p. 204; *Ethiopian Observer,* vol. III, no. 2 (1959), pp. 58–61, vol. X, no. 3 (1966), pp. 192–8; Ministry of Finance, *Budget for Financial Year 1970/1.*

some regions as much as 15 per cent of the educational expenditure is borne by local communities. Local participation in educational development has been particularly noteworthy in primary school building projets. These projects were encouraged by the Swedish International Development Authority (SIDA) scheme whereby any amount contributed by a community for school construction was matched by an equal amount from SIDA. Between 1965 and 1968 a total number of 702 classrooms were built at a cost of Eth. $3·7 million of which half was contributed by the local communities and half by SIDA. Similarly over a period of four years – 1967/8 to 1970/1 – a total sum of Eth. $12·2 million was raised out of which Eth. $5·3 million was locally contributed.[13] From the evidence of the past it can be assumed that with greater inducement local contributions to education could be significantly raised in the future. At present about 1·5 per cent of the total educational expenditure of the country comes from local community contributions.

The budget earmarked for education is allocated to two major categories of educational enterprise, formal and non-formal education. Government, private and para-statal agencies are involved in both categories and divided their educational funds between them in 1970/1 as indicated in Table 4.14.

The budget earmarked for formal education in 1970/1 was divided among primary, secondary and tertiary education as shown in Table

Table 4.14 *Summary Estimates of Education Expenditures by Government, Para-statal and Private Agencies for Formal and Non-Formal Education by Destination, 1970/1 (1971 Eth. $ thousands)*

Agency	Total	Non-Formal Education					Formal Education			
		Literacy and Adult Education	Vocational and On-the-Job Training	TV and Radio	Others	Total	Primary	Secondary	Tertiary	Total
Grand Total	141,116	1,685	13,863	357	1,130	17,035	58,178	31,756	34,147	124,081
Total Govt. Agencies	183,325	1,577	13,476	317	565	15,935	48,280	25,473	33,637	107,390
Total Para-statal Agencies	1,203	108	387	—	42	537	208	348	110	666
Total Private Agencies	16,588	—	—	40	523	563	9,690	5,935	400	16,025

Source: Kiros *et al.*, op. cit., p. 36.

Table 4.15   *Educational Expenditure, 1970/1* (1971 Eth. $ millions)

Category	Expenditure	Percentage
Primary	58	41
Secondary	32	23
Tertiary	34	24
Total Formal Education	124	88
Total Non-Formal Education	17	12
Grand Total	141	100

Source: Adapted from Kiros *et al.,* op. cit., p. 41.

4.15. For any year the bulk of this money is spent on primary education. Unfortunately over 30 per cent of the primary education budget is spent on children who drop out between grades I and III and is therefore wasted.

Finally we should note that the educational budget is apportioned between the fifteen provinces of the country. For various reasons, partly historical and partly arising from such factors as urbanisation, missionary activities, or even favouritism, some regions receive a larger share of the national educational budget. As a result glaring inequalities in educational development are observed between the provinces and among the districts within the provinces. Some of the provinces, notably Shoa, Addis Ababa and Eritrea, receive a larger share of the educational budget and as a result have the largest number of schools, teachers and school-going population in the country. Other provinces like Bale and Gemu Gofa are noticeably underprivileged in these respects because of the small share of the educational budget allocated to them. As has been suggested elsewhere, this unfair distribution of education in the country is one of the factors contributing to the periodic social discontent in the country.

IX   ADMINISTRATION AND ORGANISATION

The Minsitry of Education has control over all aspects of education in the country, including mission and private education. Moreover, the ministry has remote control over the affairs of the university in that the minister is the chairman of the university's board of governors, which is the ultimate authority over the policy matters of the univeristy and is responsible only to the chancellor. The Ministry of Education is one of the most important and oldest organs of the government and up until recently the emperor himself retained the portfolio of Minister of Education.

The Ministry of Education is headed by a minister who is a member of the Council of Ministers where he liaises with other ministers. He is the government's leader in educational affairs and decides on and promulgates major policies, plans and programmes. He is directly responsible to the emperor and all the departments of the ministry are responsible to him.

The minister is assisted by the Minister of State for Education whose functions overlap those of the minister but are more restricted. While the minister spends a good portion of his time attending to the external affairs of the organisation such as attending Council of Ministers' meetings, and other conferences, the minister of state closely follows the internal affairs of the ministry by working with the various departments and units and giving the necessry guidance and directives.

The ministry has three major departments which are headed by vice-ministers who are responsible to the minister via the minister of state. These are the Departments of Instruction, Administration, and Cultural Affairs and External Aid. The Department of Instruction is mainly responsible for the integration and co-ordination of both formal and informal education, the design, co-ordination and development of curricula, the production of teaching materials, the preparation of national examinations and evaluation of programmes and the health and physical education services and programmes. The Department of Administration is responsible for finance, supply, distribution, personnel records, registry and other matters pertaining to administration. Finally, the Department of Cultural Affairs and External Aid has a large number of functions and responsibilities, the most important of which include research, conservation and dissemination of culture and all matters relating to scholarships and external assistance.

At the provincial and district levels there are the provincial and district educational offices which are directly responsible to the Department of Instruction. The provincial educational office PEO 'is a focal point of liaison between the constituent district office and the ministry'. The officer at its head has responsibility for analysing, revising and consolidating the budgetary requests prepared by the district educational officers in the province for submission to the Ministry of Education. He also serves as an agent for the distribution of centrally organised services such as radio broadcasting and in-service training programmes. In addition he co-ordinates adult education and literacy programmes in the area.

Educational districts are in most instances coterminous with the district of Awaraja boundaries and are under the responsibility of the provincial education office. They are headed by district educational officers whose main duties include the supervision of the schools within their districts, preparing educational budgets for their areas in consultation with the directors of the shools and the smooth running of educational and related activities in their areas.

School directors hold key places in the whole organisational structure because they operate at the grassroots level. They ensure that the ministry's policies and regulations are followed, that standards are maintained and that discipline is observed. They also keep records, prepare school budgets and indents, submit plans for improvement, serve as professional advisers to their staff and participate in the various educational activities in their communities. The effectiveness of the entire administrative structure depends on the devotion and competence of the school directors and their staff.

X CONCLUSION

It is now almost eighty-five years since the Italian five-year occupation of the country was terminated and the task of national reconstruction began under Ethiopian leadership. In this task education has retained top priority because it has always been considered a condition for development. During these years a complete system of education has been built up from the kindergarten to the university level. There were at a recent count 2,371 primary schools, 436 secondary schools, 7 vocational technical institutions and 12 teacher training institutes. In all, there were some 800,000 students. Educated Ethiopians at present occupy most of the important positions in technical, administrative, business and educational fields. Despite these achievements certain critical problems have arisen which are directly connected with them.

The first problem concerns the adaptation of education to the Ethiopian culture. Despite many revisions of the curriculum to make it as relevant as possible to the needs of the country, education has remained essentially a foreign importation. The curricular revisions were essentially directed at equipping the country's youth with skills and knowledge which they could profitably use to make a living. While this was done with some success, the adaptation of the curriculum to the culture was largely neglected. The task of identifying the values and beliefs in the culture which must be incorporated in education or redefined or erased completely was never undertaken. Questions such as 'what type of an Ethiopian should the schools produce and for what type of society?' remained unsolved. As a result of this gross oversight, modern education in Ethiopia lacked direction. It produced culturally displaced individuals who felt at home neither in their own culture nor in the imported foreign culture.

Secondly, at no time was the role of education in Ethiopia examined in the context of the total socioeconomic and political order. It was assumed that the schools could go on changing and moulding the minds of the country's youth while the social order remained unchanged. Thus the schools cultivated scientific attitudes, taught about democratic institutions and transmitted egalitarian values for a society which remained pre-scientific, authoritarian and hierarchical. The school taught the opposite of what the society was and what the rulers wanted it to be. As a result the schools produced not merely cultural misfits but also enemies of the social, economic and political order. It was only when sufficient numbers of such individuals were available that they could be strong enough to pull down the social order they were taught to oppose, as they have now done.

Thirdly, education was thought of in terms of the young only and as a result all educational effort for many years was concentrated on the formal eduction of youth within the confines of the schools. The education of adults and of the masses as a whole was gravely neglected. This is shown by the high illiteracy rate of the country today and by the rudimentary stage of the literacy and adult education programmes in the country. Consequently, an unhealthy cleavage was created between the educated young and the uneducated masses. It accentuated the generation gap, and the misunderstandings between the young and the old and between parents and their children.

The fourth problem concerns the pace of educational development in Ethiopia compared with economic development. So long as the graduates from the universities, the high schools and other institutions were absorbed by the economy, a semblance of social stability prevailed. But as soon as the economy became saturated and failed to absorb the educated, as happened in later years, a grave social problem arose.

From the 1960s onwards, as the Ethiopian economy stagnated, this social problem revealed the fifth critical problem in Ethiopian education, that is, the concentration of all modern amenities, and specifically education, in the towns, and the exclusion of the country dwellers from their benefits. Yet 90 per cent of the population and 80 per cent of the labour force is to be found in the rural areas. The urban concentration of development created an unhealthy and exploitive relationship between urban and rural communities, the former enjoying most of the benefits accruing from the labour of the latter. Since the country depends so much on agriculture the neglect and deliberate suppression of the rural people inevitably produced economic underdevelopment. As long as the rural sector remained stagnant it was impossible for the urban economy to develop because whatever business and industrial activities existed in the towns depended in the last analysis on agriculture. In time the economy became increasingly incapable of absorbing the graduates from the high schools, technical institutes and even from the universities as well as those who flocked from the rural areas in search of better living conditions. Social instability increased in proportion to the increase of the number of the unemployed educated young people. This problem is well articulated by Taye Gulilate *et al.:*

A balance has to be established between the output of the educational system and the absorptive capacity of the economy. Where the education sector grows at a rate faster than the employment opportunities created by the economy, the result is an addition to the 'army' of educated unemployed – a source of social unrest and political instability. The economy's capacity to absorb the output of graduates of the educational sector depends not only on the choice of appropriate technology, wage level, supply of land, etc., but also on the growth rate of the non-educational sector. If the growth of the latter lags behind that of the educational sector, then the country will face the problem of unemployment of graduates of the educational sector and also the problem of generating funds adequate to finance the expansion of the educational sector. Education depends on the development of the economy for finance, and the generation of employment for its output, i.e. the graduates of the educational sector.[14]

This raises a crucial principle of development. Educational reform, which involves the expansion of the schools, revising the curriculum, increasing the school enrolment, and the like, is meaningless and indeed is a cause of social tension as long as these reforms are not accompanied by corresponding reforms in the economic and political organisation of the country. As long as the Ethiopian government kept on postponing the problem of rural reform and political reorganisation modern education became merely an instrument for its own destruction. Indeed, that was what happened eventually. The 1974 Revolution which tore down the *ancien régime* was spearheaded by disillusioned students who felt uncertain about their future, by young military officers who joined the army after failing at school, by dissatisfied teachers and by the large number of semi-educated young drop-outs who were crowding the streets of the major towns of Ethiopia.

NOTES: CHAPTER 4

1 E. Isaac, 'Social structure of the Ethiopian church', *Ethiopian Observer*, vol. XIV, no. 4 (1971), p. 255.
2 T. Gulilat, *et al.*, 'Education for development', *Education Sector Review*, 8 July 1972, p. 9.
3 loc. cit.
4 J. Markakis, *Ethiopia: Anatomy of National Polity* (Addis Ababa: Oxford University Press, 1974), p. 146.
5 ibid., p. 145–6.
6 A. Hapte, 'Brain drain in elementary school: why teachers leave the profession', *Ethiopian Journal of Education*, vol. I, no. 1 (June 1967), pp. 27–39.
7 Ministry of National Community Development and Social Affairs, *The Training of Manpower in Ethiopia during 1961 EC* [1967/8] (Addis Ababa: Ministry of

National Community Development and Social Affairs, 1970), p. 30.
8 B. Abdulahi *et al.*, 'Vocational technical education', *Education Sector Review*, 8 July 1972, p. 61.
9 ibid., p. 60.
10 M. Bekele, *Report on the Experimental Programme for Elementary Education* (Addis Ababa: Co-operative Education Press, January 1961), p. 161.
11 Quoted by S. Inqui *et al.*, 'Educational opportunities', *Education Sector Review*, 8 July 1972, p. 26.
12 Gulilat *et al.*, op. cit., p. 10.
13 F. G. Kiros *et al.*, 'Financing education', *Education Sector Review*, 8 July 1972, p. 33.
14 Gulilat *et al.*, op. cit., p. 16.

Chapter 5

Education in Ghana

A. ASIEDU-AKROFI

I BRIEF HISTORICAL OUTLINE

European contact with the Gold Coast, now Ghana, brought things good as well as things evil and today many people seem to share the views of Sir Herbert Stanley, that 'of the good things that it has brought we have to thank the Christian missionaries for the best',[1] that is, the schools.

Among the early 'missions' that built schools were Catholic chaplains attached to the Portuguese settlement – 'Fort São Jorge' (Fort Saint George) – built at Elmina. This school established in the castle was provided originally to cater for mulatto children born to Portuguese fathers and Ghanaian mothers. The Portuguese were followed by the Dutch and later by the Danes and English who built castles at Christiansborg and Cape Coast respectively and attached schools to them as the Portuguese had done earlier. The school at Christiansborg came to be organised by the Moravian Brethren who reached Ghana in 1737. Unfortunately the school could not endure, partly because of the high rate of mortality among the occupants of the castle.

The European activities in the eighteenth century, the spread of Christianity and, along with it, the opening of schools, were a mere footnote to the main mercantile enterprise. In the castles, therefore, the traders nearly always left the running of the school in the hands of the poorly paid chaplain, who did the best he could. Any support that he got from the castle authorities depended on particular circumstances.

Thus the castle school at Cape Coast came to be run by the Society for the Propagation of the Gospel in 1752. The little that the castle schools achieved proved to be of tremendous help to the Basle and Methodist missions who arrived in the country in 1828 and 1835 respectively. But the missionary influence proved more rewarding than that of the castle schools. At the turn of the century most of the schools in the country were under missionary control. Even though the government showed some interest in the schools and made attempts to control, or at least participate in, their administration, it was not until the governorship of Sir Gordon Guggisberg (1919–27), one of the chief protagonists of the Phelps-Stokes Report on Education,[2] that the partnership of church and state in educational matters became fully operative. Before then the schools had been almost entirely financed by the missions but thereafter the government assisted them by giving grants-in-aid because of its quest for the orderly development of the country. Under this system there were four kinds of schools:

(1) government
(2) assisted
(3) missions
(4) private.

The figures in Table 5.1 illustrate the churches' impressive contribution to education in the 1920s:

Table 5.1   *Government and Assisted Schools in Ghana (Gold Coast), 1925–7*

	1925	1926	1927
AME Zion	7	7	7
English Church	6	6	7
Ewe Presbyterian	22	31	36
Roman Catholic Mission	29	29	32
Presbyterian Mission	98	96	99
Wesleyan Mission	47	48	49
Undenominational	1	1	1
Secondary	2	2	2
Muslim	—	1	1
Total Assisted Schools	212	221	234
Government Schools	17	17	18
	229	238	252

Source: Government of the Gold Coast, *Report on the Education Department for the Period April 1927 – March 1928* (Accra: Government Printing Office, 1928), p. 10.

The development of education in the country now depended upon British colonial policy which encouraged voluntary missionary effort at primary and secondary levels. The government itself opened relatively few schools. The rapid pace of school development was arrested in the 1930s by the world economic slump. Missionary effort slackened because of severe cuts in the education budget. The government itself could not provide for management, staffing and finance, and education appeared not to be of any serious consideration. After the Second World War the British Colonial Development and Welfare Acts breathed new life into education. The period 1945–50 was marked by unprecedented expansion at all levels and by political activity which ushered in independence.

Whereas the school had been the nerve centre of Christian educational activity during the pre-independence period, the political activities in the country during and after the 1950s tended to transform the school into a nerve centre for manpower development for purposes of political stability and redemption of the African personality. Beginnings were therefore laid down for firmer state control of education. The Accelerated Development Plan of Education[3] was introduced in 1951. It must, however, be understood that state control of education means only a change in the working relationship between the missions and the Ministry of Education. The missions have continued to have an influence on education. At the moment they are represented by two people in the Ghana Education Service Council.

Despite changes in the control of education, it was not until 1961 that the whole country had a single education law. This Education Act of 1961 laid down many important features of the present system of education including free and compulsory education, the creation of local education authorities responsible for buildings, equipment and maintenance grants for primary schools, and the opening of admission to mission schools irrespective of religious belief.

II GENERAL ADMINISTRATION

In 1974 the combined professional and administrative sections of the Ministry of Education were named the Ghana Education Service. It is headed by a director-general assisted by two deputy director-generals, with twenty directors of education – one for each of the nine regions and eleven at headquarters. The service is responsible for all pre-university education including technical, commercial and vocational institutions. The headquarters house the following directorates:

(1) the Director-General's Secretariat
(2) General Administration
(3) Inspectorate
(4) Curriculum Research and Development
(5) Budget
(6) Manpower and Personnel
(7) Planning
(8) Schools and Colleges
(9) Training and Welfare
(10) Technical Education
(11) Ghana Education Service Council Secretariat.

The service also has links with the West African Examinations Council, the Ghana Library Board, the Bureau of Ghana Languages,

UNESCO, the Ghana Sports Council, the Ghana Museums and Monuments Boards and the National Archives.

Each of the nine regions of Ghana is administered by a director of education who is responsible for inspection, supervision and financing of the schools. The policy of decentralisation of education, recommended by the Mills-Odoi Commission on the Structure and Remuneration of the Public Services in Ghana in December 1967, charged the directors of the regions to be liberal in adapting the content and programmes of the schools and colleges to local conditions. The regional office is primarily responsible for the supervision of secondary schools and training colleges, commercial schools and technical institutions, while the district education office, headed by an assistant director of education, takes charge of primary and middle schools. Each education district is divided into education circuits. The professional personnel of the district education office consist of principal superintendents, superintendents and assistant superintendents. The director of education is assisted by a district education committee consisting of the representatives of the main interests in the district.

The administrative functions of the district education offices are as follows:

(1) school inspections and visits;
(2) school welfare services and relationships with other departments and organisations;
(3) organisation and staffing of district education office;
(4) preparation of district estimates;
(5) equipping the schools.

III PRIMARY EDUCATION

The organisation of primary education has two aspects: pre-primary institutions and primary schools.

Pre-Primary Institutions
Pre-primary education is very much in vogue and there are different types of schools depending on their purpose. Some aim at improving children's readiness for school and developing pre-academic skills. Some are more in the nature of day nurseries for children whose parents are ill or working. Some of those owned by individuals are run for financial gain but even so provide means for intellectual development. Organisations which sponsor pre-primary schools include the Ghana Education Service, local authorities, religious bodies and parents' co-operatives.

Primary Schools

Until 1974 when the structure of the new educational system was launched, elementary school education consisted of a six-year primary school course followed by a four-year middle school course. Thus it took ten years to complete the elementary school. At present it takes six years, starting at the age of 6 (see Figure 5.1).

Comparison between the new and old structures and content shows that:

(1) Reading, writing and calculation have become means to ends and not ends in themselves.
(2) The content of the school curriculum has vital links with the educative experiences of the home, community and work situations.
(3) The primary goal of the educational system is creative – self-expression for every child, and therefore liberation of greater diversity of personal capacities.

Curriculum

The medium of instruction for the first three years is the local language of the area where the school is situated. English is learnt as any other subject during this period but is emphasised in the fourth year so that it can be used as a medium of instruction in subsequent years. The curriculum is as follows:

Ghanaian languages: the child shall learn his own language, and in addition one other Ghanaian language.
English: this shall be learnt as a subject from the first year at school, and shall gradually become the medium of instruction as from primary class IV.
Mathematics (new).
Social Studies, including elements of geography, history, economics, sociology and civics.
Elementary Science: health education, physical and biological sciences.
Practical activities relating to animal and crop husbandry, local crafts and vocations.
Cultural Studies: religion, music (including drumming and dancing), drama, arts and crafts and home science.
Physical Education: games and sports.
Youth Programme, including practical and cultural activities, physical education, sports and community service.[4]

Education for the Handicapped

Government provides education and rehabilitation programmes for handicapped children. The programme covers the blind, the deaf and

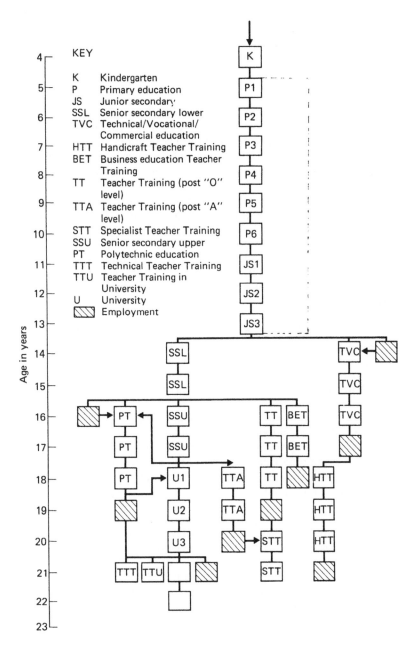

Fig. 1. *New Structure of Education*

dumb, the mentally retarded, the physically crippled and hospital schools for children who have long hospitalisation. Other bodies such as religious groups and parent–associations also sponsor some programmes. In 1976 there were 1,222 children enrolled in special schools at the primary level.

Schools for the Blind
There are two so far in the country – Akropong School for the Blind and Wa School for the Blind, both boarding. The children follow the normal school curriculum which is adapted to suit their needs. The schools also provide vocational training in typing, commercial subjects and crafts.

Schools for the Deaf and Dumb
There are eight schools of this type in the country. They provide for nursery, primary and middle school courses. In some, provision is made for children with multiple disabilities. The curriculum is the normal school one adapted to the needs of the deaf and dumb. Where they are run as day schools, parent counselling programmes are given. The middle schools offer vocational training in tailoring, woodwork and dressmaking.

School for the Mentally Retarded
At the moment the Ghana Education Service shows little interest in this kind of institution. There is only one now, run by the voluntary Society of Friends of Mentally Retarded Children and the Ministry of Health. It has two preparatory and one nursery classes.

Schools for the Physically Crippled
There are so far two managed by the Roman Catholic Mission. They are the St Joseph's Hospital School for the Crippled at Koforidua and the Orthopaedic Training Centre at Nsawam. The system of education is integrative. There is physical training but children are encouraged to attend the normal school.

Hospital Schools
The Ghana Education Service co-operates with the Ministry of Health to organise 'teach-in' schools for children who are hospitalised for a long time. These schools are mainly found in the cities with large hospitals, for example, Korle Bu Teaching Hospital, Accra, St. Joseph's Orthopaedic Hospital, Koforidua and Okomfo Anokye Hospital, Kumasi. They follow the normal primary school curriculum and are taught by certificated teachers.

Managment of Primary Schools
Schools in the education districts are managed by either local

authorities or educational units of the religious bodies. Of course, the former play a more dominant role than the latter whose responsibilities are temporary. These bodies perform the following functions:

(1) admission of pupils
(2) payment of teachers' salaries
(3) postings and transfers of teachers
(4) disbursement of maintenance grants to schools.

The management is done by general managers, local managers, supervisors, administrative and clerical staff. The local managers, who are generally ministers of religion belonging to the education units, give voluntary service, but the expenses incurred in the performance of their duties are borne by the Ghana Education Service. Except in the Northern and Upper Regions where the central government is responsible for building and maintenance of school buildings, these are the responsibilities of local governments.

Finance

All schools in the public system are financed by the government. The Education Act of 1961 made attendance at school fee-free and compulsory. However, in 1966 a textbook fee of three cedis (₡3·00) per annum was introduced. In addition every child paid 30p per annum for sports. The increases in enrolment at all levels make the financial responsibility of the government heavy as Tables 5.2 and 5.3 show.

Government expenditure patterns for financial years 1969/70 to 1973/74 indicated that Educational Expenditure has been rising by a rate of about 1·24 in total Government Expenditure. Recurrent Expenditure rose by 1·55 while Development Expenditure rose by 0·42. By 1973/74 actual education expenditure topped all other sectors in the country.[5]

Table 5.2   *Enrolment Trends by Levels, 1970/1 to 1974/5*

Level	1970/1	1971/2	1972/3	1973/4	1974/5	Multiplier 1970/1 to 1974/5
1st	1,389,804	1,415,801	1,447,205	1,455,029	1,490,667	1·07
2nd	83,935	88,056	89,865	94,781	99,481	1·19
3rd	5,426	5,990	6,391	7,466	8,022	1·48

Source: Ghana Education Service, *Digest of Education Statistics (Pre-University) 1974–75* (Accra: Government Printer, 1975), p. 9.

Table 5.3   *Percentage of Actual Expenditure of the Educational Sector in the Total Government Expenditure Programme, 1969–74.*

Financial-Year	Total Expenditure	Recurrent Expenditure	Development Expenditure
1969/70	13·85	15·81	15·16
1970/1	14·92	17·22	6·90
1971/2	14·64	16·47	7·03
1972/3	18·95	21·70	6·28
1973/4	18·08	21·20	7·61

Source: As Table 5.2.

IV   SECONDARY EDUCATION

In Ghana the term 'secondary school' is broadly used to mean post-primary institutions that provide a wide range of skills which the country's expanding cultural life and economy demand – academic, technical, commercial and vocational. It is divided into two parts – junior comprehensive secondary school and senior secondary school. The junior course covers three years and provides general education diversified with technical/vocational/commercial/agricultural courses. Entry into the junior secondary is by the common entrance examination. The senior secondary school has lower and upper divisions, each covering two years. The lower division leads to GCE O Level while the upper leads to A Level (sixth form). The O Level secondary schools include grammar schools, technical institutes, commercial institutes, agricultural institutes and vocational centres. Students with appropriate qualifications proceed to the A Level secondary schools which are provided by the grammar secondary schools and the polytechnics. Students who do not gain entrance into the universities can proceed to polytechnics, specialist and teacher education colleges.

Curriculum

The junior comprehensive secondary school curriculum comprises:[6]

A Ghanaian language
A second Ghanaian language
  or a modern/classical
  language
General science

Cultural studies – religion,
  music (including drumming
  and dancing) drama, arts
  and crafts

English
French
Social studies
Mathematics
Youth programme, including
   community service

Physical education
Agricultural science; including
   poultry and livestock
   keeping
Home science and pre-nursing

Apart from the above compulsory subjects, each student elects two of the following subjects:

Woodwork
Masonry
Metalwork
Technical drawing
Pottery
Commercial subjects
Marine science (fishing)

Automobile practice
Crafts
Beauty culture (including
   hairdressing)
Tailoring
Dressmaking
Catering, etc.

The senior secondary lower course offers:

A Ghanaian language
   (compulsory)
English language
French
Modern languages/
   classical languages
Mathematics
Science
Social studies
Literature
Agriculture
Home science

Pre nursing
Religious knowledge
Music
Art
Commercial/vocational/
   technical subjects
Cultural studies, including
   physical education
Dancing and crafts
Youth programme (to include
   community service)

Students who do not offer French for GCE are encouraged to study it throughout the course. They follow a special course in the subject.

The senior upper secondary course offers specialisation in the arts, sciences, agriculture, commercial and business education, Ghanaian languages, and music, physical education and dancing. The technical commercial and polytechnic courses are as follows:

Technical/Vocational Courses

(i) Electrical engineering
         Trades

Fashion, dressmaking and
   tailoring

Mechanical engineering trades
Automobile engineering
 trades
Building construction
 trades
Secretarial studies
Accounting
Pre-nursing
Agricultural engineering
Furniture manufacture
Beauty culture

Leather work
Commercial and industrial
 arts
Catering
Fishing
Pottery
Carving
Crop husbandry
Animal husbandry
Horticulture

(ii) A Ghanaian language
English language
 (communication)

Liberal social studies
Science
Mathematics

Commercial Courses

Book-keeping/accounts
Shorthand
Principles of office practice
Commerce

Business studies
Arithemtic
Typing and office
 machines

Polytechnics Courses

Technician diploma
Technician certificate
Advanced craft
Commercial and industrial
 arts

Full technological
 certificate
Foremanship and
 supervisory studies

Some examples of these courses are:

General engineering
Electrical technician
Electronic technician
Mechanical technician
Construction technician
Business studies
Institutional management
Refrigeration

Laboratory technician
Sanitary engineering
Plumbing
Welding
Printing
Textiles
Mining engineering

Management

Secondary schools are managed by school boards or management committees whose duties are:

(1) to see to matters of general policy;
(2) to ensure that the school operates within the limits set by national policy, for example, in matters of buildings and facilities, staff qualifications, entry age of pupils;
(3) to discuss general problems of an administrative nature arising in the school;
(4) to promote good relations between the school and the community, and between the school and parents.

Finance

The government is responsible for the financing of the secondary schools by way of payment of salaries, provision and maintenance of buildings, tuition fees, etc. Parents are, however, responsible for boarding, examination and the cost of books.

V TEACHER EDUCATION

The phenomenal expansion in schools at all levels has had a corresponding effect on the output of teachers. Further, the emphasis on technical and vocational education has broadened the content of teacher education since more practical skills have to be taught. The present trend is, therefore, the training of specialist teachers in one or two fields instead of the former omnibus type of training. The GCE has become the basic entry qualification. At the moment the categories of professional teacher education institutions are as follows:

(1) three-year advanced teacher training colleges for diploma studies,
(2) three-year post-secondary training colleges,
(3) certificate A (four-year post-primary) colleges,
(4) university for graduate teachers.

The first two categories are associated with the Institute of Education, University of Cape Coast, while the third group are organised by the National Teacher Training Council, an advisory board to the Ghana Education Service. It is expected that eventually they will be transferred to the Institute of Education.

Graduate and postgraduate professional training is offered by the University of Cape Coast which is mainly responsible for the production of graduate teachers for the educational system. These are of two categories: those who do the traditional topping-up course for one year after degree courses at either the University of Ghana, Lagon, or the University of Science and Technology, Kumasi, and those who pursue the concurrent course for four years at the University of Cape Coast.

Administration

The teacher training institutions are administered by the Professional Board of the Institute of Education, University of Cape Coast, the National Teacher Training Council and the Ghana Education Service.

The Professional Board of the Institute of Education
This consists of:

(1) the Vice-Chancellor, University of Cape Coast – Chairman,
(2) the Vice-Chancellor, University of Ghana, or his representative,
(3) the Vice-Chancellor, University of Science and Technology, or his representative,
(4) the deans of faculties, University of Cape Coast, or their representatives,
(5) Director, Institute of Education,
(6) one representative elected by each department of the Faculty of Education,
(7) the Director-General, Ghana Education Service,
(8) principals of constituent colleges.

Its functions are:

(1) to approve the courses of study of colleges in special relationship with the universities;
(2) to conduct the examinations of the Institute and to appoint examiners and subject panels;
(3) to recommend to Senate the award of certificates or diplomas to successful candidates of the colleges;
(4) to carry out any other functions as Senate may from time to time approve.

The National Teacher Training Council
The Council was established to deal with matters of common interest to the four-year post-primary Certificate A training colleges. It is responsible to the Ghana Education Service and deals with:

(1) the selection of students for training,
(2) the courses of study to be pursued,
(3) the examination for the award of certificates,
(4) research in education,
(5) in-service training for professional teachers.

The Council consists of the following members:

(1) principals of the training colleges,
(2) the dean, Faculty of Education, University of Cape Coast, and one member of his staff,
(3) representatives of the educational units which manage the training colleges (Presbyterian Church, Methodist, Roman Catholic, etc.),
(4) representatives of the West African Examinations Council,
(5) two members of the Ghana Education Service,
(6) representatives of the Ghana National Association of Teachers.

Curriculum

The curricula of the teacher education courses at different levels are as follows:

Diploma Level

French, art, physical education, home science, mathematics, science, English, business education, Ghanaian languages, music, agricultural science, technical education; students specialise in any of these subjecι

Three-Year Post-Secondary Level

Science, mathematics, English, social studies, home science, agricultural science, vocational subjects, commercial subjects, art, music; students take major and minor courses in these subjects.

Four-Year Post-Primary Level

Education, English, Ghanaian languages, cultural studies, social studies, science, mathematics, physical education, agriculture, home science, vocational subjects, commercial subjects.

Graduate Teachers

BA, B.Mus., BA Secretaryship, BA Commerce, B.Ed. Any three of the following subjects may be studied along with education for any of the degree courses stated above. The courses, however, lead to specialisation in the field of study in which the student shows proficiency: English, French, Greek, Latin, Greek and Roman civilisation, religious studies, music, Ghanaian languages, economics, mathematics, sociology, geography, history, commerce, secretaryship, etc.

B.Sc. and B.Ed. Any three of the following may be studied. The courses, however, lead to specialisation in the field in which the student shows most proficiency: botany, zoology, mathematics, physics, chemistry, agriculture and biology.

The education components of the above degree courses are as follows:

(1) psychology of human development
(2) history of education in Africa (West Africa)
(3) curriculum studies and methods
(4) psychology of human learning
(5) social foundations of African education
(6) guidance and counselling
(7) educational measurement and evaluation
(8) philosophy of African education
(9) school organisation and educational administration.

Finance

The pre-university training colleges (diploma level, three-year post-secondary level and four-year post-primary level) are financed by the government. The students' grants cover boarding and lodging expenses. Those who are on study leave are paid salaries from which they pay their college expenses.

VI UNIVERSITY EDUCATION

Ghana has three universities: University of Ghana, Legon, University of Science and Technology, Kumasi, and University of Cape Coast, Cape Coast. A fourth one is due to open in the northern part of the country. In order to avoid duplication of courses, because of the economy of the country, there is delimitation of functions. However, the delimitation is not watertight because there is reasonable overlapping in certain areas. Thus the University of Ghana, Legon, functions as a liberal arts university, the University of Science and Technology specialises in the applied sciences, while the University of Cape Coast is responsible for teacher education.

Degree Courses Available

University of Ghana

Adult Education	Geology	Swahili
African studies	History	Arabic
Archeology	Law	Nutrition and
Biochemistry	Library and	food science
Botany	archival studies	Philosophy
Chemistry	Mathematics	Physics
Classics	French	Political science
Economics	Russian	Psychology

English	Spanish	Sociology
Geography	Post-basic nursing	Study of religions
Statistical, economical	Zoology	Agriculture
and social studies	Medicine	Administration

University of Science and Technology

Practical training is an important part of the degree or diploma courses in this university:

African Studies	Chemical	Land economy
Agriculture	technology	Mathematics
Architecture	Engineering (civil,	Medicine
Art	electrical,	Pharmacy
Building	mechanical,	Physics
technology	geodetric)	Planning
		Social sciences

University of Cape Coast

The curriculum covers all teaching subjects in schools as listed under undergraduate courses in Teacher Education (see page 111).

Administration

Each of the universities is governed by a council made up of:

the Pro-Chancellor,
the Vice-Chancellor,
the Pro-Vice-Chancellor,
elected members of Senate,
elected alumni of the university
private citizens.

All the universities, however, operate under the National Council for Higher Education which is responsible for:

(1) advising the government on the development of university institutions in Ghana;
(2) recommending block allocations of funds to individual university institutions towards their running costs and grants-in-aid of capital expenditure, with such general indication as may be considered necessary as to how the allocations shall be spent;
(3) maintaining contact with the university institutions by visits and in other ways;
(4) advising generally on staff structures, rates of remuneration, conditions of appointment and service, promotions and

superannuation provision for the staff of the university institutions bearing in mind the need to relate these to the comparable arrangements and circumstances generally obtaining in Ghana;

(5) collecting, collating and making available information relating to the university institutions and publishing an annual report containing such information.

Finance

The universities are funded by the government. Grants are made to students through the Scholarships Secretariat. They cover boarding and lodging. Students who are on study leave terms are paid their salaries from which they pay university expenses. There is also a loan scheme to cover the cost of books and any other items needed by students. Undergraduate students are entitled to 300 cedis while postgraduate students can procure loans up to 500 cedis.

NOTES: CHAPTER 5

1 E. W. Smith, *The Blessed Missionaries* (London: Oxford University Press, 1950), foreword.
2 The Phelps-Stokes Commission was sponsored by the Foreign Missions Conference of North America to investigate the educational work being done in Africa and to find out how the needs of Africans were being met. The Commission was financed by the Phelps-Stokes Fund, established in 1911 for the education of negroes. Their report, published in 1922, was an epoch-making document. It was the first report that stressed sociological factors in building African curricula.
3 The Accelerated Development Plan for Education was the first outline of educational policy published by the first African government in Ghana.
4 Ministry of Education, *The New Structure and Content of Education for Ghana* (Accra: Ministry of Education, February 1974), p. 4.
5 Ghana Education Service, *Digest of Education Statistics (Pre-University) 1974-75* (Accra: Government Printer, 1975).
6 Ministry of Education, op. cit., pp. 5-9.

Chapter 6

Education in Kenya

FILOMINA INDIRE

I HISTORICAL BACKGROUND

First Phase, 1920-9

The year 1920 offers a convenient starting point in a discussion of the development of education in Kenya for two main reasons: first, in that year Kenya became a Crown colony of Britain and was no longer administered as a territorial segment of the British East African Protectorate but as a separate British territory having its own legislative council; secondly, after 1920 the authority of the Colonial Office was felt more definitely on educational matters which previously had been largely the concern of missionary societies. This was especially the case after the establishment of the Advisory Committee on Education in the Colonies in 1923. That body had great influence on the Secretary of State for the Colonies and on the development of a coherent government policy on education.

With the transition from a protectorate to a Crown colony, the multiracial composition of Kenya came to be a recurrent issue in the country's educational development. In 1908 an education board, wholly European, had been established to advise the Governor on the question of educational policy in the protectorate. In 1920 Kenya had its own education board and membership of the board reflected the multiracial population of Kenya. The board had on it representatives of the European settlers, an Indian and an Arab; ironically, although the board was set up on African soil it had no African representative. This lack of African representation on the board was in accord with the principle of racial segregation introduced in the 1909 Fraser Report. Henceforth the principle of racial segregation was to be a major factor in educational development in Kenya until the years immediately preceeding independence in 1963.

Reactions against the discriminatory policy of the colonial government resulted in a compromise policy of 'native paramountcy', 1923-39. The Indians, who by 1921 outnumbered the Europeans by more than 2:1 (22,800:9,651), demanded a halt to the discriminatory policy. This led to the 'Indian crisis' and the subsequent delegation of Indians to Britain in 1923. The political tussle between the Indians and the Europeans was intricately linked with the 'native problem'. The Africans, with an estimated population of 2·5 million, were reacting against the land allocation policy, the forced labour, the use of taxation to force contented Africans in the 'reserves' to seek employment in the European farms and the practice of missionaries representing Africans on the legislative council; against their low political, social and economic status in general. 'Native paramountcy' for Kenya and for eastern Africa north of the Zambesi was to mean that the interests of the Africans came first while those of the minority groups would be protected, but events were to show that the adminstration had little intention of implementing the policy fully and immediately.

During the era of 'native paramountcy' educational development went through three phases. During the first phase, 1923–8, the emphasis was on the rapid spread of 'bush' or catechetical schools which later developed into village elementary schools. This period also witnessed the publication of the first Education Ordinance of 1924 under the guidance of the Advisory Committee on Education in the Colonies and and the famous Phelps-Stokes Report, *Education in East Africa* (1924).

The Kikuyu Independent Schools Movement, which heralded the second phase, was formed by the Kikuyus who were dissatisfied with the quantity and quality of education provided by the missions and wanted to raise the academic standards of African schools. The movement was influenced by the pioneering nationalist struggles of people like John Owalo, who in 1910 built several independent primary schools in Nyanza and demanded a secondary school free from missionary control. Other nationalists like Jomo Kenyatta later championed the demands of the Kikuyus for compulsory education for all Africans up to standard 6, government scholarships for Africans to study at home and abroad and the opening of a Makerere-type institution in Kenya. The effects of the worldwide depression began to hit Kenya hard by 1934 and no significant advances in education were made. However, the 1931 Eduction Ordinance was introduced as a token of the implementation of native paramountcy. The Ordinance provided for the representation of the Independent Schools Movement on the local education boards and the placing of all bush and elementary schools under the control of the newly established district education boards.

The third phase of this period was ushered in by Hitler's occupation of the Rhineland in 1936 and his demands for the restoration to Germany of its former colonies. The British reaction to this was to carry out improvements in African education systems in order to strengthen their hold over their African territories.

In Kenya the colonial administration made efforts to improve the quality and to increase the quantity of the eight-year African primary schools and to improve secondary and higher education facilities for the Africans. In 1938 for the first time Africans were offered full secondary school courses at the Alliance and Mangu High Schools. In the same year Maseno became a secondary school, to be followed by Yala in 1939.

Education during the War Years

The period 1925–35 was a very difficult one for education in Kenya, but between 1935 and 1939 important proposals were made. War broke out in 1939 and interrupted the implementation of these proposals. On the positive side, the war led to a greater cash income for the people. Greater circulation of money stimulated the already intense desire for more educational services, particularly among those who had travelled to different parts of the world. Consequently, primary education expanded considerably during the war years and became a great burden to the missions which were largely responsible for education in Kenya.

Considerable advances in education were recorded in the war years. Two Colonial Development and Welfare Acts were passed by the British Parliament during this period (1939–45) – the first in 1940 and the second in 1945. These Acts provided for funds to be used for economic and social development including education in the dependencies.

The Asquith Commission on Higher Education in the Colonies, appointed in 1943, was another landmark in Kenya's progress towards securing facilities for university education.

The Postwar Years

During the period 1945–60, when the policy of 'partnership' was supposed to be in effect, Europeans continued to dominate the Ministerial Council while allowing a few Africans and Asians to hold portfolios. This period marked a phase of intense local government activity and educational development in which Africans were involved on an unprecedented scale.

A significant chapter in the history of Kenya opened in 1960 with a new constitution which assured Africans a majority on the common roll. For the first time in Kenyan history an African, Mr R. Ngala, became Minister for Education in 1961. Increasingly, English came to be used as a medium of instruction in African schools from standard 1. The Kenya Preliminary Examination became the same for all races from 1961. From 1961–4 the 'triple-four' structure of three years' lower primary, three years' upper primary and three years each for lower and upper secondary was formally replaced by the seven-year primary and four-year secondary courses. In secondary education the emphasis was placed on day rather than boarding schools. These developments and changes represented the several moves made in the three years that preceded independence to bring African education in line with European and Asian education.

The post-independence era of educational development will be discussed later in this chapter.

II ADMINISTRATION

As noted earlier, the provision and administration of education in
Kenya, as in other ex-British colonies, were pioneered by the various
foreign missions with interests in Africa. There was no government
involvement in African education by way of establishing schools for the
Africans until 1913 when the government opened an industrial school in
Machakos, although at that same time, the government already ran
different schools for the three other races in Kenya: the Europeans had
Division A schools established in Nairobi, Nakuru and Eldoret; the
Indians in Nairobi and Mombasa had Division B schools; while the
Arabs at the coast had Division C schools.

With the establishment in 1923 of the Secretary of State's Advisory
Committee on Education in the Colonies, the colonial governments
began to show more interest in African education because the
Committee in London often acted as if it were an executive body
supervising progress in Africa.

Under its guidance, Kenya's first Education Ordinance was passed.
The main purpose of the 1924 Ordinance was to provide for the
'management of education in the Kenya colony and Protectorate',[1] and
thus it 'codified' the principle of co-operation in African education
between missionaries, government, settlers and other interests. Also
provided for in the Ordinance were the issue of certificates of teachers,
registration and inspection of schools, control over their opening and
closure; and the levying of local education rates. The 1924 Ordinance
also laid down the policy for local or decentralised administration of
education. The Education Department was to be advised by district
commissioners concerning the needs of the districts since it was the
department's view that African schools were instruments in the hands of
district commissioners for the improvement of their districts and should
be supervised by them in co-operation with the department.[2] Thus, as
far back as 1924 the ground principles were laid for local administration
of education, determination of needs, supervision of schools and
inspection of efficiency. These were to be the concern and
responsibilities of the district committees.

By 1926 'school areas' were created and each area had a committee.
There was a central advisory committee which dealt with all major
policy matters and served as a link between the Governor in Executive
Council and the school area committee.

The 1924 Native Authority (Amendment) Ordinance provided for the
establishment of local native councils, later known as the African
district councils, which established district education board schools.
Thus the government became increasingly involved in the administration of schools and a dual system of administration of schools
emerged in which the local councils played a larger role in the primary

schools and the central government took charge of secondary and higher education. This administrative structure continued until six months before independence.

During the brief period of the 'Majimbo' constitution regional governments were responsible for education except for higher education and some national institutions. However, they delegated their powers in respect of primary education to local authorities in some cases.

III   FINANCE

The missionaries who pioneered the development of education in Kenya also financed education for a long time. Some received meagre grants-in-aid but only in respect of 'industrial' education. The missions continued to press for government aid. Even by 1910 it had become clear to many missionaries that it would be impossible for them to staff and finance the rapidly expanding educational system.

Under the authority of the 1924 Ordinance some local native councils began to levy rates which included education tax. However, the 1925 Grant-in-Aid Committee recommended that the time was not yet ripe for the levy of an education tax on the Africans and that the policy should be to encourage gradual local participation in the financing of education. Such participation appeared to have been successful by 1927 with the idea of self-taxation for education. This idea was most successful in North and Central Kavirondo (later North and Central Nyanza). The two districts taxed themselves at the rate of 2 shillings per head of taxable population for capital expenditure on buildings. Thus in the early period of colonial rule in Kenya education was financed largely by the missions with increasing local support and contributions.

The government reacted favourably to missionary pressure for more grants. By the first Grants-in-Aid Rules of 1925, valid until 1933, four-fifths of European and two-thirds of certified African salaries were paid. Capital grants were 50 per cent of approved costs, and loans in full or in part were given for the rest; 5 per cent of capital costs went for permanent equipment and 2 per cent of verified cost of existing buildings was given for maintenance. The capitation and boarding grants were combined into a single grant. In addition, a special merit grant was introduced in order to encourage schools to attain the highest possible efficiency. This was to be a capitation grant, subject to the recommendation of the inspector of schools and graded according to the type of schools. Bush schools received no direct grant and more aid was requested for 'special help'. The colony's educational expenditure was only 0·02 per cent of the actual expenditure in 1906. This figure rose to only 5·02 per cent in 1936.

Educational Expenditure for the Whole Country

Educational development in Kenya from 1945 went through three phases. The first phase began in 1945 and ended in 1950–1; during this period the educational percentage of total expenditure increased from 5·81 per cent to 8·58 per cent. The Education Ordinance based on the Beecher Report of 1949 inaugurated the second phase which lasted until 1956–7.

Initially European education received the largest per capita allocation of government funds, followed by Asian and finally African education. For example, in 1940 the respective figures were £25·15, £5·68 and £0·63, even though African education received the largest amount of money. By 1950 the percentage share of the education budget showed that African education received 39·39 per cent, European 32·46 per cent and Asian and others 28·15 per cent. In 1959 both these trends persisted as the figures in Table 6.1 show.

Table 6.1   *Distribution of Education Budget, 1959*

	Per Capita Expenditure (£)	Percentage of Total Expenditure
African	4·19	46·57
Asian and others	17·06	20·55
European	83·89	17·25

After independence in 1963 efforts were made to integrate the schools and to evolve a national system for financing education.

IV   PRIMARY EDUCATION

The direction and content of primary education in Kenya since the colonial period has been a source of continuous controversy. It was the subject of numerous reports by official commissions, private individuals and groups, and of often bitter public discussions. It would be impossible here to summarise the widely varying points of view that have been expressed, but the broad trend of development can be indicated.

Until 1911 little or no official attention was paid to African education. It was almost exclusively in the hands of Christian missionaries and tended to be concentrated around the major stations. In 1911 government control over education was exercised by the administration and support for mission efforts came from public funds. Despite this, for over half a century the responsibility for primary education was tossed about between the central government, the local authorities and the missions. The administration repeatedly sought to free itself from the burden by leaving it to the other two groups, but political pressures for more rapid expansion forced it to accept its responsibility.

It gradually came to be accepted that responsibility for primary education should rest in local hands. In 1931 a new Education Ordinance gave the school committee power to advise the central education authorities on the use of funds provided by the local native councils. In 1934 they were replaced by district education boards with more powers over the day-to-day operation of the schools. Represented on the boards were the local native councils and voluntary agencies. The financing of the primary schools, however, rested heavily on the local native councils.

What should be emphasised is that a major factor in the control and administration of primary education evolved around its financing. The administration was reluctantly pushed into constant expansion of allocations for education. The pressure for more educational facilities intensified during the postwar periods. Despite government efforts at control, new unaided schools sprang up everywhere, thereby increasing the number of schools demanding government's financial support. The administration sought to reduce the financial pressure by refusing to increase the list of unaided schools unless the educational expenditure of a local council did not exceed a specified amount, but the cost of teachers' salaries and building continued to rise, and the ability of the missions to increase their donations fell until a crisis point was reached immediately after the Second World War. The publication of the Ten-Year Plan in 1947 accentuated the problem with its recommendation that local expenditure for education should rise from £100,000 in 1948 to £234,000 in 1957. The plan also indicated clearly that primary education should become the complete responsibility of local government. These ideas were shared by the Beecher Report of 1949. This led local councils (which had now been renamed African district councils) to spend heavily on education. An examination of expenditure by the ADCs over representative years from 1954 until independence shows that their major financial burden was education. Between 1954 and 1959 education budgets for the councils rose from a total of £407,821 to £1,831,970, of which £703,171 fell directly on the councils.[3] Almost 50 per cent of the total expenditure by ADCs in 1959 (£3,997,669) was on education alone. this high expenditure did little to meet the popular demand for more education. As primary education expanded, the central administration felt increasingly uncomfortable about its lack of ability to give the desired level of supervision and financial administration. The lack of trained personnel forced continuing reliance on the missions which came to be resented by both central and local authorities. Without the missions, primary education could not have been carried on. The ADCs and the general public resented the presence of missionaries in education because they represented a foreign influence and because they interposed themselves between the government and the people in an area of high demand. The missions themselves complicated the situation by their own objectives. Their emphasis on evangelism diluted the value of mission education in the eyes of both the Africans and the administration.

Christian missionary control of primary schools and their ambivalent stand on matters relating to African traditions were to lead to the opening of independent schools, particularly among the Luo, the Kikuyu and the Pokomo. In a number of areas these schools remained an important feature in the school system up to independence.

Another controversy in primary education during the colonial period was that of content. Even with the comparatively slow rate of African economic development in the early years, the missions as well as the government expressed the view that primary education should be a strictly utilitarian outgrowth of an apprenticeship system. Before government endorsement of this kind of policy in 1909, early Christian missionary schools like Frere-town and the Buxton High School at Mombasa had a strong industrial bias. The Fraser Report of 1909 was the first official report to recognise an industrial curriculum as the basis of African education. It was later enunciated by the Education Commission of 1919, the Phelps-Stokes Commission of 1924 and the Beecher Report of 1949. It remained the official government policy up to independence, despite African resistance.[4]

A third major aspect of primary education was the racial stratification. Since the establishment of the British rule it was clear that each of the four races, African, Arab, Asian and European, was to run its own affairs separately. This was most pronounced in education. Each followed its own curriculum and expenditure varied from one race to another, with expenditure on African education being the least. By 1963 enrolments at primary schools for the four races was as shown in Table 6.2. By independence, however, there was a general trend towards integration.

Table 6.2   *Number of Primary School Pupils and Percentage which Each Group Constituted, 1963*

| | | Corresponding School-Age Population | |
Racial Group	*Number of Pupils*	*Total Number of Children*[1]	*Percentage of Total Children*
African	840,677	2,421,300	34·7
Arab	3,322	9,000	36·9
Asian	40,915	52,800	77·5
European	6,639	8,900	74·6

[1] It should be noted that school-age was estimated to be 5–14 years.
Source: Ministry of Economic Planning and Development, *Statistical Abstract* (Nairobi: Government Printer, 1965).

Expansion and Organisation Since 1963

As previously discussed, the expansion of primary education remained a crucial problem in the colonial era. All along it kept abreast with government projections. Many unaided primary schools continued to open through community and missionary efforts, despite government attempts to curb them. The situation did not radically change in 1963 with the achievement of independence which, in fact, heightened pressures to increase the school population and move more quickly towards universal primary education. A number of factors, however, produced a slow rate of expansion in primary education. The first of these was the report of the Conference of African States on the Development of Education in Africa, which met at Addis Ababa in May 1961. Although Kenya had not attained independence at the time of the Addis Ababa conference, it was among the thirty-nine African states that participated.[5]

The aim of the Addis Ababa conference was to provide a forum for African states to decide on their priorities and eductional needs and to promote economic and social development in Africa, and in the light of these to establish tentative short-term and long-term plans for educational development in the continent. In determining priorities, the conference assigned greatest urgency to secondary and post-secondary education. It stated that this must be put before the goal of universal primary education if for financial reasons the two were not yet compatible.[6] Primary and adult education were to be developed at the same time, with a goal of universal literacy by 1980. At the time of the conference, however, the African nations' greatest concern was for an adequate supply of skilled manpower. Expressed as percentages of the appropriate age-groups, the proposed enrolments were as shown in Table 6.3.

Table 6.3 *School Enrolments as Proposed by the Addis Ababa Conference, May 1961 (%)*

	1960–1	1965–6	1970–1	1980–1
Primary	40·0	51·0	71·0	100·0
Secondary	3·0	9·0	15·0	23·0
Higher	0·2	0·2	0·4	2·0

In accordance with resolution of the United Nations General Assembly and the Economic Commission for Africa, the ministries of education of the African countries met in Paris in 1962. They reaffirmed the high priority to be given to higher education.[7]

Against the international background of the Unesco conference, KANU in 1962 requested V. L. Griffiths, an Oxford lecturer with considerable experience in Africa, to prepare a background paper on education. Griffiths identified the two main demands of the territory upon the educational system as trained African manpower and a sense of purpose and national unity.[8] Griffiths was notably forthright in pointing out the immediate task facing Kenya in the initial phase of development. He gave the development of secondary level education the highest priority in order to meet the pressing need for trained manpower, although he recognised that this 'most urgent task' would have to be modified to some extent in order to satisfy popular aspirations, and that striking a balance between the conflicting interests was essentially a political rather than an educational problem.[9]

During this period, at the request of the governments of Kenya and Great Britain, the International Bank for Reconstruction undertook a survey of the economic development of Kenya. In its consideration of education the commission, like several of its predecessors, pointed to the bottleneck at the secondary level as the most critical education need.[10] Despite popular demands the survey did not recommend universal primary education. Local school districts were urged to take the major financial responsibility for expansion at the primary level.[11] The Hunter Report of 1962 also reinforced the idea of placing priority on highly skilled manpower. However, Hunter acknowledged that the economic demands of the state would have to be balanced against the political demands of individuals.[12]

That secondary education was to be given greater emphasis at independence was a factor that had already been realised in the late 1950s, because by that time the expansion of primary education in the 1940s and early 1950s was beginning to create a bottleneck at the secondary school level which became very pronounced at the time of independence. Thus, the new independent government in Kenya had to think about what to do with primary school leavers who could not find places in the secondary schools. Although the government did not curtail the expansion of primary education, its rate of development was reduced. As a matter of fact the increase in primary school fees in 1963 resulted in a temporary decline in primary school enrolment.[13]

The Ominde Report of 1964 was in full agreement with those priorities and endorsed the ultimate goal of universal primary education. It was, however, at pains to demonstrate that this was not financially feasible in the immediate future. The report calculated that on the most optimistic cost basis Kenya could not achieve more than 80 per cent enrolment of the eligible population in primary school by 1980. The

Table 6.4   *Primary and Secondary Pupil Enrolment,*
Percentage Increase 1961–8

	1961	1963	1965	1967	1968
Total	1·0	1·03	1·22	1·37	1·47
Primary	1·0	1·02	1·20	1·30	1·39
Secondary	1·0	1·36	2·16	4·01	4·57

Table 6.5   Number of Pupils in Primary Schools, by Standard, 1961-8

Standard	1961	1962	1963	1964	1965	1966	1967	1968
All	870,448	935,766	891,553	1,014,719	1,042,146	1,043,416	1,133,179	1,209,680
1	189,958	169,990	137,220	180,733	195,733	193,909	228,769	250,757
2	168,572	166,270	138,678	144,786	165,754	166,110	183,634	207,755
3	163,313	164,972	143,907	139,727	139,285	152,919	165,640	178,537
4	171,071	165,716	140,005	145,004	135,124	130,282	146,912	158,899
5	75,457	128,726	124,644	134,031	126,428	120,850	124,832	132,701
6	44,058	70,747	112,836	122,603	122,517	132,714	135,848	134,247
7	35,525	41,972	62,510	114,408	121,269	146,192	147,544	146,784
8	22,494	27,373	31,753	33,870	36,036	440	—	—

government was urged to concentrate on achieving a more equitable distribution of educational opportunities and on improving the quality of primary education. This reflected a desire to strengthen the content of instruction through the upgrading of the quality of teachers.[14]

As a result of the emphasis placed on higher education from 1961 to 1968, Kenya's secondary school enrolment expanded to a greater degree than its primary school enrolment as revealed by Table 6.4.

In 1961 the four-year intermediate schools composed of standards 4 to 8 were abolished in favour of a continuous eight-year primary school system which in 1967 was changed to seven. The number of pupils per class from 1961 to 1968 is shown in Table 6.5.

It is difficult to secure exact figures of the percentage of the eligible primary school population for which schooling was actually available. The figure used by the Education Commission of 1964 of 60.7 per cent in 1965 is probably too high; a more accurate overall figure would probably be 53–5 per cent.[15] In the judgement of the county education officers, the figure was somewhat lower. The problem revolved about an accurate estimate of the primary school-age population.

Average enrolment per class differed widely throughout the country. For the country as a whole it was thirty per class, but it varied from eleven in Tana River County to thirty-five in Kisii and was slightly higher in municipal schools.[16] School fees remained a barrier, especially in areas with a low rate of economic activity. In pastoral areas enrolment remained generally low since boys were seen to be more useful herding livestock than spending time in school.

On the whole Kenya maintained a good record in primary school expansion. Reviewing the recommendations of the Addis Ababa Report, a Unesco conference in 1968 noted that primary enrolment in Africa had fallen short of the targets and that there was an average wastage of 32 per cent between the first and sixth years.[17] Kenya's record of primary expansion was better than average since wastage was only 21 per cent.[18]

However, from Table 6.6[19] it is quite clear that wastage in primary education is still a serious problem, largely due to school fees. The declaration of free education in 1973 may have altered the situation somewhat but there are as yet no figures from which the trend can be gauged.

The 1970–4 Development Plan placed a high priority on universal primary education.[20] Despite its already heavy educational expenditure the government proposed to increase enrolment from an estimated 61 per cent in 1968 to 75 per cent in 1974. The Plan stated that a major instrument by which this enrolment target would be achieved was the remission of school fees. The projected increase was to involve an additional 600,000 primary school students by the end of a six-year period.[21] The Plan's projections were modified by the dramatic declaration of free education to which we shall turn later.

Table 6.6   *Projected and Actual Enrolments for Standards 1, 2, 3, 4 and 7, 1968-70*

Year	Planned Enrolment	Actual Enrolment	Drop-Outs
Standard 1			
1968	251,000	250,757	26,112
1969	266,000	253,298	27,099
1970	282,000	279,105	—
Standard 2			
1968	208,000	207,755	10,086
1969	228,000	224,645	10,314
1970	241,000	245,304	—
Standard 3			
1968	179,000	193,537	11,964
1969	200,000	197,669	10,940
1970	219,000	214,331	—
Standard 4			
1968	159,000	158,899	16,219
1969	157,000	171,573	15,865
1970	185,000	186,729	—
Standard 7			
1968	147,000	146,784	106,645
1969	148,000	150,647	104,119
1970	159,000	164,182	—

Administration and Financing of Primary Education

At independence the district education boards were abolished. The Majimbo (Federal) Constitution placed responsibility for primary education in the hands of the regional governments,[22] which had in fact administered it since the commencement of internal self-government on 1 June 1963. The powers granted to the regions reverted to a unitary form of government under the Republican Constitution on 12 December 1964. It should be pointed out that under the Majimbo Constitution some regional governments retained responsibility for financing former government schools; others passed control of education over to local authorities.[23] With the change to a federal constitution, those schools that had been handed over to local authorities by regional governments continued to be financed by those authorities. But for those that had been retained by regional governments some interim support had to be found until the central government's decision on the responsibility for primary education could be made. The government's decision to hand over administration and financing of primary education to local authorities was made early in 1965, and using powers granted under the amendments to the Education Act of 1951 the minister issued the Education (Entrustment of Functions to Local Authorities) Order.[24] On this basis the new county and municipal councils functioned in the field of primary education through their committees.

Today in the city of Nairobi and in each of the country's seven provinces primary education falls under the jurisdiction of a ministry-appointed provincial education officer. Below the provinces, to district councils and local school committees, has been delegated the responsibility for running most primary schools, and district education officers and assistant education officers are employed to function at the district level. The district education officer is actually employed by the Ministry of Education, but his assistants and primary teachers are employed by the Teachers' Service Commission.

Until the declaration of free primary education from standards 1–4, funds for primary education came mainly from two sources, school fees and grants from the Ministry of Local Government. School fees were generally uniform for all the districts. The local authorities contributed to primary education through the personal tax, but its collection became so cumbersome and difficult that the government abolished it.

On average, education accounted for about 60 per cent of county council expenditure,[25] but varied from one district to another. The heaviest expenditure went on teachers' salaries until the government was forced to take over the payment of them because of delays in payment and the counties' preference for employing untrained teachers who were generally cheaper.

Curriculum Development

Combined with the expansion programme of primary education, the government has made some efforts to reform the quality of instruction. In 1967 the Ministry of Education published the first unified syllabus for all primary schools.[26] This spelt out in great detail the subjects to be taught, the books to be used and the amount of time to be allocated to each activity.

It was stated that the function of a primary school was to give a fundamental education in respect of literacy, numeracy, manual dexterity and a general knowledge of the world.[27] It was hoped that emphasising general education would serve both the small minority who would find a place in a secondary school and the 85 or 90 per cent whose formal education was to stop in standard 7. There was no place in the curriculum for technical or vocational training, and agriculture, which was formerly taught as a separate subject, was not taught. The general attempt in the syllabus was to relate each subject to the pupils' immediate environment.

The major emphasis was given to English, mathematics and science and the 1967 syllabus noted that 'the day should start with the most mentally demanding work'.[28] Standards 1, 2 and 3 normally have thirty-five to forty periods per week of thirty minutes each. The number of periods per week in a primary school is shown in Table 6.7.

Table 6.7 *Number of Periods per Week in Primary School by Subject*

Subject	Standard			
	1	2	3	4–7
Arts and Crafts, Needlework and Domestic Science	4	4	4	4
English	4	4	7	10
Geography	—	—	3	3
History and Civics	—	—	2	3
Mathematics	6	6	7	8
Mother Tongues	10	9	5	—
Physical Education and Games	5	5	4	3
Music and Singing	1	1	1	1
Religious Education	4	3	3	3
General Science	1	3	4	6
Kiswahili	—	—	—	4
Total	35	35	40	45

The primary course in Kenya is of seven years' duration. At the end of the seventh year all the pupils in standard 7 sit the Certificate of Primary Education examination (CPE). In the 1970s as low as an average of 14 per cent passed this examination and entered the government secondary schools, another 14 per cent passed and went into Harambee (self-help) secondary schools, about 35 per cent passed and went into employment or became self-employed, while about 35 per cent repeated the examination.[29] The examination consists of a paper in English, another in mathematics and a general paper in history, geography and science. All papers consist of factual questions. The examination is used primarily as an instrument for selecting entrants to secondary schools.

Free Primary Education
At the time of the 1963 election, public demand for universal free primary education was clamorous. Political parties involved in the election campaign – specifically the KANU party – promised the nation free primary education without considering the financial implications and implementation problems.

The first step towards granting free primary education was in 1971. In this year a presidential decree abolished tuition fees for the districts located in areas described as unfavourable geographically.

These areas were largely inhabited by the nomadic people of Kenya. The districts covered by the decree were Marsabit, Idiolo, Samburu, Turkana, West Pokot, Tana River and Lamu. In other districts throughout the country a system of fees remission was formulated.[30]

In December 1973, during the celebration of Kenya's 'Ten Great Years' of independence, a presidential decree provided free education to children in standards 1–4 throughout the republic. The decree had a very dramatic effect on primary school enrolment and the announcement took planners and the entire public by surprise. In January 1974 the Ministry of Education had to reappraise its priorities in order to cope with the staggering rise in pupil enrolment. In standard 1 it rose by 1 million in place of an estimated 400,000. The total enrolment figure for standards 1–4 increased from 1·8 million in 1973 to nearly 2·8 million in January 1974.[31] Despite this rise, it is estimated that another 1 to 2 million children of primary school-age were still not attending school in 1974. It is also estimated that each year an additional 400,000 to 500,000 will enrol in standard 1.[32] Based on this estimate being correct, enrolment in primary schools was projected to reach 4 million in 1980.

Since the decree was unexpected and was not in conformity with the projected estimate of the Ministry of Education, one does not need to stress the numerous problems that faced the primary school system in January 1974. The number of existing schools could not supply classrooms to cope with the increase in enrolment and some school committees had to impose building fees on each child. The supply of equipment underwent a serious strain. There was also the problem of inadequately trained teachers.

The problem of lack of trained teachers was most urgent because at the time of the government pronouncement on free primary education Kenya was already short of properly trained teachers. In 1973 the number of primary teachers stood at 56,000, out of whom 12,600 were professionally unqualified. In 1974 an additional 25,000 teachers were needed for the new classes. By 1975 the number of unqualified teachers had risen to 40,000 out of a force of 90,000 teachers.[33] It goes without saying that this high proportion of unqualified teachers does not favour high quality of teaching in the primary schools of Kenya.

V   SECONDARY EDUCATION

The expansion of primary education in the 1940s and 1950s created a bottleneck in terms of finding places for thousands of successful primary leavers who wanted to enter secondary schools. In 1960, for example, only 12·05 per cent of the successful primary school leavers could find places. The percentage had fallen from 13 per cent in 1958 and 12·8 per cent in 1959. The new plan was to have seventeen new form 1 classes in

1961 and nine more in each of the subsequent two years. This rate of expansion was small, especially since only 0·74 per cent of the 1960 total enrolment in African primary schools attended secondary schools compared with 41·8 per cent of the European primary school enrolment, 11·3 per cent Arab and 19·46 per cent Asian primary school enrolment. How to make secondary school facilities cope with the demands of the numerous primary school leavers was thus a major problem that plagued educational planners in the early 1960s.

One of the steps taken to ease the bottleneck was the decision that from 1960 onwards more secondary schools should be day rather than boarding to permit the creation of more classes and the opening of new schools. The rationale for this decision was that boarding schools were more expensive to run while the assumption that better education could be provided in residential schools did not seem justifiable. Special attention was given to the African secondary schools were the wastage rate was very high. However, the drop-out rate not withstanding, students from African secondary schools gaining the Cambridge School Certificate increased (Table 6.8).

Table 6.8   *Expansion at School Certificate Level, Africans Only, 1958–63*

Year	No. Entered in Form 1	No. Reaching School Certificate Level	School Certificate Pass
1958	3,922	625	491
1959	4,894	799	654
1960	5,409	985	649
1961	n.a.	1,482	951
1963	n.a.	n.a.	1,255

Although we have no records for the number of Africans who entered form 1 in 1961 and 1963, the overall records show that by 1963 – the time of independence – secondary education was already undergoing a dynamic expansion. For example, whereas there were hardly more than two dozen secondary schools in 1958, the number had risen to 150 in 1963. This rate of expansion was, however, far below what was needed to cope with the demand. The famous 'Airlifts of 1959' represented an attempt to satisfy the demand. In 1959 and for some years after hundreds of Kenyan youths were sent abroad for higher education. So powerful was the rush to go abroad that proper attention was not paid to credentials. There were instances when people with no secondary education were air lifted to do post-secondary studies. There was a reported case of a waiting plane which took off with candidates other than those who had been carefully selected by the Ministry of Education!

Although Kenyans went abroad in their hundreds almost every month the demand for more secondary education facilities at home did not diminish. Thus, many Harambee schools were established in Kenya in order to cater for the many primary school leavers who could not find a place in the government-maintained schools. It is with this kind of situation in mind that the development of Harambee schools in Kenya must be assessed. In our view, the establishment of the Harambee schools was a great achievement. They met a relevant need at the time.

Until 1967 there were no unemployed secondary school leavers. It was only after this problem began to surface that the Kenya public began to get concerned about the products of their secondary school system. The need for a diversified secondary school curriculum with emphasis on applied or practical subjects became more apparent. It did not take long before individuals and groups of people began to think of a solution leading to the idea of a Harambee institute of technology that emerged strongly in 1970 and thereafter. We shall elaborate on this later. Meanwhile we shall examine the steps taken by the government to meet the need for technical secondary education.

Technical and Vocational Secondary Schools

We have seen that by 1963 there were 150 secondary schools in Kenya. The number had risen to 981 in 1973, enrolling in that year 180,000 students compared with about 30,000 in 1963. Out of the 981 secondary schools 600 were Harambee schools with an enrolment of 80,000. A year later secondary schools enrolled 195,779 pupils in forms 1–4, of whom 92,016 were in Harambee schools. In 1974 there were 7,177 students in 'A' or Advanced Level classes in Kenya. At the end of 1973, 28,094 pupils sat the East African Certificate in Education (EACE) examinations (Ordinary Level) in the fourth form. In 1975 there were 196,000 pupils in secondary schools. Of these, 92,000 were enrolled in 700 Harambee secondary schools while the rest were enrolled in some 465 maintained schools.

A careful analysis of these figures is bound to raise many questions in the minds of readers. For example, if only 7,177 students were in forms 5 and 6 in 1974 this means that only about 3,000 O Level students were able to proceed to the fifth form work. This leaves 25,000 O Level school leavers for various training schemes and general employment. Luckily for the 1973 leavers the President decreed free primary education for standards 1–4 of the primary school from January 1974. The Ministry of Education had not planned for this and was saved by the presence of a large number of unemployed secondary school leavers who had to be employed overnight as untrained teachers. It seemed for a while that Kenya's secondary school leaver problem had been solved, though the solution created problems for those responsible for teacher training.

However, the problem of unemployed secondary school leavers

remains. Since independence Kenya has been faced with the problem of the shortage of both high-level and middle-level manpower. In 1963 there were two technical and three trade schools. In 1966 trade schools were upgraded to vocational secondary schools and by 1971 there was a total of eight secondary vocational and four technical high schools. Later one of the four technical high schools was converted into a secondary vocational school. The three remaining technical high schools are at Nakuru, Nairobi and Mombasa, and they enrolled 2,200 pupils in 1974. The other nine schools later became secondary technical schools.

In addition to these maintained schools, the government assists two others and has planned to build three more. Nyeri Technical School is to be oriented towards agriculture. Technical education in Kenya is still in a state of flux and settled conditions seem not to be in sight as of 1977. Kenya Polytechnic has developed considerably since its establishment in 1961 and along with the Mombasa Polytechnic offers higher craft and technical training. The government has a huge project to expand technical education in Kenya estimated to cost over Shs 38·5 million.

In 1963 eight secondary schools offered industrial training in workshop practice, for example, carpentry and metalwork. Fifteen other workshops were built in 1966. By 1976 there were about thirty schools offering industrial education which is being expanded with aid given by the Swedish government. The Canadian government has offered to assist Kenya in this field by building a technical teachers college; the first classes began in rented accommodation at Kiamba Institute of Technology in August 1976. In spite of these and other efforts the fact that there were only 3,659 students enrolled in technical schools in forms 1–4 in 1974 means that compared to the total number of students in secondary schools technical education has a long way to develop in Kenya. Even when one adds those who were enrolled at Kenya Polytechnic in the same year, 2,547 and at Mombasa Polytechnic, 930, and those in all the 150 or so village polytechnics, about 6,000, there is no running away from the fact that technical education has grown at a painfully slow rate. There are those who say that Kenya should not produce more than the available employment opportunities; but it would be rather more tolerable to err on the side of producing more school leavers with some marketable technical skills than produce unemployables, without even any pre-vocational skills. Technical skills apart from offering more chances of self-employment, can be exported and when there are more and more people with skills the country will be forced to find a solution. The situation should, of course, be reviewed and the curriculum reformed on the basis of need at any particular moment in history. At present those who wish to improve, for example, housing in the rural areas find it almost impossible to obtain a qualified electrician or plumber, or even a really good builder or carpenter.

Kenyans should not talk about or be led into premature thinking of unemployment of skilled personnel in Kenya during the 1970s and even the 1980s. It should be easier for skilled persons to be self-employed than for those who lack any technical or commercial skills.

The Kenya Ministry of Education also sought to diversify educational offerings by expanding business education in the schools and for this ran two emergency teacher training schemes, beginning in 1971 at Kenyatta College, for prospective business studies teachers. In 1972, sixteen secondary schools were equipped with typewriters and in 1973 an additional eighteen schools were so equipped. The courses are mainly in typewriting and office routine and are preferred mostly by girls.

The third line of diversification of educational opportunities was agriculture. Building on the pioneering experience of Chavakali Secondary School in Western Province the government had expanded the programme to thirteen schools by 1967 with the help of a loan from the World Bank. In the same year the government mounted a teacher training programme at Egerton College for teachers of agriculture in secondary schools. During the 1970–4 Development Plan the Department of Agricultural Education at Egerton was planned to produce forty teachers every year in its three-year non-graduate teacher education programme. By 1972 the programme had been introduced in seventy-two secondary schools and in all primary teachers colleges.

The figures show some development in the area of diversifying secondary education in Kenya. However, the real test of success of these programmes is how many pupils in secondary school follow them and, what is more important, how many of the leavers actually continue in the various fields in higher education or training schemes or employment opportunities.

The introduction to the chapter on education in the Development Plan 1974–8 implies that there has not been much success in that direction and that attitudes towards applied subjects were so bad that it would be too optimistic to expect a sudden turnabout. However, progress has certainly been made in adding more applied subjects to the secondary school curriculum.

VI HIGHER EDUCATION

The development of higher education in Kenya was retarded by the suspicion with which both officials and settlers regarded it. It was not until the 1920s that official opinion began to take African demands more seriously and so permitted the establishment of Makerere College in Uganda in 1922 as a centre for the East African colonies. The idea of interterritoriality recurs frequently and found favour with the commission under Earl De La Warr which visited Makerere in 1937.

Although the majority report of the commission thought that the actual site was unsuitable for the development of an institution of higher learning, Makerere College, under an interterritorial council, continued to provide post-secondary education for East Africa until it became a university college in 1949 on the recommendation of the Asquith Commission of 1943.

Parallel with this latter development was a proposal initiated in 1947 for the establishment of a technical and commercial institute in Nairobi. The reasons for this move lay in the official and settler dislike of the liberal academic tradition so that they favoured a technical institution more directly under the control of the Kenya government, though such an institution managed on an interterritorial basis would be complementary to Makerere. The first intake was admitted in April 1956 to the Royal Technical College, Nairobi, and by the 1958/9 academic year the problem of duplication of courses with Makerere arose when the new college revealed that it intended to present students for the BA, B.Sc. and B.Sc. (Econ.) degrees of the University of London.

At the same time the constraints of the Makerere site were becoming apparent and the Carr Saunders Working Party of 1955 recommended the establishment of another university centre without abandoning the idea of interterritoriality, although this was further weakened by the announcement of Tanganyika's intention to establish its own university college. The Lockwood Working Party of 1959, while retaining belief in a federal university of East Africa, recommended the development of the Royal College as a university college in special relationship with the University of London and made similar recommendations in respect of the new college at Dar es Salaam. University College, Nairobi, came into existence formally on 24 May 1961.

The University of East Africa functioned on an *ad hoc* basis from 1961 with 1,364 students, a provisional council and embryonic academic management. The University of East Africa Act was formally promulgated by the East Africa High Commission in 1962 and the inauguration took place in August 1963. However skilfully the constitution of a federal university may be designed, there are always difficulties in making it work and these were compounded by the growth of national feeling and aspirations in the newly independent countries of East Africa. Thus the life of the federal university was foreshortened and came to an end in 1972. So for the development of university education in Kenya we must turn our attention to University College, Nairobi, with a passing glance at an imaginative, if haphazard, attempt to increase the number of Kenyans undergoing higher education – the famous airlifts to the United States organised by Tom Mboya. The academic attainments of the airborne students were varied and many had to enter high schools and junior colleges before they could begin degree studies. There is some dispute about the numbers actually airlifted but it must be in the region of 400–600. There were also about 1,000 Kenyans studying on scholarships in socialist countries. During the first three years of the 1960s about 44 per cent of the students from Kenya studying abroad went to Britain and 23 per cent to India and Pakistan.

University College, Nairobi

In 1962/3 further developments took place at Nairobi College: The Faculty of Veterinary Science was transferred from Makerere. The College of Social Studies, which had operated as an independent residential adult education centre since 1961, was absorbed. These two departments were merged into the Institute of Adult Education in 1963. The College of Social Studies was renamed the Adult Studies Centre in 1966. During the period 1961–7 many buildings were erected to accommodate the academic requirements of a rapidly expanding college.

In September 1963, following the inauguration of the University of East Africa in August 1963, new students enrolled for the degree and diploma courses of that university. The exceptions were the students enrolling in the Departments of Domestic Science and Land Development who continued to work for the qualifications of the University of Manchester and the Royal Institute of Chartered Surveyors respectively.

Students who had enrolled for the University of London degrees continued under the scheme until the last examinations were held in June 1966. This brought to an end a brief period of association with the University of London.

In 1965 the Institute for Development Studies was established with two divisions: the Cultural Division and Social Science Division. In 1967 the Faculty of Medicine admitted its first students.

In January 1966 a Department of Education was established in the Faculty of Arts with a close working relationship with the Faculty of Science. It started with a Postgraduate Diploma in Education class of eighteen students. In September 1966, as well as taking on a new class of postgraduate diploma students, the department embarked on a concurrent undergraduate degree programme offering service courses to arts and science students intending to become teachers. The degree which was awarded to successful students under this programme was the BA/B.Sc. (Education Option) degree. Initially the education option students commenced their education courses in the second year of their university studies, but later the Faculty of Arts accepted education as a subject and students could start reading education in their first year of university studies and continue with it for three years.

During the 1969/70 academic year a new Department of Philosophy and Religious Studies was established in the Faculty of Arts.

In 1970 when University College, Nairobi, became a national university as the University of Nairobi a number of important developments took place. The Faculties of Agriculture, Education and Law were established. The Institute for Development Studies was reorganised into two, the former Cultural Division becoming the Institute of African Studies. Meanwhile in April 1970 the School of Journalism had been established, offering initially a two-year diploma course.

Kenyatta College became a university college of the University of Nairobi with the responsibility of training graduate teachers in conjunction with Faculty of Education. The Departments of Fine Art and Home Economics were transferred to Kenyatta University College. In 1972 the Faculty of Education began offering the B.Ed. degree for students intending to go into teaching or some other educational service.

The Fine Arts Department at Kenyatta University College offers courses leading to the award of the BA and the B.Ed. degrees; the latter to those intending to go into teaching. In addition to these courses, Kenyatta College has programmes in business studies and music at the degree and non-degree levels. The Department of Home Economics also offers a B.Sc. degree and a B.Ed. degree. The University of Nairobi underwent rapid expansion particularly in the late 1960s and early 1970s. By the 1973/4 academic year the university had an enrolment of about 6,000 students. However, in the following years enrolment in the university was cut down as its admission policy underwent an internal review. The principle of admitting all those with minimum entrance requirements was discontinued. The reduction in enrolment was partly due to the fact that the problem of unemployment for some arts graduates was beginning to arise. At the same time, there were great shortages of graduates in certain professions or areas.

As an example of the cutting back on admission, the Faculty of Education, which had admitted about 800 students shared between itself and Kenyatta University College in 1973 and 1974, reduced its intake in 1975 by half. In 1976 it admitted a total of 350 students: 250 for Kenyatta University College and 100 for the Faculty of Education, Nairobi. By 1973–6 it was becoming clear that there was a need to look into the whole question of higher education and to establish the areas of greatest shortages to enable the university to plan its development. The whole sector of tertiary education in Kenya is in need of thorough study and planning.

Duplication must be avoided as much as possible. There is also a need to re-examine the use of expatriates against the long-term benefits of developing local facilities for training local manpower through aid given by those who would send expatriates. Higher education has reached a plateau in East Africa. The East African governments are to be commended for what has been achieved in a space of a dozen or so years, but there is no cause for complacency. Higher education is an expensive undertaking. The time has come now for a thorough reappraisal and the charting of a system removed from the urgency and emotional feelings of political independence. The qualitative nature of higher education is today's real challenge in East African higher education.

NOTES: CHAPTER 6

1   Education Ordinance 1924 (London: HMSO, 1924), Vol. 3, pp. 96–107.
2   Education Department, *Annual Report,* (Nairobi: Government Printer, 1924), p. 22.
3   *Journal of African Administration,* Vol. XII (July, 1960), p. 148.
4   D. N. Sifuna, *Vocational Education in Schools, A Historical Survey of Kenya and Tanzania* (Nairobi: East African Literature Bureau, 1976), p. 200.
5   Unesco, *The Addis Ababa Report on the Development of Education in Africa* (Paris: Unesco, 1961)
6   ibid., p. 10; J. R. Sheffield, *Education in Kenya, An Historical Study,* (New York: Teachers College Press, 1973), p. 68.
7   Unesco, *Meeting of Ministers of Education of African Countries Participating in the Implementation of the Addis Ababa Plan* (Paris: UNESCO, March 1962).
8   V. L. Griffiths, 'Some suggestions for an African government's educational policy in Kenya,' Oxford, 1962, mimeo., p. ii.
9   ibid., p. 1.
10 *World Bank Survey,* (Kenya, 1961), p. 300.
11 ibid., p. 227.
12 Hunter Report, 1962 Mimeo, p. 57.
13 J. R. Sheffield, *Education in the Republic of Kenya* (Washington, DC: Government Printer, 1971), p. 30.
14 *Education Commission Report* (Ominde Report) (Nairobi: Government Printer, 1964), p. 56.
15 loc. cit.
16 L. G. Cowan *The Cost of Learning: The Politics of Primary Education in Kenya* (New York: Teachers College Press, 1970), p. 31.
17 Unesco, *Conference on Education and Scientific and Technical Training in Relation to Development in Africa* (Paris): Unesco, 1968), p. 8.
18 Sheffield, *Education in Kenya,* op. cit., p. 80.
19 ibid., pp. 36–8.
20 Kenya Government, *Development Plan 1970–4* (Nairobi: Government Printer, 1969), pp. 453–4.
21 Ministry of Education, *Annual Report* (Nairobi: Government Printer, 1969), p. 4.
22 Kenya Constitution Schedule 1, *Kenya Gazette,* supplement no. 105 (10 December 1963).
23 Cowan, op. cit., p. 11.
24 *Legal Notice,* no. 74 (1965).
25 Nizar Jetha, 'The budgetary constraints in Kenya', in J. R. Sheffield (ed.), *Education, Employment and Rural Development* (Nairobi: East African Publishing House, 1967), p. 458.
26 Ministry of Education, *Primary School Syllabus* (Nairobi: Government Printer, 1967).
27 ibid., p. i.
28 loc. cit.

29 D. N. Sifuna, *Revolution in Primary Education: The New Approach in Kenya* (Nairobi: East African Literature Bureau, 1975), p. 49.
30 ILO, *Employment, Incomes and Equality: A strategy for Increasing Production Employment in Kenya* (Geneva: ILO, 1972), p. 235.
31 J. M. G. Nuhore, 'Universal free primary education – the Kenya experience', mimeo. ATEA Conference Papers, 1975, p. 3.
32 loc. cit.
33 loc. cit.

Chapter 7

Education in Lesotho

J. MOHAPELOA

I BRIEF HISTORICAL OUTLINE

In this chapter there will be scant reference to traditional forms of education because here we are concerned mainly with education as we know it today.

In order that the reader may understand why Lesotho education took the form it took, a short outline of the historical background will be given. The first schools were opened by Christian missionaries in the nineteenth century. For example, by 1860 the Paris Evangelical Missionary Society had established schools at all their central mission stations and some out-stations. In the mid-1806s the Roman Catholics had opened schools at their central mission stations; and the Anglicans were to open theirs in the 1870s. Education in Lesotho, as in other parts of Africa, is often said to be bookish. One of the reasons for this is that the missionaries, who were (and in Lesotho still are) the main providers of education, had an interest in Basotho who could read the Bible. It was also essential, the PEMS said, 'to use the natives themselves for the enlightenment of their own country'.[1] Nevertheless, the missionaries are not the only ones to blame for education that emphasises book learning. The British administrators, when Lesotho became British territory, had jobs for clerks and interpreters. In fact, it can be said in favour of the missionaries that quite early they attempted to establish vocational schools. At Roma the Sisters of the Holy Family of Bordeaux taught the girls spinning, weaving and sewing.[2] In the 1870s the PEMS established two 'industrial schools' and the Anglicans one.[3] These efforts were not supported by the government, however.

Another feature of Lesotho education which is revealed by its history is that the government involved itself as little as possible in it. From 1872 it grant-aided some schools; but this was aid without guidance and control. In the 1890s there was aid with minimal supervision. This was the time when schools were inspected by assistant commissioners and sub-inspectors of police.[4] 'An Education Department, with an Inspector of Schools, two Basotho Assistant Inspectors and a Mosotho Clerk' was only established in 1906–7.[5] But the following recommendations by an education commission appointed in 1925 show that the government was still giving insufficient direction to educational work in the country. The commission recommended *(inter alia)*:

(1) government control of educational policy;
(2) the appointment of a committee to consider the drawing up of a new syllabus and the advisability of government conducting its own examinations and issuing its own certificates;
(3) the clarification of the position of the Director of Education;
(4) a bigger staff for the Education Department.

And thirty-nine years later (in 1964) a Unesco education mission still found it necessary to point to the following as the 'areas where priority action is necessary in the next five years':

(1) the institution of a proper planning machinery;
(2) the development of secondary education;
(3) the development of teacher training;
(4) the development of technical education (including agricultural education).[6]

Among these, it considered the need for comprehensive planning the most urgent and fundamental, and a start was made in 1967, when a Unesco-sponsored education planner was appointed. Other expatriate planners followed; but at the same time Basotho were being trained, so that in 1973 a Mosotho was in charge of the Planning Unit, whose staff in 1978 consisted of an education planner, a deputy education planner, an assistant education planner (educationist), an assistant education planner (economist), an assistant education planner (special duties and research) and a facilities officer. The Planning Unit works in close co-operation with the education statistician's team.

II ADMINISTRATION AND CONTROL

To a large extent the owernship of schools determines how they are run. In this matter Lesotho is still in the nineteenth century, that is, instead of a national system of education it continues to have a grant-aided one, in which the schools are owned by voluntary bodies (usually churches) and the government assists these bodies in carrying out their educational work. Consequently, educational administration and control are shared by the government and the churches.

   Government legislates for education. But even this it only began to do in 1947, after a commission of inquiry had strongly recommended the making of an educational law.[7] Before that, Lesotho had had regulations for its schools; but they had not been based on any proclamation – the legislative method of those days. It is the government also which makes decisions on the content of education, the organisation of schools at the various levels, staffing ratios, and so on. It is responsible for school inspections, and conducts primary leaving (standard 7) and teacher training examinations. In the latter case the examinations are actually conducted by the National Teacher Training College; but one can say they are conducted by the government because it is one of the few government educational institutions. Educational expansion (for example, how many new schools should be opened and where they should be sited) is also a matter for the government.

The churches are the proprietors of the vast majority of the schools and supply most of the furniture and equipment. The schools are run by school managers usually assisted by school committees. Many secondary schools are run by school committees or boards of governors. The teachers in these schools are church employees, and are responsible to school managers, most of whom are ministers of religion. But an interesting arrangement has been made here by means of which these employees of the churches receive their salaries direct from the government. As there has to be close co-operation between the churches and the government, the Ministry of Education provides the churches with funds for the employment of liaison officers designated educational secretaries. These officials are the link between the churches and the government on educational matters. They represent the churches on the bodies which are advisory to the Ministry of Education such as the Central Advisory Board on Education. They appoint the managers of their schools and ratify the employment contracts of teachers in church schools on behalf of the churches.

In relation to the amount of work it has to do, the Ministry of Education has, up to now, been rather small; but it is being reorganised into several departments and sections with specific functions.

I shall now discuss the various levels and kinds of education. In doing this, I shall follow the usual order from primary education upwards; but I shall discuss teacher education before secondary education. The reason for this is that teachers were being trained in Lesotho before it had any secondary education, and up to quite recently primary school teachers were trained on the completion of their primary education. The order, therefore, will be (1) primary education, (2) teacher education, (3) secondary education, (4) technical and vocational education, (5) higher education and (6) non-formal education.

III PRIMARY EDUCATION

Lesotho has a seven-year primary course, and the stipulated age of first entry is 6–7 years of age, but many over-age children are to be found in the schools, just as there are a considerable number of under-age ones. Of the 23,763 boys enrolled in 1975, for example, 5,732 were under 6 years while the ages of some 9,018 ranged from 8 to 20 years and over. A similar grouping of the girls' ages produced this result: under 6 years, 7 452; 8–18 years, 6,954; total, 26,453.[8] The organisational, teaching and even disciplinary problems caused by this kind of age-range are easy to imagine.

During the past ten years the primary curriculum has undergone some changes. The aims in making these changes have been (a) to integrate the areas of learning, and think less in terms of subjects, (b) to streamline the curriculum by omitting non-essentials and concentrating on communication skills, numeracy and a practical introduction to science, and, of course, (c) to relate the pupils' learning to their experiences. The integration and streamlining carried out in 1967 was not very successful, however, because one still finds four 'subjects', namely, Sesotho, English, mathematics and science; and where an attempt was made to integrate areas of study, the subjects have tended to retain their identity. For example, 'social studies' is made up of geography and history, each with its own syllabus, and under the label 'skill' are to be found arts and crafts, gardening, handwork, music, needlework, physical education and writing.[9]

I shall later discuss this apparent failure to help the child in the Lesotho primary school to see life and see it as a whole. Before I do that, I shall mention some of the problems facing the schools.

Small (often one-teacher), scattered schools

In the uplands the terrain makes it difficult for schools to be 'consolidated' and still be within easy reach of all the children. In the lowlands for a long time this problem, on a smaller scale, was due to rivalry between the missionary bodies which were managing the schools.

Poor physical conditions

What a commission of inquiry said about these as long ago as 1905 is still largely true, namely, that 'the school buildings are generally ill-adapted to their purpose, and are badly equipped in respect of furniture and other school material'.[10]

The pupil/teacher ratio

In many cases teachers are faced with classes far in excess of what could be regarded as a class of normal size. Between 1965 and 1975 there was never a year in which there were fewer than forty-four pupils per teacher, and the ratio could be as bad as fifty-nine pupils to one teacher. It was stated in May 1978 that 'since 1973, the ratio of pupils to teachers has stabilised around 52·5 to 1'.[11]

The quality of the teaching staff
Here we shall only consider the teachers' qualifications and their effectiveness. In 1977 31 per cent of the teachers were untrained. Of the 2,974 trained teachers, 1,729 or 58 per cent had primary education plus three years' training; that is, they were underqualified. The underqualified and the totally untrained teachers together constituted 71 per cent of the teaching force.[12] While it may be true that good teachers are born, not made, it has to be conceded that the effectiveness of the teacher is largely influenced by how well he is trained. This effectiveness is also influenced by his dedication, which in turn is affected by his status in society. The Lesotho primary schoolteacher has ceased to have the high status he formerly enjoyed. This is mainly because materially he compares unfavourably with the civil servant, the doctor, the lawyer, and so on. In spite of this, however, he is still, on the whole, very conscientious. With better pre-service training, and better conditions of service, he would be more effective because he is dedicated.

Wastage
Gross wastage, which is defined as the difference between the first grade of the cycle of education and the final grade, is 71·5 per cent.[13] According to a study made in 1976 by the Statistics Unit of the Ministry of Education, one out of three pupils entering primary school completes the seven-year primary course (see Table 7.1). But because girls can perform their domestic duties and still attend school, while boys may be withdrawn to herd livestock, there are fewer drop-outs among girls than among boys. One of the causes of this wastage could be the fact that not all primary schools offer the full seven-year primary course. In 1977 only 414 of the 1,074 primary schools provided it. The rest taught up to the fourth year only.

Table 7.1   *Promotion and Drop-Out Profiles, 1976*

Grades	Promotion (Standard 1 = 1,000)	Drop-Out
I	1,000	242
II	758	55
III	703	81
IV	622	52
V	570	91
VI	479	69
VII	410	99
Total	311	689 (All Grades)

Source: Ministry of Education, *A Case Study Evaluating Educational Wastage* ED/Y/1 (Maseru: Ministry of Education, 1977).

I now return to a brief discussion of some of the defects of Lesotho's primary education, dealing mainly with its objectives, the teaching procedures and associated matters.

The objectives have always been unexceptional. In 1946, for example, the Clarke Commission stated that:

> The overmastering purpose of any system of education for the Basuto (Basotho) is so obvious that it leaps to the eyes at once. It may be stated as the development and organisation of all possible resources, material and human, to secure the maximum of self-sufficiency; to train a people that can stand and cohere and defy the forces of disintegration, whatever its ultimate destiny may be.

To this the following specific objectives were added:

(1) insistence on the highest attainable level of general education;
(2) the advancement of the capacity of the people to increase the wealth of the country;
(3) the preservation and strengthening of the basis and resources of family life.[14]

In its introduction to the 1957 syllabus for primary schools the then Department of Education described the 'aim and purpose of primary education' in similar words. This education was to enable the children 'to lead a full life not only as individuals but also as members of the community', and to 'afford an adequate background' for those going on to secondary and tertiary education.[15]

The Ministry of Education and other educators in Lesotho hold advanced views on teaching methods. For example, in the 1967 syllabus they advised teachers that in mathematics the 'sums' must be 'useful', that is, they should be related to the pupils' daily experience. Mechanical work should be preceded by practical work; but the mechanical work itself must lead to problem-solving. Further, to make mathematics real, in addition to basing their examples 'upon what is familiar to the children in their daily lives', teachers must give their pupils work that is 'related to practical projects such as [those which] arise in craft work, gardening, domestic science, family budgets, wages, taxation, etc.'. Much stress is laid on pupil activity and groupwork. The teacher is given considerable assistance. The science syllabus, for example, includes both content and teachers' notes, and pupil activity is described in detail. The teachers are given suggestions on how to conduct physical education, music and art lessons.[16]

The weakness of the system is that in many cases these objectives and procedures are still the ideal. In many schools the position is still as it was in 1964 when a visiting mission wrote:

The syllabus for each subject has been carefully drawn up and is revised from time to time . . . The gradual progress from the child's immediate experience and environment to wider issues, and the emphasis on child participation and active learning, are all marks of a syllabus conceived and drafted in an enlightened manner. Unfortunately, the syllabus is far ahead of the conditions in the schools . . . Performance in the schools differs lamentably from the enlightened aims and methods embodied in the syllabus.[17]

I have been careful to use the words 'in many cases' because, although one still encounters rote learning, efforts continue to be made to bring about learning that results from reasoning and understanding. Teachers, individual schools and groups of schools (notably the 'experimental schools') are engaged in this work of reorientation of teachers and modernisation of procedures. The Ministry of Education's 'Experimental Primary Schools Project', which is a by-product of a scheme for the upgrading of untrained primary teachers launched in 1966, is an attempt to bring about a modern approach to the work of the primary school by the in-service training of not one or two members of staff but the whole staff of the school. It also aims at developing 'strategically located schools which could serve as local demonstration and resource centres'.[18]

Much has still to be done (by establishing teachers' centres and in other ways) to eradicate unsatisfactory teaching procedures. For example, one finds it difficult to blame a teacher who has abandoned his training college idealism about activity methods, experimentation, and so on, if such a teacher is in a school with no teaching aids. His enthusiasm is often dampened by having to teach in a school which does not (because it cannot) help him to purchase ready-made aids or materials to make his own. Therefore, it must be one of the principal aims of the educational system of Lesotho both to produce teachers who are fully aware of the learning experiences their pupils need and to make it possible for them to provide those experiences. The energetic, inventive teacher, who devises ways of procuring and making teaching aids, should be supported. It is also an encouragement to such a teacher to find that there is a stock to which he can add, or that his task is to modernise and bring about variety.

Finance

This brings us to the financing of primary education. The 1978 seminar on education, to which references have been made, was told that 'in 1976 education received 26·1 per cent of total Government budgetary expenditure. Of the 26·1 per cent about 53 per cent went into primary education, all of which went to teachers' salaries.' For the purchase of equipment and teaching materials the schools depend on the fees paid by

Table 7.2 *Public Expenditure on Education, 1973–6* (R thousands)

	1972/3 r	1973/4 r	1974/5 r	1975/6 r
Recurrent				
Administration	116·3	125·8	183·4	213·4
Inspectorate	120·7	182·0	158·3	181·3
Technical and Voca-tional Education	83·9	80·9	95·2	98·3
Teaching Service Unit	—	—	—	78·5
Teacher Training	100·1	106·5	35·2	117·3
Primary Education	1,410·2	1,432·7	1,424·8	3,479·8
Secondary Education	357·0	370·2	428·7	1,116·6
Higher Education	597·8	717·7	912·8	1,349·9
Total Recurrent Expenditure	2,786·0	3,015·8	3,258·4	6,631·1
Capital				
Administration	—	—	25,000	50,000
Technical and Voca-tional Education	—	41,000	520,000	1,163,000
Teacher Education	—	—	73,000	513,000
Primary Education	—	—	26,300	8,000
Secondary Education	217,217	336,950	128,470	469,500
Higher Education	71,250	—	—	25,000
Total Capital Expenditure	288,467	377,950	772,770	2,228,500

Source: Ministry of Education, *Annual Report, 1974/75* (Maseru: Ministry of Education, 1976), p. 47

the parents and on grants from private agencies. In order that the government should be able to assist with this, the share of the budget allocated to primary education would have to be increased; but this would mean decreasing the provision for secondary, technical, teacher and higher education.[19] What this means is that primary education is inadequately financed in spite of the fact that between 1972/3 and 1975/6 the amount provided for recurrent expenditure has more than doubled. It has risen from R 1·4 million to R 3·5 million (see Table 7.2).

The problems of financing primary education will become more severe rather than easier if only because of the growing enrolment figures. In 1977 the total primary school enrolment was 226,019; and the projected figure for 1980 was 238,445. It is unlikely that it will fall. It did so in 1971 when the length of the primary course was reduced from eight to seven years; but it has been rising steadily since.

In addition there is a shortage of professional advisers for the primary schoolteachers. I am referring, in particular, to inspectors who can visit the teachers and spend some time working with them in their schools.

Such visits would serve a twofold purpose, namely, to give untrained teachers a kind of on-the-job training, and to help trained teachers update their understanding of the purpose of education in the context of their society and, as a result re-examine and adjust their methods of teaching. It has been said that 'the inspector of primary schools should regard himself as a "mobile teachers' college" and his work as an extension of that done by the colleges themselves'.[20] To be able to play this role effectively, the inspector must see his teachers as often as possible, and his visits to them should not be short and fleeting. Unfortunately, the Lesotho inspectorate cannot do otherwise. For example, although in 1977 there were seventeen assistant education officers in post, only ten to twelve were available at any one time for the inspection of the 1,080 primary schools. Because some of the 190 school days are used for end-of-term examinations and preparations for them it is estimated that in any given year 40–50 per cent of the schools are not visited.[21] To remedy this situation, the size of the inspectorate was doubled in 1978.[22]

IV   TEACHER EDUCATION

Until 1974 primary schoolteachers were trained at seven small, church-run colleges. The course for teachers intended for the lower primary schools (i.e. standards 1 to 5 or 6) led to the Lesotho Primary Teachers' Certificate (LPTC). This was a three-year, post-primary course. For prospective higher primary schoolteachers there was a two-year Primary Higher (PH) course of training to which the holders of the Junior Certificate (JC), a certificate earned after the successful completion of three years of secondary education, were admitted.[23] The LPTC was phased out in 1974, and now all primary schoolteachers undergo training after JC. The duration of the course of training is three years.

One of the seven colleges offered a two-year post-Cambridge Overseas School Certificate (COSC) course for teachers in junior secondary schools. Other junior and senior secondary schoolteachers worked for the certificates, diplomas and degrees of the University of Botswana, Lesotho and Swaziland (UBLS).

Since 1975 the training of the primary and junior secondary schoolteachers has been consolidated. The courses are now given at one institution financed and run by the government. This is the National Teacher Training College (NTTC). The college offers the following courses:

(1) the Primary Teachers' Certificate programme (PTC)
(2) the Advanced Primary Teachers' Certificate Programme (APTC)

(3)   the Secondary Teachers' Certificate programme (STC).

The entrance qualifications are:

(1)   PTC – a satisfactory Junior Certificate
(2)   APTC – completed (junior) secondary education plus a successful teaching record
(3)   STC – completed secondary education with satisfactory performance in the Cambridge Overseas School Certificate Examination.[24]

In both the APTC and STC programmes there is provision for a compulsory subject specialisation and an optional specialisation. The major subjects which may be selected for specialisation are English, Sesotho, development studies, agriculture, home economics, commercial studies, mathematics, science, social studies and professional studies. The optional specialisation may be selected from the major subjects or from the following ancillary courses: arts and crafts, music, religious education, health education and physical education.

The second year of each of the three courses (PTC, APTC and STC) is an internship year, which the students spend teaching in selected schools under the supervision of the college staff.

The college also offers in-service courses. These range from 'the lower certificates to upgrade underqualified and unqualified teachers to the highest . . . professional certificate'.[25]

During 1975/7 enrolment in pre-service and in-service courses was 787, broken down as in Table 7.3.

One of the innovations of the NTTC is the production of self-instructional materials. These are single-topic units, each with a specified objective (or objectives) and designed in such a way that it can be completed without the assistance of a teacher and there is 'allowance for students working at different paces'. It is claimed that

> Through the development of self-instructional materials, the College is placing a sizeable portion of its curriculum in objectively-defined and well-organized topics. These topics . . . provide the College with curriculum topics for materials development that are orientated to Lesotho.[26]

To achieve this, the authors of the materials visit schools to familiarise themselves with real life conditions. Further, 'a field list is undertaken to assess cultural sensitivity and appropriateness for local conditions. Units are revised on the basis of this field list.'[27]

Before 1975, when the college opened, the only place for the training

Table 7.3 Teacher Training Enrolment, 1975–7

| Intake | Pre-Service | | | | | | In-Service | | | | Totals | |
| | PTC | | APTC | | STC | | Primary | | Secondary | | | |
	M	F	M	F	M	F	M	F	M	F	M	F
1975	17	20	2	11	12	16	—	—	—	—	31	47
1976	55	100	7	24	45	49	12	87	6	5	125	265
1977	44	138	17	19	37	64	—	—	—	—	98	221
Total	116	258	26	54	94	129	12	87	6	5	254	533

Source: *Mid-Project Review, NTCC* (Maseru: Ministry of Education, 1977), p.1.

of secondary schoolteachers, junior and senior, was the Roma campus of the University of Botswana, Lesotho and Swaziland.[28] To say this is to say that the level of training was virtually non-existent, a somewhat extravagant way of drawing attention to the frustration the teacher educators of the National University of Lesotho and its forerunner, the UBLS have felt because of the difficulty they have had in recruiting trainees and (having enrolled them) retaining them, and their disappointment when those who have completed their courses have either taught for short periods and left for more lucrative jobs or been immediately snatched by government ministries other than that of education. This is a serious matter because a recent survey has revealed that between 1964 and 1975 the UBLS produced only seventy teachers for Lesotho's sixty-two secondary schools, as may be seen in Table 7.4.

Table 7.4 *Output of Qualified Teachers from UBLS, 1964-75*

Initial Qualifications	B.Ed.	BA. + CCE.[1]	B.Sc.+CCE[2]	PCE[3]	CSE[4]	T. CERT[5]
Numbers	2	22	4	5	4	33

Notes:
[1]BA. + CCE = Bachelor of Arts and Concurrent Certificate in Education
[2]B.Sc. + CCE = Bachelor of Science and Concurrent Certificate in Education
[3]PCE = Postgraduate Certificate in Education
[4]CSE = Certificate in Secondary Education
[5]T. Cert. = Teachers' Certificate
Source: C. Hudson and P. E. Khabele, 'Tracer study: a critical survey of secondary school teachers trained for the Lesotho educational system by the University of Botswana, Lesotho and Swaziland from 1964 to 1975', unpublished paper, Faculty of Education, National University of Lesotho, 1976.

The NUL Faculty of Education (like the UBLS Faculty of Education before it) has twelve forward-looking objectives from which these three excerpts are taken:

(1) to educate secondary teachers in the understanding and skills necessary for them . . . to contribute, by constructive proposals and innovation, to the improvement of the education system as a whole;

(2) to educate experienced primary and secondary teachers and other educational workers so that they may
(*a*) occupy posts of professional leadership,
(*b*) contribute to the overall improvement of the education system . . .

(6) To provide an integrated programme of short courses, workshops and conferences for secondary teachers, training college personnel leaders in primary education and, where feasible, educational workers in other sectors of national development, in such a way that the programme is related to the policies and priorities of the Ministry of· Education while, at the same time, encouraging innovation and development of the teaching profession.[29]

One fears, however, that these aims, which if pursued energetically could lead to the production of educators and not mere classroom practitioners, will count for nothing until education is accorded its rightful place in the university. The very fact that the only full-time courses offered by the Faculty of Education were *in addition* to other courses (BA, CCE and B.Sc. + CCE) means that for the students 'the real thing' was those other courses. Such an attitude was responsible for unsatisfactory work being done. Put another way, this attitude led to the production of poorly trained teachers with very little motivation. That is changing, however. In the 1977/8 academic year the B.Sc. + CCE was replaced by a B.Sc.Ed. degree which integrates content courses with professional studies and aims at the improvement of science education. A BA Ed. degree will replace BA & CCE in 1978/9.

The enrolments in the education programmes of the Faculty of Education of the National University of Lesotho during the 1977/8 academic year show that, in view of the comments made earlier on wastage, it will be a long time before NUL can produce enough teachers for Lesotho's secondary schools. The enrolments were as shown in Table 7.5.

Table 7.5   *NUL Faculty of Education Enrolment Figures, 1977/8*

Programme	Number of Students by Years				
	1	*2*	*3*	*4*	*Total*
CCE[1]	31	43	46	40	159
B.Sc.Ed.[2]	6	8	—	—	14
CPE[3],[5]	—	12	—	—	12
Dip.Ed.[4],[5]	—	19	—	—	19
B.Ed.	—	11	—	—	1
M.Ed.[5]	—	1	—	—	1
Total	37	83	46	40	206

Notes:
[1] CCE = Concurrent Certificate in Education
[2] B.Sc.Ed. = Bachelor of Science in Education
[3] CPE = Certificate in Primary Education
[4] Dip.Ed. = Diploma in Education
[5] CPE, Dip.Ed. and M.Ed. are part-time programmes.
Source: Student Record Office and Faculty of Education, NUL.

Because the structure of the teacher education programme at NUL is undergoing change the courses as at June 1978 will merely be listed. They are grouped under the various programmes thus:

(1) *Postgraduate Certificate in Education, Concurrent Certificate in Education*
   Human development, educational policy, educational psychology,

introduction to teaching, educational resources, educational planning, school management, on-campus (mainly micro-) teaching practice, in-school teaching practice, introduction to science education, introduction to mathematics education, curriculum studies in the following teaching subjects; African languages, English, mathematics, science, history, geography, religious education, development studies.

(2) *Certificate in Primary Education*
English for primary education, mathematics for primary education, primary education policy, primary teacher education, supervision of primary schools, curriculum studies in *one* of the following: African languages, English, mathematics, science, social studies and environmental studies.

(3) *Diploma in Education*
Education, curriculum studies in 2/3 primary/secondary school subjects.

(4) *Bachelor of Education*
Educational policy and planning, philosophy of education, psychology of education, statistics and research methods; project, and *one* of the following: teacher education, educational administration, adult education, agricultural education, curriculum studies.

V SECONDARY EDUCATION

Lesotho has a five-year secondary course, the first three years of which lead to the award of the Junior Certificate (JC) and the remaining two to the Cambridge Overseas School Certificate (COSC). The JC course is controlled by the Examinations Council of Botswana, Lesotho and Swaziland and the COSC by the Cambridge University Examinations Syndicate.

The structure of the Junior Certificate course is determined by the Examinations Council which, through its subject panels, decides on the content of the subjects to be taught; but the Lesotho Ministry of Education tries to ensure that what is taught (and how it is taught) is what Lesotho needs. For example, in 1973, a compulsory 'core curriculum', consisting of Sesotho, English, mathematics, science and, 'in some cases', development studies and practical skills was introduced. It was then stated that

The curriculum ensures that every pupil studies basic subjects necessary for higher education and at the same time ensures that he will have sufficient practical subjects to prepare him for situations in real life and to make school experience meaningful.[30]

In addition to this, a curriculum diversification programme, intended for both JC and COSC, was launched in 1974 under the title 'The Training for Self-Reliance Project'. The project had the following three purposes:

(1) to expand the Lerotholi Technical Institute from 120 students to 560, and upgrade it to a fully fledged polytechnic;
(2) to introduce practical subjects in six pilot schools;
(3) to launch a community outreach programme using the new facilities of these schools.[31]

Progress is being made with this programme, and more secondary schools are being brought into the Training for Self-Reliance Project.

The secondary school, like the primary school, is beset with problems, the most difficult of which is staffing. One of these difficulties, the comparatively small number of Basotho graduate teachers, is the result of competition between the schools on the one hand and the civil service and the private sector on the other for qualified university graduates. It is because of this and because secondary teachers have not been produced in anything like sufficient numbers that in 1975 among the 611 secondary schoolteachers there were 251 expatriates; of the local teachers only 50 were graduates while 113 held lower teachers' qualifications, and some 197 teachers were unqualified.[32] These calculations are somewhat misleading, however, because (i) not all graduates are qualified, (ii) there may be some expatriates among the unqualified teachers, which would mean there are more than 251 expatriates, and (iii) there may be expatriates among the holders of lower teachers' qualifications. Poor staffing and other inadequacies are reflected in the low educational quality of the products of Lesotho's secondary schools.

VI TECHNICAL AND VOCATIONAL EDUCATION

Progress has been slowest in this sector. During the nineteenth century, as mentioned earlier, missionary bodies established small vocational schools; but it was only in 1906 that, as a result of the initiative taken by Paramount Chief Lerotholi, the government opened an industrial school at Maseru. This is still the only government-run institution of this kind in the country. The establishment of the school did not signal the strengthening and development of vocational education, however, and most of the money provided for educational work continued to be used for the expansion of primary education. During the financial year 1973/4, for example, recurrent expenditure on primary education was 47·51 per cent of total recurrent expenditure on education, while that on

Table 7.6   *Expenditure, by Sector, as Percentage of Total Expenditure on Education (Recurrent), 1971–3*

	1970/1	1971/2	1972/3	1973/4
Administration	2·13	3·73	4·17	4·17
Education (Inspectorate)	3·21	3·82	4·33	6·03
Technical and Vocational	3·48	3·34	3·01	2·68
Teacher Training	4·33	4·33	3·59	3·53
Primary Education	59·31	50·92	50·62	47·51
Secondary Education	12·89	14·76	12·82	12·28
Higher Education	14·65	19·10	21·46	23·80
	100·00	100·00	100·00	100·00

Source: Annual Report of the Ministry of Education and Culture, 1973, p. 39.

vocational education was 2·68 per cent.[33] How expenditure on vocational education compared with expenditure on other sectors is shown in Table 7.6.

In spite of this modest expenditure on technical and vocational education, there has been some expansion in recent years. One example of this is the rising enrolment at the Lerotholi Technical Institute which has gone from 126 in 1974 to 392 in 1978. This institute, which offers training at both post-JC and post-COSC levels, has seen a number of interesting developments since 1973. The technician training school, formerly under the Ministry of Works, has become part of it and gives training in civil engineering and draughtsmanship. In 1973 Gold Fields of South Africa Ltd and the government of the Federal Republic of Germany helped the LTI to give training in basic engineering which would lead to general mechanics and automotive training. This development was followed in 1974 by the introduction by the same two bodies of new courses in plumbing and sheet metal work. Consolidated Gold Fields Ltd of London co-operated with the GSA to upgrade the instruction that was being given in carpentry and joinery, brickwork and electrical installation. Two more courses were introduced in 1976. These were a basic electronics course and an industrial arts training course. In 1977 a commercial training school, for the production of clerks, accountants, copy typists and secretaries, was opened.

In addition to the full-time training described above, LTI organises short in-service courses as, and when, requested by the government or the private sector. It also runs a night school for the upgrading of artisans and other skilled workers in and around Maseru.[34]

At three church training centres which go by different names – a vocational school, a trades school and a technical school – lower-level training is given in some of the trades named above and in basic agriculture, domestic science and cookery.[35] There is also a flourishing home economics school and several less ambitious vocational schools for girls.

The form of vocational education which should have had precedence in a country like Lesotho, agricultural training, can be said to have begun to receive serious attention in 1955, when the School (now College) of Agriculture was established. At this college, as at the LTI, development is gathering momentum. The output of 1978 and the expected output of 1979 illustrate this by showing an increase from 63 to 104.

At present all the students of the Lesotho Agricultural College are trained to enter the Ministry of Agriculture as extension staff. When the college opened in 1955 it admitted boys only; but with the inception of the rural domestic economy course for girls in 1964, it became coeducational. Since 1975 girls have been admitted to both the rural domestic economy and agricultural courses. So today the college offers two courses to which boys and girls are admitted if they are in possession of a good JC. These are the Certificate in Agriculture and the Certificate in Rural Domestic Economy. In 1977 a third course, the Diploma in Agriculture, was introduced. Entrants to this course must have a good COSC or a first-class Certificate in Agriculture. Before they are admitted to the college, all applicants (certificate and diploma) must also perform satisfactorily at an interview. The duration of each of the three courses is three years.

The college seeks to make its training as practical as possible. Three of the ways in which this is done are (*a*) conservation studies, (*b*) farm development and (*c*) workshop practice. In (*a*) the college runs an 'outreach' programme in twenty-five selected schools scattered throughout Lesotho, where pupils are given practice in the application of simple low-cost conservation and anti-erosion measures. Among the farm development projects is the 'Lesotho Village'. Here the students establish small-scale enterprises that can be copied by groups of farmers. Most of the building, for example, the construction of the piggery, the cattle kraal, calving boxes and calf pens, has been done by the students. This ties in with the work done in the workshops, where the students are taught basic skills in working with wood, stone, brick and metal so that, as extension officers, they can *show* the farmers how to erect simple structures or repair their implements instead of merely *telling* them that these things need to be done.[36]

VII   UNIVERSITY EDUCATION

Up to 1945 all, and from 1945 most, students who wanted to follow university courses went to institutions outside Lesotho. In 1945 the Roman Catholic Church established Pius XII University College at Roma. The college prepared its students for the awards of the University of South Africa.

In 1964 Pius XII College became the autonomous, three-country University of Botswana, Lesotho and Swaziland,[37] awarding its own degrees, diplomas and certificates. In 1975 Lesotho withdrew from UBLS and established the National University of Lesotho. Both UBLS and NUL were development-oriented, because in the 1960s and the 1970s the view had become generally accepted that universities should be closely associated with, and indeed engender, the 'development both of individuals and countries'.[38] Thus the 1976 Development Plan of NUL recommended, among other things:

(1) the appointment of a committee to study the cost implications of establishing a faculty of agriculture;
(2) the appointment of a committee to study the cost implications of establishing a faculty of engineering/technology;
(3) the establishment of a teaching programme leading to a B.Sc. in earth sciences;
(4) the establishment of a national research council;
(5) the establishment of an institute of Southern African studies;
(6) the introduction of new non-degree programmes to meet national needs.[39]

But one fears that for the following reasons NUL will find it difficult to make its education truly education for development. First, its being embedded in the Republic of South Africa makes contact between it and universities with a similar philosophy very difficult. Secondly, because its geographical situation makes the staff and students feel somewhat academically isolated, there is a staff turnover which does not make for continued progress. Thirdly, its staff development programme is adversely affected by the failure of some prospective university teachers sent abroad for further studies to return to Lesotho. Finally, its resources are limited.

The foregoing notwithstanding, an examination of NUL syllabuses and acquaintance with the research and other activities of its departments (e.g. the participation of the Department of Economics in the preparation of Lesotho's Second Development Plan) show that the university is always seeking ways of fulfilling the functions spelt out by the National University Act, 1976, which include the following:

> to provide educational facilities . . . for persons who, being eligible, seek the benefit of such facilities and to give instruction and training to such persons in such branches of knowledge as will most effectively improve their education and prepare them for service to their community; to promote by research and other means the advancement of knowledge and its practical application to social and technological problems primarily within Lesotho and more generally in Southern Africa.

There are several degree and sub-degree courses which can be said to prepare NUL students for 'service to their community'. An example is the business management component of the accounting and commerce course:

> Business and management in other cultures. Current management issues in Lesotho (survey of worker and management attitudes). Functional area problems in a small business (case study). Entrepreneurship and management (biography of an entrepreneur). The community concept of business for Africa.[40]

There are community- or work/profession-oriented courses in several departments, for example, education, law, statistics, and some of these are conducted under the aegis of the Institute of Extra-Mural Studies (IEMS), such as the Certificate in Business Studies and Diploma in Business Studies. The IEMS also organises a variety of short courses, formal and non-formal, for farmers, businessmen, members of co-operatives, women's organisations, and so on. In addition, it is the arm of the university which helps bodies wishing to do so to hold conferences, seminars and workshops at the university.

The National University of Lesotho is a young institution. Therefore it is only tentatively beginning to venture into postgraduate work in a few disciplines; and so far it has established only a few professional departments and faculties. For senior degrees and for training in medicine, pharmacy, dentistry, engineering, architecture and even agriculture Basotho students have to be sent to other countries.

VIII   NON-FORMAL EDUCATION

For a number of years there was a section in the annual report of the Ministry of Education which described the work being done in community development and adult education.[41] The lead in these each-one-teach-one activities which were going on in social welfare, nutrition and hygiene was taken by women's organisations. Later the government, through its Department of Community Development, ran courses, conferences and seminars 'whose aim was both to sensitize communities to their problems and to help them find ways of solving these problems'[42]. The British Council and the United States Information Service also made their contribution through their libraries and by making their halls available for educational and cultural activities.

It will be noticed from this account that, as the designation of the kind of education given indicates, the aim was to assist the grown-up, and little or no attention was given to the adolescent who had never gone to school or whose schooling had been interrupted. When, in 1966, with the establishment of the Lesotho Institute of Further Education, something began to be done for these young people, the education given to them was not of the non-formal kind whose content and methods of teaching were determined by the real life purposes for which they needed it. Nevertheless, the Lesotho Institute of Further Education (LIFE) corrected this, when it began functioning, by conducting evening classes for all who wanted them and arranging for educational broadcasts by Radio Lesotho. It also co-ordinated evening and radio tuition with the work of correspondence colleges operating in Lesotho. But such was the pressure for formal secondary education that LIFE has now ceded its buildings and facilities to an ordinary secondary school.

That Lesotho has now grasped the nature and importance of non-formal education is proved by the reference made to it by the Education Study Commission of 1976 and the 1975–80 Development Plan. Both the commission and the Plan have observed that the Ministry of Education has only recently involved itself in adult and non-formal education and that this involvement has been marginal. During the period 1975–80, however, a section responsible for adult and non-formal education was establised in the Ministry of Education. This section will maintain contact with agencies engaged in this work 'and ensure that their respective activities are so planned as to minimize overlap and maximize impact.' In addition, there will be an interministerial council to co-ordinate non-formal education activities.[43]

IX CONCLUSION

This short account of education in Lesotho shows that, as elsewhere in Africa, Christian missionaries were the pioneers; and this, to a certain extent, influenced the kind of education given as well as the nature of its development. For example, after primary education, teacher education had to be the first sector to be developed because the missionaries required teachers; and when the British annexed Lesotho their clerks and interpreters were often recruited from among these teachers.

For a long time Basotho sought secondary (later university) education outside Lesotho. This meant that the education they received was not necessarily geared to conditions in their country. Therefore the process of adapting secondary and tertiary education to the needs of Basotho is only beginning. A few examples, drawn from secondary and university education, have been cited. Others could be drawn from, say, the training of nurses, para-medicals of various kinds, and so on. This process of review and reconstruction is seen in such activities as the creation of primary and post-primary curriculum development units, the refashioning of teacher and university education and the expansion and upgrading of technical and vocational education in all its forms.

If, therefore, Lesotho's education has long remained imitative and somewhat irrelevant, it is purposefully giving itself a new character. This ·was the objective of the 'dialogue' held with the people at village level in 1977 and 1978 which led to the national seminar of May 1978. The hope is, therefore, that before long it will become the education of the Basotho for Lesotho. But, in the spirit of the 1976 University Act, to this end to the words 'more generally . . . Southern Africa', appearing in the Act, should be added 'and humanity'.

NOTES: CHAPTER 7

1 V. Ellenberger, *Landmarks in the Story of the French Protestant Church in Basutoland During the First Hundred Years of its Existence, 1833/1933* (Morija: Morija Printing Works 1933), p. 15.
2 Lesotho Ministry of Education, *Annual Report of the Permanent Secretary* (Maseru: Ministry of Education, 1966), pp. 3–4.
3 J. M. Mohapeloa, *Government by Proxy: Ten Years of Cape Colony Rule in Lesotho, 1871–1881* (Morija: Morija Printing Works, 1971), pp. 93–4.
4 Ministry of Education, *Annual Report,* 1966, p. 5.
5 ibid., p. 6.
6 Unesco, *Basutoland Educational Planning Mission* (Paris: Unesco, 1964), p. 2.
7 Basutoland, *Report of the Commission Appointed by His Majesty's Secretary of State for Dominion Affairs to Enquire into 'the Recommendations upon Education in Basutoland'* (Pretoria: Government Printer, 1946), pp. 27–8.
8 Lesotho Ministry of Education, *Annual Report, 1974/75* (Maseru: Ministry of Education, 1976), p. 100.
9 See Lesotho Ministry of Education, *Syllabus for Primary Schools* (Maseru: Ministry of Education, 1967), pp. 21–3 and 34–60.
10 E. B. Sargant, *Report on Education in Basutoland 1905-6* (London: Longmans Green, 1906), p. 39.
11 'An appraisal of the education system', a background paper for the Seminar on Education in Lesotho held at Maseru, 15–19 May 1978. In one place this paper says: 'In 1977, this ratio ws 53 pupils to one teacher for the country as a whole. But there were areas in the country where a single teacher had to cope with about 150 pupils in a single class. In 1977 there were 11 classes of that size. About 140 classes had more than 100 pupils in them. 1,449 classes contained between 55 and 99 pupils.'
12 See note 11.
13 Information supplied by the educational statistician.
14 Basutoland, *Report of the Commission Appointed by His Majesty's Secretary of State for Dominion Affairs to Enquire into and Make Recommendations upon Education in Basutoland* (Pretoria: Government Printer, 1946), p. 12.
15 Basutoland Education Department, *Syllabus for Primary Schools* (Maseru: Ministry of Education, 1957), p. 1. The 1967 syllabus repeated this aim almost word for word, substituting, of course, 'Lesotho' for 'Basutoland'.
16 Ministry of Education, *Syllabus for Primary Schools* (Maseru: Ministry of Education, 1967), pp. 1–68.
17 Unesco, *Basutoland Educational Planning Mission* (Paris: Unesco, 1964) p. 2.

18 S. Vivian, *A Handbook on In-Service Teacher Training in Developing Countries of the Commonwealth* (London: Commonwealth Secretariat, 1977), p. 67.
19 See note 11.
20 W. A. Dodd, *Primary School Inspection: New Countries,* quoted by J. K. Matsaba in 'Role, objectives, organisation and techniques of the Lesotho school inspectorate', unpublished M.Ed. thesis, NUL, pp. 76-7.
21 Information supplied by the officer in the Ministry of Education in charge of the scheme for the development of the inspectorate.
22 Information given at the seminar held in May 1978.
23 Primary schools no longer have the classifications 'higher' and 'lower' because the aim is that eventually all such schools should teach from standard 1 to standard 7.
24 'Papers for the mid-project review, NTTC' (Maseru: Ministry of Education, 1977), ch. 3.
25 S. Anzalone, 'To build a college: NTTC – the first year,' mimeo. (Maseru, 1976), p. 4.
26 Anzalone, op. cit., p. 4.
27 Anzalone, op. cit., pp. 14-15.
28 The Roma campus became the National University of Lesotho in October 1975.
29 National University of Lesotho, *Special Handbook on Academic Regulations and Syllabuses, 1976/77,* p. 42.
30 Ministry of Education, *Annual Report,* 1973, p. 11.
31 Ministry of Education, *Annual Report,* 1974/5, pp. 13-14.
32 Ministry of Education, *Report of the Education Study Commission, 1976,* (Maseru: Ministry of Education, 1976), p. 24.
33 Ministry of Education, *Annual Report,* 1973, p. 39.
34 Informant, Mr S. M. Mokete, Director, Lerotholi Technical Institution.
35 Ministry of Education, *Annual Report,* 1974/75, p. 27.
36 Informant, Mr K. Younger, Principal, Lesotho Agricultural College.
37 Before the independence of Botswana and Lesotho in 1966 the name was the University of Basutoland, Bechuanaland Protectorate and Swaziland (UBBS), but for convenience I have used the better-known name, the University of Botswana, Lesotho and Swaziland (UBLS).
38 University of Botswana, Lesotho and Swaziland, *Education in Transition: The Report of the Polytechnic Mission,* (1973), p. 58.
39 National University of Lesotho, *Development Plan,* 1976, pp. 1-2.
40 *National University of Lesotho Calendar, 1977/78,* p. 121.
41 This section has disappeared from recent reports.
42 Ministry of Education, *Annual Report,* 1966, p. 50.
43 Ministry of Education, *Report of the Education Study Commission,* p. 43; Kingdom of Lesotho, *Second Five-Year Development Plan, 1975/76-1979/80,* Vol. 1, pp. 184-5.

Chapter 8

Education in Liberia

MARY BROWN SHERMAN

I BRIEF HISTORICAL OUTLINE

Introduction

The Liberian nation usually traces its beginnings to settlement in the 1820s by blacks from the New World under the auspices of the American Society for Colonizing the Free People of Colour of the United States of America[1] and the various state colonisation societies which sprang up in relation to it. However, the ethnic groups which they met in the area had migrated from the Sudanic region of the continent and settled in the area, the Grain Coast, more than two hundred years earlier. Interaction between these two groups of people over the years has yielded the Liberian nation as we know it today.

The early migrants to the area had their own means of educating their young, the best known and most widespread being the regularly organised system of the secret societies, PORO and SANDE, the 'bush schools' – which were found among ten of the sixteen major ethnic groups in the area and also in Sierra Leone and Guinea. Such education prevailed until the settlers from the New World arrived and introduced Western education shortly after their settlement in 1822. From that period the education indigenous to this part of Africa coexisted with the introduced Western system of education.

Throughout the nineteenth century and well into the twentieth these two systems of education competed for children. Their aims differed sharply as they quite naturally were geared to the respective societies which they served.[2]

Attempts have been made to recognise the significance of the indigenous schools and to co-operate with them. However, it is the introduced system of education which has been adopted by the nation as its own, and the challenge remains to integrate the two systems, using the best of both. Thus the next paragraphs will be devoted mainly to the nation's adopted school system.

II ELEMENTARY EDUCATION

As might be expected, the initial emphasis was on elementary (primary) education and from 1822 to 1839 only elementary schools existed. They were run by individual settlers who were already members of Christian churches. From 1833 the church missions began to work directly in Liberia and to play a dominant role in education.

For most of the nineteenth century the schools served the few rather than the masses, drawing their pupils from the children of settlers, recaptured Africans and those local people who happened to live within the confines of the new settlements. In 1868, more than forty years after the initial settlement and twenty years after independence, there were less than thirty schools, averaging less than twenty pupils per school.

Educational growth was slow because the American Colonization Society which had sponsored the settlements and was responsible for the government until independence in 1847 was indifferent to development, particularly educational development. Moreover, there was a high percentage of illiterates among those who migrated from the New World and the few who had some education had a low level of education.[3] In addition, many of these immigrants were poor.

It was not until the 1880s, about forty years after independence, that a struggling government began a sustained effort in the field of education which led to an enrolment in the 1920s of nearly 10,000 students, approximately one-third in government schools. Dramatic changes did not take place until William V. S. Tubman became President in 1944 and initiated policies leading to social development. The masses began to yearn for education and the government responded by opening schools in various parts of the country and making education free at the elementary level.[4] By 1951 there were 24,526 students enrolled in the nation's schools – more than double the figures of ten years earlier. Slightly more than 95 per cent of these students, or 23,494 were at the elementary level.

The quantitative rise in enrolment continued at an ever-increasing rate through the 1950s and 1960s and into the 1970s, stimulated by the consolidation of public schools in the Monrovia area in 1965 under the Monrovia Consolidated School System. However, not enough schools were provided to accommodate the children of school-age. Moreover, problems of quality became accentuated, as was reflected in high wastage. Most children enrolled were in the lower elementary grades, including pre-grade and kindergarten.

It must also be understood that many of the pupils were over-age while a smaller number were under-age, with the result that in spite of increased numbers the proportion of the 6–11 year age-group in school probably remained at about 20 per cent.

Given this quantitative growth at the elementary school level (for figures see Appendix B), the question of quality became of special concern in the 1970s when efforts were made to match quantity with quality in the educational development of the country.

III SECONDARY EDUCATION

High school education was begun by the Protestant church missions in response to their need for local people with a higher level of education to assist in carrying out their functions. In April 1839 the first of these institutions was launched in Monrovia by the Methodist mission – the Liberia Conference Seminary, later called Monrovia Seminary and from 1898 the College of West Africa. This institution operated for short and irregular periods between 1839 and 1847.[5] Other church missions followed between the late 1840s and the early 1860s with schools concentrated in Monrovia and Cape Palmas and enrolling a small number of students, mainly boys.

The outstanding effort during this early period was the Alexander High School of the Presbyterian mission which opened at Monrovia in 1849 under the Rev. Harrison Ellis of that mission and operated by fifteen consecutive years, maintaining a high standard. Among its outstanding products was Edward Wilmot Blyden, who entered the school shortly after he emigrated to Liberia in 1851, and his contemporary, Hilary Wright Johnson, who became President of Liberia in the 1880s. Other important institutions during this period were the Cape Palmas Seminary of the Methodist mission, opened in Cape Palmas in 1857, and the high school of the Episcopal mission, also opened in Cape Palmas at Mount Vaughan in 1850, the Orphan Asylum for Girls in 1855 and the Hoffman Institute in 1862.

A principal function of these schools was to train ministers, teachers and other leaders for the respective church missions. They operated either irregularly or for short periods. Moreover, limited enrolment remained a major problem: admission standards were high, elementary schools were neither widespread nor firmly rooted, teachers were scarce and physical facilities were sparsely distributed.

On 23 January 1862, when Liberia College formally opened its classes, there were only two high schools in the country – the Alexander High School and the high school at Mount Vaughan. There were less than fifty students enrolled in these schools. Thus, the college had to establish what was called a Preparatory Department (High School Section) to ensure its supply of entrants to the college. This department served only boys until 1885 when a Female Division was opened. Numbers in the Preparatory Department remained small up to the close of the century. In 1901 the number enrolled was 118.[6]

Meanwhile, between the 1860s and 1900 there was little progress in the mission schools which had been established and there was no expansion of their work. During the 1870s the work of all the church missions in Liberia declined following the aftermath of the Civil War which occurred in the United States of America, 1861–5. The Government had to fill in the gap left by these missions, but its main efforts were in the area of elementary education.

It was only in the 1900s that efforts in high school education were renewed. The work of the Preparatory Department of Liberia College was supplemented by the few mission high schools which were then in existence. There were further developments in the 1930s and 1940s as government turned its attention to the four remaining counties, taking over existing high schools or establishing a public high school to supplement the work it was already doing at this level of education in Montserrado County.

Yet the growth of high school education was exceedingly slow. For one thing, too few people were graduating from elementary schools – less than 300 in 1949. Moreover, the rural areas of the country were still without a public high school. By 1951 there were only nine high schools in the country enrolling 874 students – not quite 5 per cent of the total number of students enrolled in the republic during that year.

The next ten years were to be the period of dramatic rise in the high school population as government took a major responsibility for education at this level. Also by 1962 there was a change in the structure of education in the country which became six years of elementary school and six years of high school. Records for that year showed more than sixty high schools in the country and an enrolment of 5,574 or approximately 7 per cent, of the enrolment of elementary and high school students. On the whole, there was a remarkable increase in primary and secondary enrolment in the 1960s.[7]

Despite the quantitative growth indicated above, middle-level manpower needs of the country are not being met. Numbers graduating from the high school are still inadequate. Besides, the present high school programmes are too general for the diversified manpower needs of the country. The challenge of the 1970s is to diversify offerings in the senior high school to permit a concentration sequence, that is, a broad junior high school education followed by some specialisation in the senior high school.

IV   TECHNICAL EDUCATION

One of the weakest areas in the Liberian education system is that of technical/vocational education. During the nineteenth century practically nothing was accomplished in this area. The Christian missions which dominated education in the country were so preoccupied with Christianising and 'civilising' that they neglected vocational education. Moreover, most of the New World settlers had no training or interest in this area since they came from a background which looked down upon the tutoring of manual skills in schools. Those who had technical skills such as building trades and agriculture passed these on through apprentices, although there was apparently no organised apprenticeship system. However, in some societies with sub-sistence economies the indigenous schools continued to pass on to those who attended them the age-old technical skills which were still required.

Some changes came during the first three decades of the twentieth century, but these efforts were small compared with the needs of the country. Probably in response to the concern of the then bishop of the Protestant Episcopal mission Samuel David Ferguson, for the church to become self-supporting, it was considered essential for students to learn to support themselves, and the schools established by this mission during this period began industrial and mechanical training. Ferguson felt that a great mistake had been made for the church to have given attention exclusively to intellectual and moral training.

The outstanding effort during this period was the Booker T. Washington Agricultural and Industrial Institute which was established in 1929 in Kakata, about 70 kilometres (45 miles) from Monrovia. The institute was established from funds left by Mrs Olivia Phelps-Stokes who was desirous of perpetuating the name of Booker T. Washington by founding in Africa an institution similar to Tuskegee Institute. Thus right from the start the school placed more emphasis on industrial training than academic training. It was controlled by a foreign board of trustees which consisted of representatives from the various contributing organisations which included the Phelps-Stokes Fund, Tuskegee Institute, colonisation societies, church missions and the Firestone Company. It also had a local board on which several church missions were represented, the Government of Liberia and prominent individuals. Government provided 1,000 acres of land and a small annual subsidy of $5,000 for the first twenty years, then raised this subsidy to $7,500 in 1950 and $11,500 the following year. The running of the institution continued under the original arrangement until 1 July 1953, when it passed into the hands of the government of Liberia.

With the rapid economic changes which took place in the country during the 1950s and 1960s, the demand for people with technical/vocational training became exceedingly great and with more expatriates being hired for jobs in industry, the limitations of offerings in the country in this area became glaring. A few secondary schools in different parts of the country began to diversify their offerings to include vocational courses, and the William V. S. Tubman High School was established as a comprehensive high school offering vocational training as one of its streams. However, Booker T. Washington Agricultural and Industrial Institute remained the major vocational effort, expanding its enrolment to over 700 in about eleven areas and providing about 120 graduates per year. The other two major efforts were:

(1)   the Liberian Swedish Vocational Training Centre (LSVTC),

established in Kekepa, Nimba County, in 1964, under the joint
management of the government of Liberia and the mining
company, LAMCO, with the assistance of the Swedish
government;
(2)   the Bong Mines Vocational Training Centre, a private vocational
school established in 1965 at Bong Mines, about 105 kilometres
(65 miles) from Monrovia.

The LSVTC enrols about 120, has offerings in the following areas of
specialisation – auto mechanics, heavy duty mechanics, electricity and
woodwork – and an annual output of between twenty-six and forty.
Bong Mines Vocational Training Centre is even smaller. It enrols about
forty, has offerings in three areas of specialisation – auto mechanics,
electro-mechanics and machinery – and an annual output of about
twelve students, seeking to supply its own needs.
    Despite all of these efforts, development in the technical/vocational
area has not kept pace with developments in other areas of education in
the country. Secondary general education developed far more rapidly in
the 1960s and 1970s. While total enrolment at the secondary level in
1972 was 21,411, only about 908 were in the vocational schools. In 1974
there was a little change in these figures as 1,087 enrolled in the three
vocational institutions. There are no definite figures for those enrolled
in vocational courses in the few high schools which offered such courses.
However, enrolments in those high schools have been estimated to be
about 500. The limitations in this area represent a major drawback to
development and emphasise the need for the establishment of more
vocational high schools. For rapid development it is essential to open
comprehensive high schools with vocational streams as well as technical
schools or vocational training centres with facilities for specialised
training at higher levels.

V   TEACHER EDUCATION

Development in this area has been extremely slow and constitutes an
even greater limitation on national development of technical/
vocational education. Throughout the nineteenth century and well into
the twentieth, the attempts at training teachers were limited to course
adjuncts in academic high schools and institutes for short duration.
Institutes were organised as far back as 1900, but it was the late 1930s
when these institutes began to function on a regular annual basis, first in
Monrovia, and later in other parts of the country.
    Improvement in these efforts on a systematic and sustained basis took
place when in March 1947, the William V. S. Tubman School of Teacher
Training was founded as a co-operative venture of the government of

Liberia, the Methodist church mission and the Episcopal church mission. It was a normal school programme, admitting high school graduates and offering academic and professional courses to prepare them for teaching in elementary schools. Those who enrolled - thirty in number – were in-service teachers. In 1950 the government of Liberia assumed full responsibility for support of the school, a full-time dean was appointed and the programme was expanded to four years. The school was chartered for the awarding of degrees. During that year the first degrees were awarded to nine persons, six male and three female, all in elementary education.

In 1951 that school was merged with Liberia College and several other schools to form the University of Liberia. Offerings in the area of secondary education began in that year, for the school became part of a university which offered opportunities for specialisation in the following basic areas: English, social science, science and mathematics.

In keeping with social and economic developments in the 1950s, enrolment in the College rose rapidly during the decade. By 1959 it had reached 112 – 88 men and 24 women. Meanwhile, collegiate programmes in education were established at the Maryland College of Our Lady of Fatima in Harper, Cape Palmas, in 1953[8] and at Cuttington College and Divinity School in Suacoco in 1957. By 1960 136 degrees in education had been awarded in the country.[9]

The 1960s saw other developments: establishment of junior teacher training colleges which were short-lived, and the introduction of teacher training at the secondary school level. Two rural institutions for training elementary teachers at the higher school level were established. The duration of the training was three years, so that on completion the students attained the status of high school graduates with professional training. Between 1963 and 1969 these two institutions produced 447 graduates. With the much smaller numbers which graduated in education from the collegiate institutions during the 1960s, meeting the needs in the country for trained teachers remained a major problem.

Not unrelated to the problem of output from these institutions is that of intake. Government's failure during the 1960s to implement the proposal made in May 1960 for the certification of teachers and administrators, plus the fact that salaries for teachers did not keep pace in the 1960s with salaries in other fields which require personnel with comparable training, made the teaching field unattractive. Naturally, no sizeable numbers opted for the demanding training this area entails. Thus there were fluctuating and even declining enrolments at the collegiate institutions during this period. Besides, there was neither expansion of facilities at the institutions training elementary teachers at the high school level, nor opening of additional institutions of this type.

Apart from the development of the training institutions beginning in the late 1940s, there were other attempts to meet the needs for trained teachers which flourished during the 1950s, but declined or were abolished during the 1960s. These were:

(1)   The two-week institutes held during the long vacation period each year. These had been operating on a regular basis since 1937. In 1952 they were extended to four weeks and their nomenclature changed to vacation schools. They provided basic content courses and professional education courses, mainly for teachers at the elementary and high school levels. Many teachers benefited from these programmes, but there were sticky problems which were not resolved and in 1969 these vacation schools were discontinued.

(2)   The Extension Schools which began in 1955 with pilot programmes in Montserrado and Maryland Counties and later were extended to all other counties and the three provinces – then the eight major geographical divisions of the country. These schools operated in the evenings during the regular academic year and were attached to existing high schools. The principal of the high school was responsible for the extension classes which provided high school education and limited professional courses. Extension education classes were discontinued except for one or two centres in the late 1960s.

Thus, in the 1970s the training of teachers for the nation's schools was left with the William V. S. Tubman Teachers College of the University of Liberia and Cuttington College and Divinity School for teachers earning degrees, and with Zorzor Rural Teacher Training Institute and Kataka Rural Teacher Training Institute for teachers earning certificates of high school standing.

For the collegiate institutions, there was a spurt in enrolment in 1973 when salaries for holders of the B.Sc. degree in education rose by about a third. But, as nothing further was done towards implementing the proposed salary scale for teachers, certification of teachers and retirement benefits, enrolment did not rise further. In 1975 the Teachers' College of the University of Liberia enrolled 153 and the Education Division of Cuttington College enrolled 40. The intake of pre-service teachers at the rural institutes declined since only Kataka admits pre-service teachers while Zorzor concentrates on reorientation and upgrading of in-service teachers. This is unfortunate indeed when measured against the needs of the country for trained teachers. Using 1974 figures, more than 60 per cent of the elementary and secondary school teachers need upgrading, professional training, or both.

The note of hope, despite limitations of numbers, is that the two collegiate institutions as well as the rural institutes have added new dimensions to their respective training programmes. Research, extension and community orientation are important features. However, expansion of offerings to include areas not presently offered, for example, training and technical teachers in areas in secondary teaching such as agriculture, home economics, business and French are urgent.

VI HIGHER EDUCATION

Collegiate education began in the country with the formal opening of Liberia College on 23 January 1862. However, this too was plagued by the problems of an inadequate supply of students and a dependence on foreign financial support which was withdrawn in 1879. In the following years the college's fortunes fluctuated and from 1874 to 1902 it produced no graduates.

On the accession of William David Coleman to the presidency of the nation in 1898, after serving the unexpired term of Joseph J. Cheeseman, one-half of the export duty on piassava, then a principal export product, and one-half of the proceeds of sales of land and all escheated property, were earmarked for the support of Liberia College. Thus the government took a direct interest in the operation and control of the college which reopened for work on 21 February 1900.

For the next fifty years the college struggled for existence with a single curriculum which was a general liberal arts programme and annually put out a small number of graduates, mostly men. Then, with the rapid economic growth which the country experienced during the 1950s, basic changes were made. In 1951 the University of Liberia was established, with Liberia College and the William V. S. Tubman School of Teacher Training which had been established in 1947 as its two degree-granting colleges. The Law School was added in 1954 and the College of Forestry in 1957. Thereafter the efforts to broaden and strengthen the institution continued. The high school which was a heritage of Liberia College and the other specialised schools of a similar level added in the 1950s were separated from the institution. The College of Agriculture established in 1962 was merged with the College of Forestry in 1967 to become the College of Agriculture and Forestry. Programmes in economics and business administration were initiated in the College of Liberal and Fine Arts (Libera College). In 1971 the College of Medicine, which had been established outside the university in 1968, was incorporated as a college of the university, and in 1972 the College of Business and Public Administration was established. In 1974 the Division of Science, started in the 1950s as part of the College of Liberal and Fine Arts, became the seventh college, the College of Science and Technology, consisting of the Divisions of Science and Geology, Architecture and Engineering.

Over the years enrolment rose gradually – from one student who entered for classes in 1862 but was held back until 1864 when twelve students enrolled and instruction began, to one hundred in 1950, nineteen of whom were girls. Prior to 1950, girls in college were a rarity.[10] With the establishment of the university in 1951 the spurt began. Between 1950 and 1956, the enrolment more than doubled – to 259. By 1968 it had passed the 1,000 mark and in 1974, it stood at 1,713.

The other higher education venture was launched by the Protestant Episcopal mission, also in the nineteenth century, in 1889, at Cape Palmas. Like Liberia College, Cuttington College established a Preparatory Department from its beginning. Its other two departments were the Theological and the Higher Departments. It began with twenty-one students in the Higher Department and seventy in the Preparatory. The college ran steadily for forty years, admitting only male students, but it was closed in 1929. From the various and often conflicting accounts, the reasons summarised for this closure of the college are: change in the leadership from Liberian to American, beginning of depression in the United States of America and controversy over textbooks. It was twenty years later – 1949 – when the college reopened, but at a completely different site, Suacoco, Bong County. It admitted female students in 1950, the second year of the new era. Again, funds for capital development, this time on the new 607-hectare (1,500-acre) tract of land donated by the Government of Liberia ($200,000), and for operating expenses, were provided by the Protestant Episcopal mission.

During its early years Cuttington had a five-year collegiate programme based on a classical curriculum and theology. Probably after 1900 it sought to operate on a limited basis an Agricultural and Industrial Department and in 1906 held a horticultural and industrial show, but it is not clear how sustained this attempt was. Prior to 1922 it seems that certificates of proficiency were awarded. It was in 1922 that the school was chartered to confer degrees.[11]

The period of rapid economic and social change in the country – in the 1950s and 1960s – also influenced developments at Cuttingtor College. This was reflected in the type of offerings, the size of enrolment and the number of girls who entered the college. During this new period degrees were offered in the liberal arts and science, in agriculture beginning in 1955 and education beginning in 1957. The programme in agriculture was discontinued in 1966 as the University of Liberia extended into this area. In 1963 other programmes were added in keeping with developments in the country. The new programmes were business and economics, and a collegiate programme in nursing run in co-operation with Phoebe Hospital of the Lutheran Church.

From 1949 to 1962 its enrolment grew from the twelve students, all male, who entered in 1949 to 134 in 1962, including forty-one women representing a female ratio of approximately 2:1. The 1974 enrolment was 349.

Thus it can be seen that higher education has been characterised by a significant rise in enrolment since 1950. Over the last ten years this rise has been at the rate of approximately 15 per cent per annum. Enrolment among the various disciplines has not, however, been in line with national needs. A major challenge of the years immediately ahead is the correction of this tendency.

VII   NON-FORMAL EDUCATION

From the foregoing sections, it can be seen that for many years the adopted school system was extremely limited in terms of numbers it served. Throughout the nineteenth century and well into the twentieth schools in the indigenous system prepared the vast majority for a living in a small-scale, pre-industrial society.

Economic and social changes which began in the 1920s and which were accelerated by the end of the Second World War affected the provision of alternatives to formal schooling. The informal system of individualised apprenticeships continued but the field of business training was opened up by private individual effort, which continued until the last decade, though it was increased, supplemented by government provision of commercial courses in high schools and the vocational high school.

Adult literacy classes in Liberian languages and English were begun in 1950 under both mission and government auspicies on a small scale. For about ten years from 1954 the Fundamental Education Centre at Klay provided an outstanding adult education programme training rural development workers. Other extension programmes have been provided more recently by the Ministry of Agriculture and the Ministry of Labour, Youth and Sports with various objectives such as preparing adults and youths for employment, training in agriculture, animal husbandry, business and domestic arts.

The Basic Craft Training Centre set up in 1972 with the assistance of the International Labour Organisation aims at turning over-age school drop-outs into rural maintenance workers in building, electrical and metalwork, and at training instructors.

Sustained efforts are required to permit imaginative new projects to be launched to meet the demands of people moving from the subsistence to the cash economy. The training projects provide the necessary education for gainful employment thereby facilitating life in an industrialising, urbanising and modernising society.

VIII   ORGANISATION

As pointed out earlier, there are two school systems in Liberia. The indigenous school system has to some extent been losing against the forces of modernisation and urbanisation as less and less people opt for attending *only* the indigenous schools. Duration of the sessions of these schools are known to be becoming shorter (PORO reduced from about seven years per session to about three and SANDE from about three years per session to approximately one year; and in special cases sessions of either were only a few months long) so that youths might be exposed to both school systems, the conflict in value systems notwith- standing.

Liberian educators are beginning to give thought to how these schools can be integrated. A few alternatives have been proposed, but none adopted. In fact, no alternative has been seriously studied and assessed. Meanwhile, most people are yearning for such education as the adopted school system provides.

The latter system is what Robert Ulich would describe as 'single ladder' rather than 'bifurcated', for there is a straight movement from the elementary level to college, the possibility existing for entering the four-year college from any type of secondary school programme. There is no sharp cut-off between the levels. Although a national examination system was instituted in 1960 with examinations given at the terminal grades for each level (sixth for the elementary, ninth for junior high school and twelfth for senior high school), the examinations do not serve as formidable barriers to movement from one school level to another. The school grades of the students weigh heavily in determining promotion – 75 per cent as against 25 per cent for the national examinations. The examinations for grade VI have since 1972 been temporarily discontinued.

This adopted system is organised into three levels:

(1)   elementary, preceded by kindergarten for children of pre-school age and pre-grade for over-age children who need to learn to speak English, the language of instruction of the schools, before they enter grade I;
(2)   secondary, usually referred to as high school;
(3)   college.

The number of years allotted to each level has gone through changes. Until 1959 there were eight years of elementary school, four years of high school and four years of college, the 8–4–4 system. Kindergarten, which was not widespread and hardly considered part of the public school system, and pre-grade which ranged from one to three years, were often not represented as part of the system. Since 1959 there have been six years of elementary school, six years of high school (three junior high and three senior high) and four years of college. Kindergarten has been more widespread and a few public kindergartens established, but the pre-grades occupy a dubious place, with strong suggestions for abolishing the arrangement. Thus, it is not uncommon to represent the system as K–6–3–3–4.

The school ages for these levels are

kindergarten	5 or slightly below
elementary	6–11
high school	12–17
college	18–22

but entering and leaving school at these ages happens more in theory (i.e. on paper) than in practice. For instance, although the law specifies ages 6–16 as compulsory school-age, it is not uncommon to find students dropping out of school before they attain 16 years of age, or students entering elementary school much older than the specified 6 years school-age. For various reasons, for example, insufficiency of schools and teachers, imbalance in the distribution of schools between urban and rural areas, cultural resistances to schooling and low financial earnings of many parents, many children enter elementary school as late as their teens, pushing up the age for completing this level as well as high school and college for those in this category who continue. From data collected in 1973 covering more than half the students enrolled in schools, the median age in grade I was 10 years for boys and 9 years for girls; in grade XII, 21 and 19 years respectively.[12] Entry to kindergarten is much stricter – 5 years or slightly below.

Like the political and economic systems of the country, the educational system is highly centralised. All schools and educational institutions, with the exception of the chartered higher educational institutions, are under the direct oversight of the Ministry of Education. Centralisation has resulted in some degree of co-ordination of the national education effort and the distribution of schools over wider areas of the country, although more has to be achieved in these respects.

Within the centralised school system is the Monrovia Consolidated School System which was introduced in the 1960s as an experiment in decentralisation, though without autonomy. This system brings together all public schools in the city of Monrovia under a superintendent and a school council responsible for its operations. But involvement is more with co-ordination of the work of the schools and decisions relating to personnel, subject, of course, to review by the Ministry of Education. The Monrovia Consolidated School System draws its finance from the central government and not from funds provided by the city through taxes, uses the prescribed curriculum and textbooks of the ministry and follows the school calendar set by the ministry for all schools at the elementary and secondary levels.

Schools are designated by type as

(1) *Government:* Schools wholly financed and administered by government, tuition free at the elementary and secondary school levels, with an annual registration fee of $5.00 at the secondary school level. Fees at the tertiary level are negligible.

(2) *Non-Governmental:*

    (*a*) Mission schools – operated by church missions and often a legacy of the nineteenth century.

    (*b*) Concession schools – situated in the Concession areas, financed and operated by the Concessions in keeping with their responsibility to government for people working in these areas whose children must be provided with free education up to junior high school. Provision for schools is usually a stipulation of Concession Agreements and a superintendent of the Concession school works closely with the Ministry of Education in the administration and supervision of schools in each Concession area.

    (*c*) Private schools – supported mainly from tuition fees and funds provided by private individuals. Such schools are extremely few.

    Non-governmental schools are subject to the same regulations of the Ministry of Education as governmental schools. In fact, practically all of these schools which do not fall under the sub-category 'Concessions' receive subsidy from the government either in direct cash allotments, teacher(s) paid by government, or free use of government school buildings.

At the elementary school level, particularly the lower elementary (grades I–II), classrooms are usually self-contained, that is, a single teacher teaches all subjects to a given class. Where there is acute shortage of staff, a single teacher is likely to teach all subjects to more than one class. Recently, there has been a movement towards the teacher teaching a particular subject or two, to several grades, particularly in the upper elementary grades IV–VI.

At the high school level the teacher teaches subjects in his area of specialisation or minor field of study to various classes. However, due to staff shortage and inadequate qualification of a sizeable number of teachers at this level, a teacher is likely to teach a subject or two outside his major or minor area of specialisation.

Most high schools are academic or what may be called general secondary. There are a few specialised high schools with offerings in each of the following areas: general secondary, commercial, vocational. A good example of a comprehensive high school is the William V. S. Tubman High School of the Monrovia Consolidated School System, a public high school with an enrolment of about 1,000. Two similar comprehensive high schools have been planned and soon will be under construction, both in a rural area – in Voinjama, Lofa County, and Swedru, Grand Gedeh County.

Collegiate education is of four years' duration, with the first two years given over to general education and the last two to specialisation, an arrangement similar to the American four-year college. The higher educational institutions generally award the first degrees, the exceptions being the professional degrees in law and medicine awarded by the University of Liberia. Both the Law School and the College of Medicine admit students on completion of college or after two years of college work.

Limitations of facilities and pressure of numbers have led to three school sessions per day – morning, afternoon and evening. The evening session has evolved for working adults at the elementary and secondary school levels, but mainly at the secondary school level. Statistics for 1974 show about 84 per cent of evening schools at the secondary school level.

The academic year covers the period from late February or early March to early December, and for the elementary and secondary schools the school year is divided into two semesters. Each semester is again divided into three six-week periods making a total of eighteen weeks per semester. The collegiate institutions begin in early March and have two semesters of approximately sixteen weeks, ending in early December. There is a mid-year vacation of two weeks in July and an end of the year vacation of approximately three months – early or middle December to late February or early March. School is held Monday to Friday each week for about five to six hours per day for institutions below the collegiate level.

Promotion is not automatic and the system is characterised by numerous failures and repetitions.

IX   ADMINISTRATION AND CONTROL

Through much of the nineteenth century the various Christian missions which operated schools in Liberia were controlled by the foreign division of their boards with headquarters in the United States of America and representatives in Liberia to implement the policies formulated in the USA. Reports were sent by these representatives to their boards, but hardly any information on their schools was available in Liberia. The change began in 1869 when the law was enacted providing for county commissioners of education who gathered information on schools in each county and reported this information semi-annually to the Secretary of Interior, the cabinet member whose department was then responsible for education. The Secretary of Interior in turn reported annually to the national legislature. Thus, the legislature was kept informed as to the state of education in the country.

The move towards centralisation took on momentum with the turn of the century. In 1900 the Bureau of Education was established by law and responsibility for education given to it. The General Superintendent of Public Instruction and Common Schools, as the head of the bureau was called, was to 'superintend the operation of Public and private schools, and see that the school laws are enforced.'[13] In 1921 the General Education Act Act was passed, consolidating and amending the various education Acts and raising this bureau to cabinet rank with the nomenclature Department of Public Instruction. Responsibility for the oversight of all schools and educational institutions below the collegiate level was vested in the Secretary of Public Instruction, a member of the President's cabinet. Control has since then remained centred in this department which has grown over the years, endeavouring to meet the challenges of the growing size and complexity of the nation's educational venture, and has changed in nomenclature in 1962 (to Department of Education) and in 1973 (to Ministry of Education).

The biggest changes in this agency of government, as with the national educational venture, have come since the 1950s. These changes have been largely in the expansion of the central office, more clerical staff but less professional and technical, and an even smaller expansion of the administrative and supervisory personnel in the field.

Presently there are four bureaux within the Ministry of Education:

(1) Bureau of Administration
(2) Bureau of Instruction
(3) Bureau of Planning and Research
(4) Bureau of Science and Technical Education.

Two deputy ministers, one for Administration and the other for Instruction, and two assistant ministers, one for Planning and Research and the other for Science and Technical Education, head these bureaux.[14] These ministers co-ordinate the work of the various divisions which fall under their respective bureaux, each of which is headed by a director. At the head of the ministry is the Minister of Education.

In the field, the supervisor of schools is the official responsible for education in each country. He is aided by one assistant supervisor of schools or more and an inspector of missions, the latter concerned with non-governmental schools. There are presently in the country nine supervisors, twenty assistant supervisors and nine inspectors of missions. They function under the Deputy Minister for Instruction and concentrate on administrative problems, giving little attention to supervisory problems.

Control has been exercised through attempts to enforce educational laws; formulation of educational policies; collection, analysis and compilation of statistics and other information; prescription of textbooks; development of curriculum; licensing of teachers; employment and dismissal of teachers; and regulation of the academic year. A major step in control came with the institution of the national examinations in 1960, already discussed briefly. Effective control from this centralised point has, however, been decidedly handicapped by difficulties of transportation and communication and an insufficient number of administrative and particularly supervisory personnel.

At the head of each elementary and secondary school there is a principal, except in the teacher training institutes where he is known as a director, who administers it, usually with the assistance of a board. The scope and authority of this administrator is severely restricted, especially in the public schools, as he does not have the authority to appoint, promote, or dismiss school personnel but only to recommend such actions through the Supervisor of Schools to the Minister of Education who alone has such authority.

The higher educational institutions, the University of Liberia and Cuttington College and Divinity School, are controlled by independent boards of trustees, constituted in keeping with the respective charters of these institutions. Each of these institutions is headed by a president who is the executive officer of the board. The Minister of Education is *ex officio* on the board of the University of Liberia and thus has some effect on policies governing the institution. Also, there is within the Ministry of Education a Division of Higher Education and Textbook Research which aids in linking the higher educational institutions with the lower schools in the educational system.

X   CURRICULUM

In the indigenous schools curriculum content was related to the environment and the real life experiences of the people the schools served. This content varied from skills connected with exploiting the environment such as farming, hunting, fishing, to artistic skills such as singing, dancing, drumming, handicrafts, to subjects such as history, law and religion.

Cutting across the lines of physical, moral and intellectual development, the curriculum provided both general instruction to equip all for basic economic self-sufficiency as well as specialised training in given areas for those who showed the aptitude.

On the other hand, the Western schools introduced during the nineteenth century were alien transplants. What was taught in them was accordingly unrelated to the Liberian environment and life therein. The Christianising – 'civilising' – theme dominated life in the nation and the curriculum of schools. At all school levels there was emphasis on Bible reading and Christian teachings. Some knowledge of the English language, the medium of instruction and also a school subject, was given.

In addition, at the lower elementary level stress was on reading, writing and spelling, and at the upper elementary level, along with these, arithmetic, geography and grammar. In the high schools the classical languages, Latin and Greek, were introduced. In some high schools music was included as well as theory and practice of teaching. For a short period during the nineteenth century there was also instruction in the local language which dominated the given area, for example, Grebo in the Cape Palmas area. Social learnings growing out of and related to the Liberian environment were not a part of the curriculum; nor were technical skills necessary for exploiting the environment. Such education, divorced from real life, was associated with books and involved to a large extent memorisation.

Because the missions provided most of the schools in the nineteenth century they largely determined the curriculum. Even after the establishment of the Bureau of Education in 1900 and the gradual increase in government control of mission schools, it was not until 1953 that a national curriculum was prescribed for the elementary schools. Earlier in the twentieth century a mere listing of textbooks had sufficed.

Several versions of the 1953 curriculum were produced in subsequent years and in 1962 a syllabus for junior and senior high schools. At both the elementary and high school levels the curriculum made a minimal provision for studies related to Liberia, but the textbooks were largely foreign and so the values and content of the curriculum continued to be mainly foreign. Among other limitations of the curriculum produced during this period were the following:

(1) Concentration was on the four basic subjects – language arts, social studies, mathematics and science. Neglected were arts, music, business, industrial, agricultural and vocational subjects.

(2) Concentration was on *what* should be taught and not *how,* and consequently little attention was given to the preparation of teachers for implementation of the curriculum.

The move towards industrialisation and urbanisation after 1950 and the rapid economic and social changes which occurred in the country during that period highlighted the weaknesses of the curriculum as well as other shortcomings of the school.

In 1970 the Department of Education sponsored the first national conference to review the curriculum, which was followed by a series of smaller conferences. Focus was on curriculum content and organisation, teaching personnel, teaching materials and facilities needed to implement the curriculum. In progress since 1972 is a curriculum revision exercise in which various institutions are involved in attempts to rectify some of the major weaknesses of the curriculum.

Flexibility is of paramount importance so that content and organisation will be responsive to the environment and needs of the students. For example, at the elementary level there is to be general education for all plus variations based on the location of the school and the needs, abilities and potential of students. Liberian languages, long neglected in the schools, are to receive attention. The dominant Liberian language of the area where the school is located is to be introduced within the first three grades and continued through the upper elementary grades, replacing French at the upper elementary level. Instructional materials for teaching eight out of the total of sixteen major Liberian languages are being developed. An integrated approach is to be used in grades I to III but a separate subject approach in grades IV to VI. At the upper elementary level there is to be a different emphasis for children of normal school-age as against over-age children – the former continuing the expressive arts begun in the lower grades and the over-age exposed to pre-vocational courses.

At the secondary level, the curriculum in the junior high school is to provide for exploration and identification of aptitudes and talents. Consequently, provision is to be made for educational guidance and vocational exploration. In addition to these are the basic subjects – language arts, mathematics, social studies, general science and ethics, health and nutrition, a Liberian language and French. Provision is also made for flexibility to enable the school to provide additional work for required courses or programmes for enrichment.

The senior high school is to be characterised by differentiation and concentration, so that students may be qualified to pursue further education in various specialisations or prepared to enter the world of work.

At present there is an oversupply of students in secondary general education. Efforts are being made to diversify through provision of additional comprehensive high schools where the student may either:

(1) enter an academic stream where he will concentrate on
    (a)   science/mathematics
    (b)   social studies
    (c)   liberal studies
    or pursue general studies with no concentration;
(2) enter a vocational stream with concentration in
    (a)   agriculture
    (b)   building trades
    (c)   pre-engineering
    (d)   business education
    (e)   home economics.

The production of skilled craftsmen will take place in vocational training centres, where there will be greater emphasis on on-the-job training than can be provided in the vocational stream of the comprehensive high school. The curriculum is specialised, covers three years of study, and is geared to producing skilled personnel in:

(1) building trades,
(2) engineering trades,
(3) agriculture,
(4) home economics,
(5) commercial/business.

Some teacher training (pre-service and in-service) to qualify persons for teaching in elementary schools is presently carried on in high schools, but it is planned that for pre-service training students will be admitted after completion of high school and take a year or two of post-secondary training. The programme for in-service teachers at the secondary school level will continue to facilitate upgrading of the many unqualified teachers at this level.

Yet another concern in the curriculum revision exercise is how material is presented. Innovative approaches to meet varying needs are being encouraged and tried. Further, steps are being taken to produce trained teachers for the implementation of the revised curriculum.

The tertiary level has been affected too. Although institutions at this level are autonomous and, therefore, have not been subject to the curriculum revision exercise, some members of various faculties have been involved in preparing curricular materials for the lower levels and have worked with the national committee which has been co-ordinating curriculum revision. Further, these institutions have been adjusting their curriculum in keeping with changes which occurred on the national scene. As may be expected, teacher education has been a major point of focus. Efforts are being made to modify not only curriculum content but also methodological approaches and types of curricular materials utilised in the education of teachers. The active involvement of students-in-training in their own education as teachers is a growing reality.

Curriculum at the tertiary level until recently was rooted in the classical tradition at both Liberia College and Cuttington College which began their work in the nineteenth century. A programme of general studies led to the Bachelor of Arts degree, and through the fourth decade of the twentieth century there was hardly any change.[15] The subjects taught were the classical languages – Latin and Greek – and for a short period Arabic at Liberia College; the English lanuage and literature; intellectual and moral philosophy; social sciences, mainly outside the Liberian experience; mathematics; and science. The duration of the course was four years. At Cuttington alone there was a Theological

Department which offered theological training, and Hebrew was taught in addition to Latin and Greek.

The basic pattern of a four-year college has been retained, but since the 1950s, there has been emphasis on specialisation, broadening and varying of offerings. Moreover, the entire programme has been spelled out in terms of semester hours and grade points. It consists of general education followed by specialised training which includes education, science, forestry, agriculture, economics, management, nursing, theology and engineering.[16] Further, there was expansion in the Bachelor of Arts degree programme so that degrees are awarded in various specialisations in the humanities and social sciences. Degrees are also awarded in law and medicine; however, completion of a first degree is preferable and not less than two years of college essential for entering these professional programmes which last for three years and five years respectively.

Another development is the inclusion in the curriculum of a growing number of courses dealing with Africa in general and Liberia in particular. Also, theoretical courses in various disciplines are related to the Liberian experience. In varying degrees, depending on the field of specialisation, the curriculum has been adjusted to include practical experiences and research and to reflect community orientation and growing involvement in extension, all of which make studies relevant to the Liberian environment and experience.

The challenge of the 1970s is the production in substantial numbers of textbooks, supplementary reading materials and other instructional aids based on the Liberian experience, which can be used at this level and also at the secondary and elementary school levels.

XI   FINANCE

Like the educational system itself, educational finance is centralised. Funds for all publicity supported education is budgeted by the central government from general revenues. This includes expenditures for all government schools, subsidies to non-governmental schools and scholarships (foreign and local). The remaining funds for education come mainly from Concessions and religious groups but also from grants from bilateral and multilateral sources, loans to government, tuition and fees, and the minimal contributions from private individuals.

This centralised system of educational financing dates back to the second decade of the twentieth century, influenced by two developments:

(1)   the passage of the General Education Act in 1912 which established the Department of Public Instruction;

(2) the establishment by law in 1914 of a unitary system of inter-
     nal revenues which made school revenue a part of general
     revenues.

During the last decades of the nineteenth century government began
increasingly to assume responsibility from the county commissioners of
education for the financial support of education, but funds remained
meagre for years.

It was not until the economic changes which occurred in the country
during the 1950s and 1960s that substantial amounts could be
appropriated for education. In 1960 6·6 per cent of the national budget
of $22,500,000, or $1,475,243, was budgeted for education. This amount
rose substantially during the next few years and by 1968 $5,752,622 or
12·1 per cent of the total national budget was appropriated for
education. Of this amount $5,886,460 went to the Department of
Education and $861,645 to the University of Liberia.[17]

Between 1965 and 1974, in absolute amounts, there was considerable
rise in the education budget, but the percentage of the national budget
assigned to education remained relatively unchanged at around 12 per
cent. With the pupil population increasing at a much higher rate than
the budgeted expenditure the amount spent per pupil dropped,
adversely affecting quality in the schools. Moreover, there were
considerable demands for capital outlay for new structures and for
improving old ones and for the more costly types of education –
vocational/technical and science-oriented. The educational system was
severely constrained.

Another major problem relates to distribution of educational
expenditure whether considered in terms of purposes of education or
levels and types of education. Ministry of Education figures over the
period 1971–4 show the highest percentage of expenditure from the
basic education budget on personnel services (64·9 per cent in 1971, 65·6
per cent in 1972, 69·7 per cent in 1973 and 67·1 per cent in 1974). This is
understandable, but it is surprising indeed to find the next highest
expenditure on foreign scholarships (15·1 per cent in 1971, 15·5 per cent
in 1972, 12·9 per cent in 1973 and 9·9 per cent in 1974) and the lowest
expenditure on equipment (1·1 per cent in 1971, 0·4 per cent in 1972, 1·6
per cent in 1973 and 1·0 per cent in 1974).[18] Further insight into the
problem is gained when expenditure is viewed by functional category
as was done by the Minister of Eduction for the 1974 appropriation for
education which was 12 per cent of the national budget (see Table 8.1)[19]

When such basic needs are considered as the numbers out of school
for whom some education should be provided, the demand for
improvement in the quality of the teaching force, particularly at
elementary level, the outlay required if curriculum and instructional
materials development is to assume its rightful role, it is clear that a

Table 8.1   *Education Budget Distribution, 1974 ($)*

Elementary education	2,800,000
Secondary education	1,400,000
Higher education	2,400,000
Student educational aid	1,200,000
Central administration	1,200,000
Vocational/technical education	900,000
Teacher education	800,000
Supervision	400,000
Miscellaneous programmes (textbooks, library services, and subsidies to schools and social organisations)	100,000
Out-of-school education	70,000
Curriculum and instructional materials development	60,000
Total	11,330,000

substantially larger percentage of the national budget must be devoted to education if education is to make the impact it should on national development.

NOTES: CHAPTER 8

1 This society is better known as the American Colonization Society.
2 See M. A. G. Brown, 'Education for a developing Liberia', the First Christian W. Baker Annual Lecture of Cuttington College and Divinity School, Suacoco, Bong County, Liberia, November, 1971, pp. 3 and 4.
3 M. A. G. Brown, 'Education and national development in Liberia, 1800–1900', PhD thesis, Cornell University, 1967, pp. 45–56.
4 Although the General Education Act of 1912 provided for free eduction in all public schools below college, there was some charging of fees until 1944 when a law was passed prohibiting the collection of fees in public elementary schools. See Bureau of Planning and Research, Ministry of Education, 'The impact of the free tuition policy for Liberian public secondary schools in 1972 and implications for educational planning', mimeo., 1973, pp. 1–2.
5 It was closed for much of the period between 1847 and 1878, and operated for short and irregular periods between 1878 and 1896, after which sustained efforts characterised the work of the institution.
6 A. A. Hoff, *A Short History of Libera College and the University of Liberia* (New York: Consolidated Publications).
7 For the enrolment figures for secondary schools over the period 1960–74 see Appendix C.
8 This institution is discussed here only and not again under higher education because it operated an afternoon programme and offered degrees only in eduction. Its collegiate section ran for twenty years, closing in 1972.

9   These were distributed as follows:

The William V. S. Tubman Teachers' College,	
University of Liberia	92 (65 male, 27 female)
The Maryland College of Our	
Lady of Fatima	35 (15 male, 20 female)
Cuttington College and	
Divinity School	9 (7 male, 2 female)
Total	136 87 49

10 No girls enrolled in Liberia College during the nineteenth century. The first class of
    girls, four in number, graduated from the college in 1905. The other years in which
    girls graduated prior to 1950 were: 1925 – one, 1928 – one; 1931 – one; 1935 – two;
    1945 – one; 1947 – two; 1949 – one.

11 A full discussion on Cuttington College can be found in Melvin Justinian Mason,
    'The role of Cuttington College and the development of Liberia', doctoral thesis,
    Michigan State University, 1965.

12 M. Von Rundstedt, 'Statistical analysis of age-grade structure of students in
    elementary and secondary education in Liberia, 1973', NECP/5, National
    Consultative Conference on Educational Policy and Planning, Monrovia,
    September 1920, mimeo., 1974, p. 1.

13 Anonymous, 'The Department of Public Instruction, its origin, organization,
    functions and duties', mimeo., n.d., appendix I, p.9

14 There is also an Assistant Minister for Instruction. But it must be noted that the
    administrative arrangement referred to is a recent development in which each
    bureau in this organisational scheme, set forth in 1972, is headed by an assistant
    minister, with one deputy minister giving overall assistance to the minister. It should
    be noted further that these four bureaux replaced an earlier organisation of three
    consisting of: (1) Administration; (2) Instruction; (3) Unesco and other Special
    Programmes.

15 Cuttington College for most of its early years awarded no degrees and consequently
    followed a different pattern. See Mason, op. cit., n. 11 above.

16 The engineering programme, established in 1974, is the exception as far as
    duration of studies leading to the first degree is concerned. It extends for five
    years rather than four.

17 B. B. Azango, 'Expenditure on education in Liberia', NEC/68/Ref. 6, National
    Education Conference, Monrovia, November 1968, Mimeo., p. 1.

18 Annual Report of the Minister of Education to the National Legislature covering
    the period 1 January 1974 to 31 December 1974, mimeo., p. 43.

19 ibid., p. 42.

Appendix A   School-age population ages 6–16 years by sex, counties, and territories, 1974 national census provisional figures

County or Territory	Age in Years	School-Age Population			Population – All Ages		
		Total	Male	Female	Total	Male	Female
Bomi	6—16	14,845	7,653	7,192	62,141	32,262	29,879
Bong	6—16	56,261	28,368	27,893	194,191	95,252	98,939
Bassa	6—16	32,779	17,433	15,346	123,179	62,077	61,102
Cape Mount	6—16	14,342	7,690	6,652	56,604	29,600	27,004
Grand Gedeh	6—16	19,924	10,230	9,694	71,825	33,854	37,971
Kru Coast	6—16	8,193	4,453	3,740	27,134	13,298	13,836
Lofa	6—16	42,679	21,282	21,397	180,737	86,491	94,246
Marshall	6—16	4,971	2,448	2,523	20,732	10,752	9,980
Maryland	6—16	18,966	9,901	9,065	64,485	32,052	32,433
Montserrado	6—16	95,630	50,071	45,559	357,124	193,012	164,112
Nimba	6—16	69,594	35,368	34,226	249,702	122,203	127,499
Rivercess	6—16	8,262	4,644	3,618	27,747	13,800	13,947
Sasstown	6—16	2,858	1,594	1,264	9,952	4,877	5,075
Sinoe	6—16	16,550	9,123	7,427	57,647	29,270	28,377
Country Total	6—16	405,854	210,258	195,596	1,503,200	758,800	744,400

Source: Ministry of Planning and Economic Affairs.

Appendix B: *Elementary Education, Enrolment by Sex and Graduates, 1960-74*

| Year | Number of Pupils | | | Number of Graduates[1] |
	Total	Male	Female	
1960	58,613	41,861	16,752	n.a.
1961	68,641	52,060	16,581	764
1962	74,191	54,112	20,079	n.a.
1963	70,088	48,966	21,122	1,367
1964	78,539	55,673	22,866	1,928
1965	83,571	59,850	23,721	2,808
1966	110,252	77,068	33,184	2,644
1967	108,030	74,859	33,171	3,374
1968	120,101	n.a.	n.a.	3,735
1969	130,309	88,709	41,600	3,883
1970	120,245	80,680	39,565	4,714
1971	128,768	n.a.	n.a.	n.a.
1972	139,045	91,089	47,956	4,974
1973	148,730	n.a.	n.a.	5,879[2]
1974	149,687	96,658	53,029	6,720[2]

Notes:
1 Figures on graduates are available only after the national examinations were instituted in 1961. In 1962 no national examinations were given due to change of the school year and return to the original.
2 Estimated, as the national examinations at this level, sources for these figures were temporarily discontinued in 1972.

Sources: B. B. Azango, 'Developments in elementary and secondary education in Liberia', NEC/68/Ref. 2, National Education Conference, Monrovia, 13–16 November 1968, mimeo; Department of Education and Ministry of Education, *Annual Report,* 1969, 1970, 1974; Division of Statistics, Ministry of Education, 'Statistics of education in Liberia', 1970, 1972 and 1974, and other information supplied.

Appendix C: *Total National Budget and Public Appropriation for Education, 1971-4 ($ millions)*

	1971	1972	1973	1974
National Budget	71·2	81·6	83·0	96·0
Ministry of Education	7·4	8·4	8·2	8·9
University of Liberia	1·5	1·4	2·1	2·4
Total Education	8·9	9·8	10·3	11·3
Total Education as % of National Budget	12·5	12·0	12·5	12·0

Source: Table 1, Annual Report of the Minister of Education to the National Legislature covering the period 1 January 1974 to 31 December 1974, mimeo. p. 42.

Chapter 9

Education in Mali

AHMADOU TOURE

I HISTORICAL BACKGROUND

Educational developments in Mali were greatly influenced by the wider issues of the country's historical experience so that we may say that educationally as well as politically there was a colonial system and a Malian national system of education in the post-independence era after 1960. However, this division with two periods should not obscure the fact that in pre-colonial times Mali had evolved its own indigenous education system which was greatly influenced by Islamic education which flourished throughout the Sudan in the Middle Ages.

It is unfortunate that with the establishment of the colonial school system educational advances made through the indigenous and Qur'anic systems were completely wiped out.

The Colonial School System

The colonial school system emerged when Mali was governed as part of the entire French Sudan. At that time there was no national school system peculiar to each member state; rather there was a uniform system encompassing the whole French colony of the Sudan. Thus, when the first school was established in Kayes, the ancient capital of the French Sudan, it was meant to serve the entire territory and not just the area where the school was located.

The colonial school at Kayes established in 1886 was known as the 'school of hostages' because the pupils were children of the traditional chiefs. They had been taken from their fathers and held as hostages to prevent them from instigating rebellions against the colonial authority. While in school the pupils were taught to respect and appreciate French ideals and French culture and, of course, to speak French. In 1910 the name of the school was changed to the School for the Sons of Chiefs and Interpreters.

With the change of name the school assumed the special responsibility of producing from among the children of the traditional chiefs a nucleus of native aristocracy who would eventually propagate the French way of life throughout the country. The children were taught to despise their culture, to be ashamed of their language and to see French, instead, as the language of light, the symbol of virtue and civilisation.

All the colonial schools established thereafter followed the guidelines of the Kayes school. In 1916 a professional school was opened at Bamako which became the capital of the territory that same year. In 1924 the school was removed to the premises of what was to become the upper primary school. The Bamako school was named 'Terrasson de Fougères School' in honour of Governor Terrasson. That school remained for a long time the highest place of learning in Sudan.

However, as more schools were opened, a system emerged having the following types of school:

(1) *Elementary Schools* This type of school was of four years' duration – two years for the preparatory classes and two years for the elementary classes. These schools were located in the major towns and in the populous villages.

(2) *Regional Schools* Regional schools were of six years' duration comprising:

- preparatory classes for two years,
- elementary classes for two years,
- intermediate classes for two years.

At the end of the intermediate classes the pupils sat for an examination leading to the award of the Primary and Elementary Studies Certificate. Each major town had a regional school.

(3) *Upper Primary Schools* Each territory in French West Africa had one of these schools which accepted only the best pupils from the regional schools. It was only in 1947 that the school was made open to all the pupils who passed the elementary school certificate examination. This examination was usually taken at the end of elementary education, i.e. after the first four years of schooling.

Graduates of the UPS constituted the first recruitment pool for the country's manpower needs.

(4) *High Schools* This category of school can be equated with present-day secondary education and they were very few in number. They included:

(a) The School for the Sons of Chiefs and Interpreters which produced native schoolmasters;
(b) Veterinary Surgeons' School;
(c) Rural Training School of Katibougou;
(d) Higher Technical School of the Sudan, which was later turned into the Public Works Schools. These schools were directly under the control of the federal government of French West Africa and were open to qualified persons in different

parts of the territory irrespective of the location of a particular school. Classified under the Public Works Schools were:

(i)   Medical School and School of Pharmacy at Dakar, Senegal,
(ii) Rural Training School at Dabou, Ivory Coast,
(iii) Teacher Training School at Sebikotane, Senegal, which was later transferred to Goree Island and took the name William Ponty.

In concluding this discussion of the colonial school system, it is pertinent to make special reference to the motives evident in the establishment of the colonial schools and the type of curriculum offered by those schools.

From the very beginning it was quite easy to see the colonising goal of the schools. In fact, the French colonial authority was quick to realise the importance of the school as a major agent for ensuring the consolidation of colonial authority in the Sudan. The school was used as a means of assimilating the African into the French culture; for ensuring his total rejection of things African and his total submission to colonial rule. In essence, the schools helped to 'educate' the African away from his society and to condition him to French ways of life, culture and values. The young African in school had to differentiate himself from his kith and kin; he wore French clothes, spoke French and lived French.

The school curriculum was decided by officials in the Ministry of the Colonies in France. Consequently, French history, French civilisation, French language and French hymns were considered good enough for the African schoolchild. In fact the African was not considered as having a civilisation. Similarly, the textbooks were foreign, written in French by French authors.

The aim of the colonial schools can be summed up in a statement credited to Governor Roume:

the colonial duty in the field of education is twofold – one, it is to produce native trained staff who must be auxiliaries in every field and assume the status of a carefully chosen elite. The other task of education is to bring the masses through schools nearer us in the colonial country and to transform the natives' system of living.

The political function of the colonial schools was to make the natives appreciate colonial efforts and institutions and to make them think French. Economically, education was conceived as a means of producing a class of consumers. Thus, the cardinal concern of the colonial schools was simply to teach people to read, write and calculate.

The inadequacy of the colonial educational programmes is reflected in the abysmally low level of manpower development in Mali during the seventy-five years of colonisation. For example, at independence, only one person out of every ten could read and write; twelve children out of every hundred went to school; technical and middle-level staff were grossly limited in number. As for high-level manpower supply, the educational programmes did nothing about it. Consequently, on the attainment of independence, the country had only three veterinary surgeons, eight medical doctors, ten lawyers, seven engineers and three pharmacists for a population of 4,300,000 persons.

Such was the educational picture of Mali at the time of independence. The educational planners in independent Mali had to carve out a system of education truly Malian which reflected the national aspirations of the young country.

The first consideration in the task of building an independent national educational system was the political and cultural decolonisation of the people through the medium of the schools – the same agent used by the colonisers to perpetuate their colonial interests in the Sudan. The next consideration was to tailor educational development towards an overall national growth, particularly in the economic sphere. The production of middle- and high-level manpower for the country's labour force became an important responsibility of the educational institutions. To achieve this goal, the educational planners rightly felt that the liberation of the people's minds from colonial 'hangovers' was a prerequisite. Hence the educational reform that followed soon after independence.

The Malian School

Independence in 1960 ushered in a general revival of nationalist feeling among the generality of the people. From that time on, attempts were made to develop a truly Malian system of thinking and living. Everyone was urged to shake off the yoke of colonisation and to think and behave Malian. Towards this end, a general reform of education was embarked upon between 1960 and 1962, the product of which was a Malian school system distinct in character and purpose from the colonial school system. In the post-colonial era education was seen as a sure weapon of nation-building, development and modernisation.

The first step taken by the educational reformers was to interest parents in sending their children to schools. Parents responded to this call positively and henceforth they sent their children to school voluntarily, as opposed to the colonial period when parents reluctantly sent their children. 'Rush to school' became a popular slogan in the reform.

The second step taken by the reformers was a direct consequence of the first: the provision of more school buildings. As a result of the rush to school, enrolment soared; new schools were opened while more classes were added to existing ones.

Despite the increase in schools, demand for education far outweighed what could be provided in terms of physical buildings, materials and staff. The limited resources notwithstanding, ten years after the educational reform, primary school enrolment rose from 66,208 in 1962 to 229,879 in 1972, representing an increase from 12 per cent enrolment in 1962 to 20 per cent in 1972.

In general, the reform of education aimed at:

(1) mass education in which quality is not jeopardised;
(2) education able to provide, within the shortest possible time and with minimum expenditure, all the managerial staff that the country needed for its different plans of development;
(3) education which preserves and perpetuates a culture that is distinctively Malian;
(4) education whose content is based upon the Malian ideals but which at the same time respects universally acceptable values;
(5) education which decolonises the mind.

II ORGANISATION

Since 1962 education in Mali has followed the lines laid down by the reform of 1960–2. However, the first seminar on national education and the meeting of education leaders at Bamako in December 1964 introduced some modifications. On the whole, however, the structure of education and the spirit which the reform infused into it remained unchanged.

The educational structure since 1962 is as follows:

(1) fundamental education
(2) teacher education
(3) technical, professional and general secondary education
(4) higher education.

Until 1973 these different branches of education were under the control of one ministry: the Ministry of National Education and Science. From that year, the ministry was divided into two, as follows:

(1) Ministry of Fundamental Education, Youth and Sports
(2) Ministry of Secondary and Higher Education, and of Scientific Research.

III FUNDAMENTAL EDUCATION

This is the first nine years of schooling divided into two cycles. The first cycle is of six years' duration, consisting of:

(1) two classes of initiation (first and second years),
(2) two classes of aptitude (third and fourth years),
(3) two classes of orientation (fifth and sixth years).

The second cycle is merely an extension of the first and it lasts three years, divided into seventh, eighth and ninth.

In the reform of 1962 no examination was needed at the end of the first cycle to enter the second cycle. However, some few years ago such an examination was introduced. Thus, at the end of the sixth year pupils sit for the Certificate Ending the First-Cycle Studies, equivalent to the former Certificate of Elementary Primary Studies. At the end of the second cycle the pupils sit for the Certificate of Fundamental Studies (CFS), equivalent to the Certificate Ending the First-Cycle Studies in France. Table 9.1 shows school enrolment in the country's primary

Table 9.1   *Comparative Enrolments,*
1960/1 and 1970/1

	1960/1	1970/1
Enrolment in first year of schooling	19,401	57,368
Enrolment in last year of schooling	479	8,594
Enrolment in public schools	61,363	213,851
Enrolment in private schools	7,460	16,068
Total enrolment	68,823	229,879

education institutions and the first cycle of secondary education 1960–1 (before the reform) compared with enrolment for fundamental education 1970–1 (after the reform). It should be remembered that the former course was ten years as opposed to the latter's nine.

Apart from the general increase in school enrolment, the post-educational school reform era also witnessed a shift from the boarding system to the day system in the secondary schools. Non-residential day

Table 9.2   *Rate of Enrolment by Region for*
the Two Cycles, 1970/1

Regions	School-Age	Enrolled Pupils	% Increase Rate
Kayes	223,000	34,224	15·34
Bamako	274,000	70,285	25·65
Sikasso	270,000	30,689	11·36
Segou	226,000	30,311	13·41
Mopti	296,000	28,145	9·50
Gao	182,000	29,858	16·40

schools permitted larger intakes, thereby absorbing an increased number of primary school leavers eager for secondary education. The limited financial resources of the country and the need to keep students longer at home were factors in favour of day secondary schools.

It is important to note that the craving for education after independence was nationwide, as shown in Table 9.2. School enrolment increased in all the six regions of Mali, although the capital city Bamako recorded the highest increase.

IV   SECONDARY EDUCATION

Two kinds of secondary education exist in Mali; the purely academic secondary education offered in the grammar schools and the technical education offered in the technical secondary schools. Technical schools prepare students for middle-level positions in commerce and industry.

Entry into the secondary schools depends on performances in the competitive entrance examination held annually for holders of the CFS. Thereafter, students are assigned to either the secondary grammar or the secondary technical on the basis of aptitude.

The period of studies in the grammar schools is broken into two stages: a general education stage, followed by the higher stage in which three subject areas are offered for specialisation – literature, biological sciences and pure sciences. Usually the schools prepare students for higher education and not directly for employment.

Two examinations are conducted in the grammar schools, one at the end of the second year and the other at the end of the third year. These examinations are referred to as the first and second parts of the Baccalauréat. Success in both examinations is necessary to qualify for university education. For this reason the Baccalauréat examinations are considered very important and are taken very seriously by aspirants for university education. It is encouraging to note that success in the Baccalauréat has increased in the last ten years. In 1975 53 per cent of candidates were successful in the first part and 66 per cent in the second part.

V   SECONDARY TECHNICAL EDUCATION

The primary aim of technical education is to provide as quickly as possible a competent technical labour force necessary for the country's development, but at the same time care is taken to ensure quality. Thus the curricula of technical schools and the instructional programmes are carefully drawn up and revised from time to time to ensure high standards.

Unfortunately, lack of qualified teaching staff constitutes one of the main problems in the secondary technical schools. In a developing country, the training of qualified personnel for the technical and professional areas of the economy is essential.

Some of the professional, technical and vocational schools are described below.

(1) *Central School for Industry, Trade and Administration*
    This school attracts a great number of pupils, probably because the school is a four-year one, which is relatively shorter than the period of the general secondary schools. It trains people for middle-level positions in the administration, justice, industry, commerce and electro-mechanics.

(2) *Centre for Vocational Training*
    This school trains staff at the intermediate level to satisfy the need for qualified personnel in the public and private sectors of the economy. The training period is two years for pupils who have the CFS and three years for those without it.

(3) *Secondary School of Health*
    This school has a three-year course and trains staff nurses, midwives and sanitary workers. The curriculum is broad so as to give pupils a combination of the theoretical and practical learning experiences needed for effective functioning in the different areas of public health.

(4) *Rural Polytechnic Institute*
    This school, located at Katibougou, provides different courses in agriculture and stock-breeding. It includes a section for veterinary training at Bamako under the name of Assistant Veterinary Surgeons' School. The major course offerings are appropriate and relevant to the country's economy which is essentially agricultural and pastoral.

VI TEACHER EDUCATION

There are four types of teacher education institutions:

(1) Pedagogical Institutes of General Education (PIGEs)

There are four of these, located at Bamako, Sikasso, Dire and Kayes. They offer a two-year course for the award of the diploma which certifies teachers for the first cycle of fundamental education.

The establishment of the pedagogical institutes is one of the great achievements of the educational reform of the 1960s which not only provided the aims of education for the country, but also made suggestions for the realisation of those aims.

The smooth running of the pedagogical institutes is of great importance to the administration of education because a steady flow of qualified teachers into the schools depends on them. For this reason the curriculum has been structured to ensure a sound training in all the branches of knowledge.

(2)   Secondary Teacher Training Schools

These are the school for boys at Badalabougou (Bamako) and the girls' technical training school at Banankoro (near Segou).

These schools offer the following subjects: literature, history and geography, biological sciences, language, music, drawing, mathematics, physics, chemistry and physical training. The girls' technical training school, in addition to these subjects, has a section for domestic science.

(3)   Centre for Practical Orientation

In pursuance of the government's policy of relating fundamental education to local needs, the Centre for Practical Orientation was established with the assistance of a United Nations special fund to train teachers in agriculture and stock-breeding.

(4)   National Institute of Fine Arts

This institute trains teachers for the second cycle with specialisation in painting, music, sculpture and dramatic art.

Teacher education is of primary concern to the government of Mali and the rate of enrolment in the country's teacher training institutions bears testimony to this fact. A comparison of the enrolment figures in the teacher training institutions 1959/60 and 1971/2 demonstrates the efforts of the Malian government to expand teacher training facilities (Table 9.3).

Table 9.3   *Enrolment of Fundamental Education Teachers in Training, 1959/60 and 1971/2*

	1959/60	*1971/2*
Teachers of first cycle	1,049	1,954
Teachers of second cycle	37	1,400

Source: Schools Statistics of the Republic of Mali.

VII   HIGHER EDUCATION

The history of university education in Mali is comparatively recent. Until 1962 when the reform of education started, the training of high-level staff for every sector of the country's economy was done abroad – particularly in France. Such a practice was considered unsatisfactory for a country trying to rid itself of colonial vestiges. Consequently, the 1960 educational reform recommended the establishment of a university in Mali, primarily to provide technical and professional training for the country's high-level manpower needs. The proposed university was also to undertake scientific research, and sponsor studies in the general areas of scientific, social and cultural development. The training of teachers at the university level for the country's schools was another significant responsibility of the proposed university. The interests of the industrial, administrative, health and agricultural sectors were also to be its concern.

Thus, between 1962 and 1972, five schools offering courses at the university level were established. These were:

(1)   National Teacher Training College
(2)   National College of Administration
(3)   National College for Engineers
(4)   College of Medicine
(5)   Rural Polytechnic Institute.

The first four of these colleges were located in Bamako while the fifth was at Katibougou.

(1)   National Teacher Training College

The establishment of a teacher training college of a university standard was made possible by a United Nations Development Programme (UNDP) aid to the government of Mali in 1962. The college started a new university teacher education programme which had courses in the humanities, the sciences and, of course, education. It trained teachers for secondary schools.

To qualify for admission prospective students must possess the Baccalauréat while teachers of fundamental education must pass the competitive entrance examination.

The course is of four years' duration, at the end of which, the Certificate of University Teacher Training College is awarded. In the fourth year emphasis is on methodology and pedagogy. Thereafter, student-teachers undergo probation for nine months in a grammar school or in a secondary teacher training school. In addition, the student is expected to write a dissertation on any aspect of teaching or educational problems to demonstrate his research skills and aptitude for teaching. The students' performance in all these areas – coursework, probation and dissertation – are considered for certification and grading.

The number of teachers trained in this college increases from year to year thereby permitting the progressive replacement of foreign teachers in the country's schools whose services are often too expensive and less efficient. The college's enrolment of Malian students has risen from 18 in the session 1962–3 to 446 in 1973–4.

(2)   National College of Administration

This college is open to students with the Baccalauréat who, in addition, must pass a competitive entrance examination. The College's areas of studies include law, administration and economics.

(3)   National College for Engineers

This college was originally known as the Higher Technical School of the Sudan and later named the School of Public Works, The National College for Engineers, as it is now called, is a four-year school offering specialisation in engineering, mines and geology, electro-mechanics and topography.

(4)   College of Medicine

This college trains doctors, pharmacists and dental surgeons. The course is of five years' duration. Entry into the college is highly competitive for holders of the Baccalauréat or its equivalent.

(5)   Rural Polytechnic Institute

Holders of the Baccalauréat who wish to specialise in agronomy or stock-breeding are admitted. There is usually a short-cycle course and a long-cycle course.

VIII   POSTGRADUATE EDUCATION

Postgraduate education in Mali is directed towards scientific research and at present is available only in two institutions.

(1)   The Higher Teacher Training Centre

Located in the same building as the Teacher Training College, this centre was established in 1970 to prepare teachers for the country's post-secondary institutions.

It was established with the help of Unesco which also provides research materials necessary for the preparation of doctoral theses. The course is of three years' duration. During the first year the students continue to teach, for a reduced number of hours, in grammar schools or other secondary schools. After the first year students sit for an examination and only successful students continue their studies at the centre. During the last two years students teach as assistants in the colleges, in addition to their regular studies at the centre.

The establishment of the centre has put a check on the practice of training people abroad for teaching positions in the country's colleges. However, visiting professors still come twice or thrice a year to supervise the students' theses. Successful completion and defence of a thesis is compulsory for the award of the doctoral degree.

The first students to be awarded the PhD graduated in 1973 and the second set of PhD graduates passed out in 1975.

For the 1973 thesis examination, an international panel of reputable professors from American, European and African universities was set up. In 1975 students wrote theses in the areas of mathematics, statistics, geometry, animal physiology, microbiology, comparative literature and applied linguistics.

(2) Previsional Productivity and Management Institute
One of the aims of the institute is to promote the study and adaptation, in the African context, of the various techniques of previsional productivity and management in firms. It also trains managers.

The institute enrols persons who hold a university degree and pass a pre-entry test. People already working in firms are also enrolled.

Figure 9.1 gives a comprehensive summary of the Malian school system.

IX ADMINISTRATION

The Ministry of National Education was formed in 1972 by the merger of two separate ministries.

(1) The Ministry of Fundamental Education, Youth and Sports
This ministry is headed by an Education Secretary who is assisted by an administrative staff usually referred to as the Education Secretary's Department staff. Directly subordinate to them are the Departments of Basic Education and of Youth.

The Fundamental Education Department, which also comes under this ministry, serves as a liaison between the ministry and the fundamental school inspectors in the different regions who supervise schools in their areas. Each fundamental school, first or second cycle, is directed by a headmaster.

The Department of Youth and Sports is headed by an inspector who is responsible for all youth activities in the country.

(2) The Ministry of Secondary and Higher Education and Scientific Research
This ministry also is headed by an Education Secretary with a similar departmental staff.

This ministry is divided into:

Fig. 9.1. *The Malian School System*

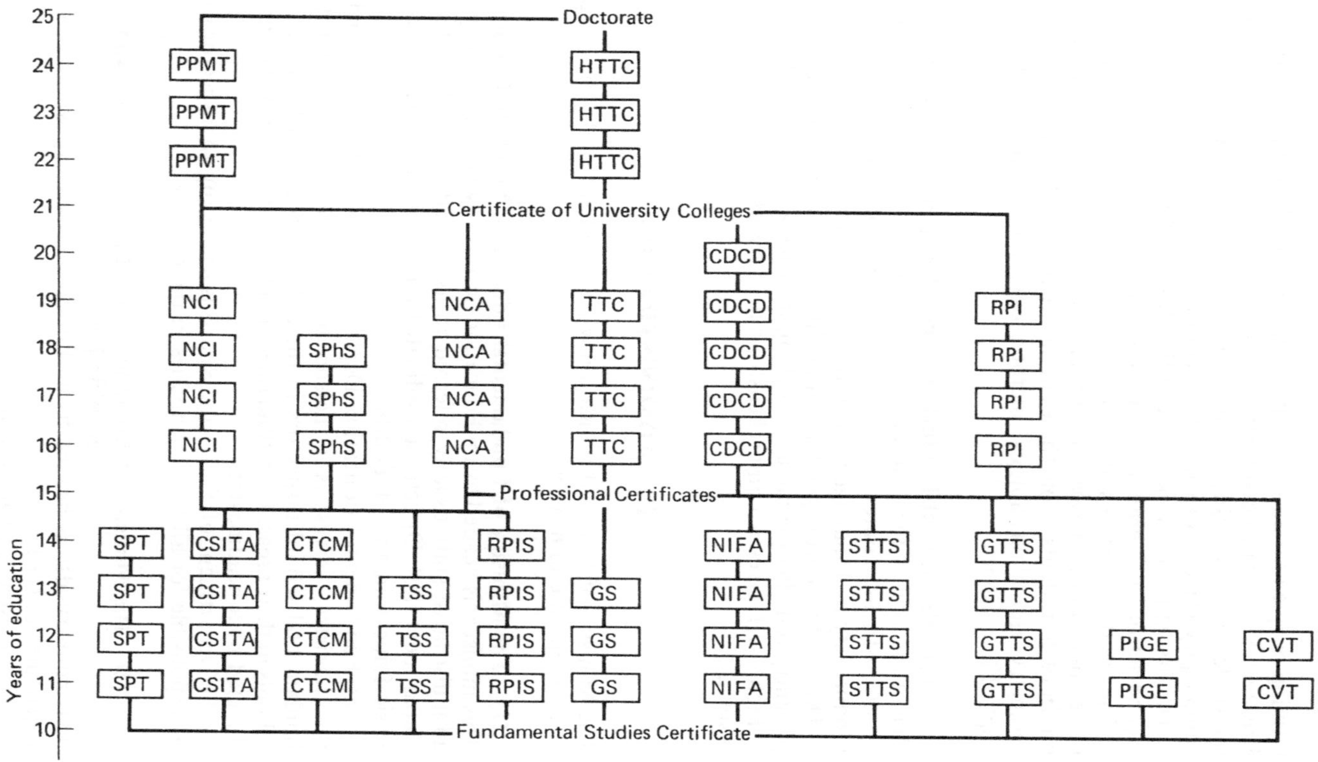

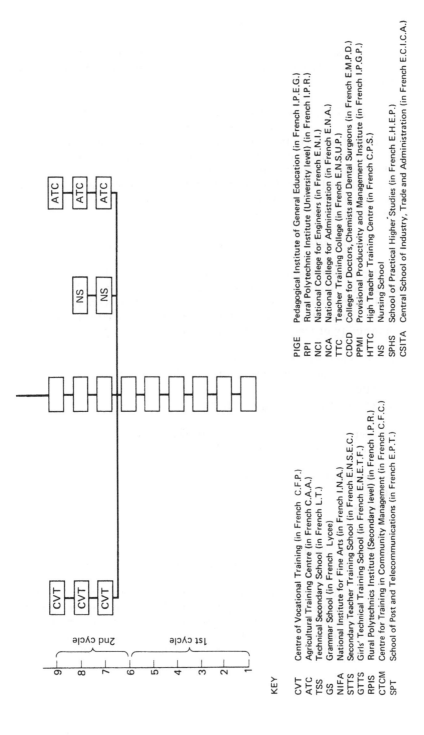

KEY

CVT   Centre of Vocational Training (in French C.F.P.)
ATC   Agricultural Training Centre (in French C.A.A.)
TSS   Technical Secondary School (in French L.T.)
GS   Grammar School (in French Lycee)
NIFA   National Institute for Fine Arts (in French I.N.A.)
STTS   Secondary Teacher Training School (in French E.N.S.E.C.)
GTTS   Girls' Technical Training School (in French E.N.E.T.F.)
RPIS   Rural Polytechnics Institute (Secondary level) (in French I.P.R.)
CTCM   Centre for Training in Community Management (in French C.F.C.)
SPT   School of Post and Telecommunications (in French E.P.T.)

PIGE   Pedagogical Institute of General Education (in French I.P.E.G.)
RPI   Rural Polytechnic Institute (University level) (in French I.P.R.)
NCI   National College for Engineers (in French E.N.I.)
NCA   National College for Administration (in French E.N.A.)
TTC   Teacher Training College (in French E.N.S.U.P.)
CDCD   College for Doctors, Chemists and Dental Surgeons (in French E.M.P.D.)
PPMI   Provisional Productivity and Management Institute (in French I.P.G.P.)
HTTC   High Teacher Training Centre (in French C.P.S.)
NS   Nursing School
SPHS   School of Practical Higher Studies (in French E.H.E.P.)
CSITA Central School of Industry, Trade and Administration (in French E.C.I.C.A.)

The Department of Higher Education and Scientific Research

All the university colleges and the research institutes come under this department.

The Department of General, Secondary, Technical and Vocational Education

This department controls the greatest number of schools. In fact all aspects of secondary education come under its administrative umbrella. It also controls private education as a sub-department.

The responsibilities of this department include general supervision of all secondary institutions and the organisation of examinations for each level of education.

The Department of the National Pedagogical Institute and Teacher Training

This department was created after the 1962 reform and it performs the specialised function of school materials production and supplies; including appropriate textbooks and teaching materials relevant for the new curricula. Furthermore, the department is charged with the responsibility of teacher training as a whole, including:

    research and experimentation,
    production and adaptation of school records and documentary
        materials,
    disseminating school information.

The department's responsibilities are discharged, first, in the institute itself through the following branches:

    research and experimentation
    production
    training
    library
    printing
    vocational guidance
    audio-visual aids with school broadcasting and television.

Secondly, at the training schools – the main concern here is to ensure the juxtaposition of theory and practice in the various teacher training programmes. Researches into educational practices are also sponsored to find ways of adapting teaching methods to Malian conditions. The Institute organises short-term in-service courses for schoolmasters.

X CONTROL

At each level of education, control of schools is vested in school inspectors appointed for their sound knowledge of educational problems in general.

At the fundamental level, for example, the ministry appoints inspectors to take charge of fundamental schools in each of the six regions of the country. There is a senior inspector for each school area.

The inspectors ensure the smooth running of schools under their control. In addition to this role, the inspectors are expected to give expert advice and suggestions for the improvement of teaching methods. While for the first cycle of fundamental education inspectors are generalists, that is, school inspectors as distinct from subject area inspectors, for the second cycle inspectors are subject specialists, thus, for example, inspectors for French, English, natural science and mathematics.

Secondary education inspectors, for their part, supervise teachers in their subject areas both for the advancement of quality teaching and for curriculum innovations. They also take part in the organisation of final examinations. These inspectors are in the department of general, secondary, technical and vocational education; they are appointed from among teachers in the Teacher Training College.

At the university level control is in the hands of the head of the institution assisted by a council of heads of academic studies and a research department.

XI FINANCE

Education takes about 30 per cent of the country's budget and 65 per cent of this allocation goes to fundamental education alone.

Despite this huge government investment in education, the quality and quantity of education is not satisfactory. The country still suffers from lack of sufficient schools to enrol those eager for education. There is a shortage of teachers for all levels of school; young school leavers refuse to take up teaching because of the poor conditions of service. The schools are poorly equipped while the need for more school buildings is felt throughout the country. To supplement the government's annual budget for education, pupils' parents sometimes get together to build and equip schools.

School administrators and ministry officials often attribute the fall in the standard of education to lack of sufficient funds.

As may be seen from Table 9.4, at the general, secondary, technical and vocational levels the bulk of the funds goes to supply materials to pupils. Mali is one of the very few countries in Africa where the

Table 9.4   *Ministry of National Education Expenditures, 1971/2
(thousands of Malian francs)*[1]

| Type and Level | 1971/2 | | |
of Education or Service	Personnel	Material	Total
Department staff	45,500	115,400	160,900
Fundamental Education			
Department: first cycle	1,508,100	135,100	1,643,200
second cycle	2,380,000	93,000	2,473,000
Centre for Practical Orientation	8,600	12,800	21,400
General secondary education	258,600	246,900	505,500
Technical education	132,100	169,900	302,000
Higher education, National Institute of Pedagogy	198,800	166,900	385,700
Youth and sports	164,200	14,500	178,700
Total	5,058,400	1,150,800	6,209,200
Scholarship and family allowances			706,100
Sum total			6,915,300

Note:
1   450 Malian francs = US $1.
Source: National Budgets, 1971/2.

government offers free tuition and boarding to pupils. However, the present scholarship and boarding systems are being changed.

Expenditure on higher education is the greatest. This is due to the fact that not only is university education free, but also each university student receives an allowance equal in value to an average civil servant's pay. This situation constitutes a major problem for the education planners.

Chapter 10

Education in Nigeria

ONYERISARA UKEJE AND J.U. AISIKU

I BRIEF INTRODUCTION

Our concern in this chapter is to trace the history of Western education in Nigeria, highlighting some relevant historical antecedents that have helped to shape its development at different stages. In our treatment of the subject, the mode of introduction of Western education into the country, its content and method, major landmarks, problems and progress will serve as essential signposts in the historical terrain of Western education in Nigeria from 1842 – the year of its introduction – to date. Our focus on Western education should not be taken to mean the absence of other forms of education in the country. In fact, traditional African education and the Qur'anic system predate Western education; and each system constitutes a separate and viable subject of study.

Fafunwa, for example, has given what we regard as an inspiring introductory inroad into the nature of traditional African education.[1] More elaborate and comprehensive study of that aspect of education is needed, not only for Nigeria, but for Africa as a whole. While recognising the importance and prevalence of the traditional system of education in Nigeria, we will concentrate our attention on the Western system in this chapter.

The Early Beginnings of Western Education

The introduction of Western education into Nigeria dates back to the year 1842, when on the invitation of some Yoruba immigrants from Sierra Leone who had settled in Badagry some 50 kilometres west of Lagos, the Wesleyan Methodist Missionary Society sent the Rev. Thomas Birch Freeman from Cape Coast where he had been the superintendent of the Methodist mission. By 1860 the big four missionary societies in Nigeria – the Wesleyan Methodist, the Church Missionary Society, the Baptist and the Roman Catholic – had established stations. Others that followed include the Qua Iboe of Northern Ireland in 1887 and the Primitive Methodist Society in 1872. The missionary societies founded schools whenever and wherever they established stations. This was the earliest means of proselytising.

Colonial Government and Education in Nigeria, 1891–1951

The story of the British imperial government in Nigeria started in the year 1851, when after a flat refusal by the then King Kosoko of Lagos to sign a treaty with the British for the abolition of the export of slaves from the Lagos Island he was attacked and defeated by them after some strong resistance. His uncle, Akintoye, who helped the British to defeat him, was made king in January 1852.

In the treaty signed with the new king and his chiefs, it was clearly stated that education would not only be permitted but encouraged. However, the then colonial government in Nigeria did nothing in the education field for the first twenty years of its administration.

It was only in the year 1872 that the colonial government made available the sum of £30 to each of the three missionary societies involved in educational activities in Lagos – the CMS, the Wesleyan Methodist and the Catholic – to support their educational activities. This marked the beginning of the system of grants-in-aid to education which formed the major educational financing policy of the colonial government and was subsequently adopted by the governments of the first Republic of Nigeria. In 1877 the grant was increased to £200 per year for each of the three missions. The grant-in-aid stood at this amount until 1882.

In 1899 the first government primary school was opened in Lagos for the education of Muslim children. In 1903 the first Department of Education in the country was established. The department was headed by a director assisted by four Europeans, designated superintendents, and some West Indian and African teachers.

Following the creation of the Colony and Protectorate of Southern Nigeria in 1906, an Education Ordinance for the new territory was enacted in 1908. In 1909 the first government secondary school in the country – Kings College, Lagos – was founded. By this time the total number of government schools (primary and secondary) stood at forty. But most of these schools, though founded by the colonial government, received from time to time some financial support from the local chiefs.

By the year 1912 there were altogether fifty-nine government primary schools in the territory. About ninety-one mission primary schools were receiving government grants-in-aid at that time. By the same year there were one government secondary school and four assisted mission secondary schools in Lagos. There were in addition to these several unassisted mission and private primary schools and five unassisted secondary schools in the then Colony and Protectorate of Southern Nigeria. Thus, by 1912, there were in the whole Colony and Protectorate of Southern Nigeria 150 primary schools under government control with a total enrolment of some 16,000 pupils while at the same time some 20,000 pupils were enrolled in unassisted mission and private schools. There were also three voluntary agency teacher training institutions, one of which was assisted. Thus, at that time, the government had not a single teacher training institution and the missions provided not less than 75 per cent of all educational facilities.

The school system varied as each mission operated its own educational system. However, the first Nigerian education code of 1926 standardised the school system into the following:

Infant: Classes 1 and 2
Primary: Standards 1 to 6
Secondary: Forms 1 to 6.

This was, in effect, a system comprising eight years of primary and four years of secondary education. This system was regarded unsatisfactory and in 1930 E. R. J. Hussey, the first Director of Education for Nigeria, proposed a 6-6 system comprising six years elementary school of infant classes 1 and 2 and primary standards 1 to 6; and a secondary education comprising middle schools of two years duration and secondary forms 1 to 4. The Hussey school system was not accepted by the mission schools.

The 1947 Memorandum on Education tried to harmonise the school system into junior primary of infant classes 1 and 2 and elementary classes 1 and 2, and senior primary of elementary classes 3 and 4. The Northern Provinces however, retained until 1953 their own system of four years of elementary schools followed by five years of middle consisting of Remove and Middle 1 to 4. With regionalisation of the country in 1951, regional school systems emerged. The Western Region operated a 6-6 system, Eastern Region a 7-5 system, Northern Region 7-6 and Lagos continued the 8-6 system. The school system has since been standardised into a 6-5 system throughout the country.

Qur'anic Schools

It should be noted that while the Christian missions confined their evangelistic and educational activities to the coastal and southern parts of the country, Islam with its Arabic influence was already firmly established in the northern part. Thus, while Western education became the prevalent and dominant type of education in the south, Qur'anic education remained, for many decades, the only kind of formal education in the north and when the Christian missions began to penetrate into the north, they were to limit their activities to the non-Muslim areas. Lord Lugard, the first High Commissioner for the Protectorate of Northern Nigeria, declared, in 1902, an education policy which specifically advised the Christian missions to direct their activities to the non-Muslim areas of the north.

Consequently, Qur'anic schools, essentially for religious instruction and for the reading of the Qur'an, flourished in the north. In 1913 there were some 19,073 Qur'anic schools with an enrolment of 143,312 students. Shortly after the British conquest small Western-style schools were opened in provincial capitals under the aegis of residents, but it was not until 1909 that such a school was established by the government just outside the walls of Kano at Nassarawa. By 1913 the school had an enrolment of 300 pupils. By 1922 the Katsina Teachers' College was opened. Training centres for elementary school teachers were also opened at Bauchi and Katsina. In 1928 another centre was opened at Toro. By 1931 there were twenty-nine Western education schools in the north run by the native administrations with a total enrolment of 1,931 students, excluding schools run by the voluntary agencies.

Another landmark in the history of colonial education in Nigeria was the impact of the Advisory Committee on Native Education in the British Tropical African Dependencies, as it was called when it was established in 1923. One important example of this impact was the Education Ordinance introduced in 1926. The Ordinance made provisions for a board of education consisting of a director of education, a deputy director, an assistant director and not fewer than ten representatives of the missions and other voluntary agencies working in the Colony and Protectorate of Southern Nigeria.

In 1927 a scheme for the creation of supervisory personnel was created. By this scheme all school agencies were to appoint full-time supervisors of schools. The government was to indemnify the agencies for the salaries of the supervisors and other expenses connected with their work. In the same year (1927) the colonial government made an important addition to its list of schools when it founded Queen's College, Lagos, a secondary school for girls. In 1929 two government training colleges were established, one at Ibadan and the other at Umuahia.

In 1930 a system of visiting teachers was created as another supervisory and controlling device to ensure high standards. These were government teachers who visited schools, particularly unassisted schools, to render some help, though they often failed to help and the visits were more like military inspections than an educational experience.

In the year 1929 the Departments of Education of the Colony and Protectorate of Southern Nigeria and the Protectorate of Northern Nigeria were combined to form one Department of Education for Nigeria. E. R. J. Hussey was appointed the first Director of Education for the country in 1930.

In 1946, soon after the end of the Second World War, Nigeria introduced a Ten-Year Development Plan. The educational aims of the plan were to provide:

(1) a type of education more suitable for the needs of the country;

(2) better conditions of service for teachers employed by missions and other voluntary bodies, in order to provide a better-trained and more contented staff;

(3) more adequate financial assistance to mission and other voluntary educational bodies;

(4) financial assistance to native administrations to maintain an efficient staff of teachers and expand education in their areas;

(5) controlled expansion within financial limits.

After the Second World War there was rapid educational expansion due to the efforts of private voluntary agencies, tribal unions and individuals.

At places like Onitsha, Ibadan and Lagos, private primary and secondary schools sprang up almost overnight. Some eight private secondary schools in Onitsha alone were opened between 1939 and 1947. Thus in 1947 the primary school population in the south stood at 600,000, while in the north the figure was 70,000. By 1951 the total primary school population throughout Nigeria rose to 1,002,559 and the number of primary schools was recorded as 9,108. There were at the same time 93 secondary schools with a student population of 31,425. There were also 39,573 teachers working in all types of schools throughout the country but only 11,032 of these possessed degrees or teaching certificates.

Development during Representative Government, 1951–60

In 1951 Nigeria was divided into three regions – Northern, Western and Eastern. Education became a regional function. Each region possessed its own department of education and enacted regional education laws, all of which came into effect in 1952. The education law in each of the regions made provision for the establishment of a regional board of education and a Ministry of Education headed by a minister. There was a tremendous educational expansion during this period, perhaps as a result of regional rivalry. In January 1955 the Western Region, for instance, introduced what came to be popularly known as the universal primary education (UPE) scheme – a scheme which made primary education non-fee-paying. The impact of this scheme on primary school enrolment in that region was impressive and immediate. Primary school population, which had risen from 240,000 in 1947 to 457,000 in 1954, skyrocketed to 811,000 in 1955! This figure rose to 982,755 in 1957.

Two years after the introduction of the UPE scheme in the Western Region, in February 1957, the Eastern Region launched its own scheme. Primary school enrolment rose to 1,209,167 that year, compared to 320,000 some ten years earlier. Unfortunately this scheme ran into problems only a year after its introduction and had to be modified on a three-year non-fee-paying and a three-year fee-paying basis. Thus, on comparative terms, particularly in relation to its lifespan, the Western Region scheme was more successful.

The Northern Region, which did not follow the other two regions in the free education scheme, also recorded a remarkable increase in primary school enrolment during the same period. In that region primary school enrolment rose from 66,000 in 1947 to 205,767 in 1957.

The role of individuals like Chief Obafemi Awolowo, Dr Nnamdi Azikiwe, Chief S. O. Awokoya and others must be emphasised as contributory to the educational boom of post–1950. Chief S. O. Awokoya, then Minister of Education, Western Region, was reported to have declared in a parliamentary debate: 'Educational development is imperative and urgent. It must be treated as a national emergency second only to war. It must move with the momentum of a revolution.'[2] Against such background initiative and parliamentary support, education expanded at all levels. Secondary school enrolment increased from 9,908 in 1947 to 55,235 in 1960. There were only 161 secondary grammar schools in the whole of the country in 1955. This had risen to 325 in 1960. Although little happened in the area of higher education during this period (1951–60), the voice of dissatisfaction over the inadequacy of higher education facilities in the country was loud enough to evoke public and government concern. Towards the end of the period under review, specifically in April 1959, the federal government set up a commission to conduct an investigation into Nigeria's needs in the field of post-secondary school certificate and higher education over the next twenty years: 1960–80. Thus, it can be seen that the foundations for the proliferous higher education expansion of the 1960s were laid in the 1950s. However, only one higher educational institution, opened in October 1960, was added to the existing ones – University College, Ibadan (1948), and the Colleges of Arts, Science and Technology at Zaria, Ibadan and Enugu. This was the University of Nigeria, Nsukka.

EDUCATIONAL DEVELOPMENT DURING THE POST-INDEPENDENCE ERA 1960–79

II PRIMARY EDUCATION

The pace of educational expansion set in motion in the mid-1950s by the launching of the UPE scheme in the former Western Region and later, partially, in the former Eastern Region seemed to have lost its momentum in the 1960s. The number of primary schools, for example, declined from 15,703 in 1960 to 14,976 in 1964. The Civil War (May 1967 to January 1970) further aggravated the decline.

Another development which slowed down the pace of primary school expansion in the 1960s was the apparent shift in emphasis from quantity to quality. This shift was manifested in the merging of schools, particularly in the then East-Central State, ostensibly to increase efficiency. However, in the opening years of the 1970s, as a result of the end of the Civil War, the number of primary schools rose again. In 1971, the number of primary schools rose to 15,324 with an enrolment of 3,894,539. In 1973 the corresponding figures were 14,502 schools with 4,662,400 enrolment. On the whole, primary school enrolment increased from 2,912,618 in 1960 to 4,662,400 in 1973 – an increase of 62 per cent in thirteen years.

The 1975–80 Development Plan ushered in a most profound boom for primary education in the country. The plan explicitly stated: 'Universal Primary Education is a pre-requisite for equalization of opportunities for education across the country in all its known facets.'[3] Hence the federal military government introduced, in September 1976, a system of free universal primary education (UPE) throughout the federation. Under the scheme, primary education will continue to be of six years' duration throughout the country. Children aged 6 or who will be 6 before the end of the calendar year for which admission is sought are qualified for enrolment.

Table 10.1   *Primary School Enrolment and Annual Increases for the Nineteen States, 1975/6 to 1977/8*

States	*1975/6*	*1976/7*	% *Increase*	*1977/8*	% *Increase*
Anambra	641,775	873,800	36·1	907,252	3·8
Bauchi	—	201,700	—	329,600	63·4
Bendel	606,115	676,400	11·6	743,370	9·9
Benue	245,802	535,100	117·7	686,900	28·4
Borno	159,187	220,200	38·3	360,100	63·5
Cross River	603,228	741,400	22·9	768,290	77·7
Gongola	—	218,000	—	340,300	56·1
Imo	759,213	938,400	123·6	1,034,790	10·3
Kaduna	218,204	472,400	116·5	636,000	34·6
Kano	—	341,800	—	565,380	65·4
Kwara	181,050	236,500	30·6	319,020	34·9
Lagos	339,359	374,200	10·3	404,000	8·0
Niger	—	107,400	—	179,860	67·5
Ogun	—	286,900	—	299,000	4·3
Ondo	332,611	404,900	21·7	490,000	21·0
Oyo	599,094	817,900	36·5	866,400	5·9
Plateau	147,873	317,400	114·6	463,500	46·0
River	—	416,000	—	405,908	2·4
Sokoto	136,977	206,200	50·5	301,000	46·0
Total		8,386,400		10,104,670	20·5

Source: Background paper for the National Conference on Manpower Constraints to Nigeria's Economic Development, National Manpower Secretariat, September 1978.

It was estimated on the basis of 100 per cent enrolment that 2,300,000 children would be enrolled in primary class 1 in the 1976/7 session. Thus a total primary school population of 7,400,000 was expected for that year. However, the actual enrolment for 1976/7 was 8,386,400 (see Table 10.1). It was further projected that by 1982, the terminal year for the UPE first cycle, primary school population would be around 14,100,000, but judging from the present actual annual enrolment increase of about 2 million and considering the fact that 10,104,670 were actually in primary schools in the 1977/8 school year, actual school enrolment in 1982 should far exceed the estimated 14,100,000.

A total sum of ₦300,000,000 has been allocated by the federal military government to cover capital expenditure alone for the UPE scheme during the Plan period 1975/80. From analysis of the figures in Table 10.1 one can conclude that the government's huge investment in primary education is already showing positive dividends, at least in terms of number. Although no figures were obtained from some states in the 1975/6 school year, the year immediately preceding the introduction of UPE, a comparison of the 1975/6 and 1976/7 figures on a state-by-state basis justifies this conclusion.

III   SECONDARY EDUCATION

Secondary education consists of the secondary grammar; technical and vocational; commercial; the secondary modern introduced by the government of former Western Region in 1955 and now phased out; and the teacher training colleges. Secondary grammar schools are the most popular (see Table 10.2) and these schools prepare students for higher education, though many of their pupils go on to vocational training and employment. The technical, vocational and commercial secondary schools are expected to prepare students for middle-level job positions while the teacher training colleges prepare teachers for primary schools. The modern schools existed in the former Western Region (which included what is now Bendel State) but they are now either replaced by other types of secondary schools or closed down. In this first part of the section on secondary education, the focus will be in the grammar type.

Secondary grammar school enrolment showed some modest increase during the period 1960-73. In 1960 there were some 325 secondary grammar schools in the country, enrolling altogether some 19,883 students. The number of such institutions increased to 1,327 in 1964 with an enrolment of 205,002. In 1971 the number of schools declined to 1,234, partly as a result of the Civil War and partly because of the merging of some schools in the war-affected areas. Despite the decline in the number of schools, enrolment increased that year to 343,313, and in 1973 the figure rose to 448,908 in some 1,499 schools. Thus, secondary

Table 10.2   Number of Secondary Schools, Students and Teachers, 1960–74/75

Year	Secondary Grammar				Technical and Vocational				Teacher Training			
	No. of Schools	No. of Students	No. of Teachers	Student Teacher Ratio	No. of Schools	No. of Students	No. of Teachers	Student Teacher Ratio	No. of Schools	No. of Students	No. of Teachers	Student Teacher Ratio
1960	883	135,434	6,735	20·0	29	5,037	351	14·4	315	32,339	1,829	17·7
1961	997	168,238	8,070	20·8	31	6,023	379	15·9	295	31,054	1,940	16·0
1962	1,156	195,499	9,779	20·0	32	7,241	410	17·7	287	30,926	2,057	15·0
1963	1,240	211,879	10,905	19·4	31	7,355	442	16·6	266	32,339	2,052	15·8
1964	1,327	205,012	10,753	19·1	39	9,911	573	17·3	257	31,054	1,910	16·3
1965	1,382	209,015	10,855	19·3	63	12,646	760	16·6	195	30,926	1,925	16·1
1966	1,350	211,305	11,644	18·1	73	15,059	789	19·1	193	30,493	1,837	16·6
1967	—	—	—		—	—	—				—	
1968	852	166,876	8,443	19·7	59	—	—		114	22,783	1,340	17·0
1969	564	137,458	8,159	16·8	54	—	—		105	25,128	1,342	18·7
1970	1,155	310,054	14,091	22·0	66	13,645	845	16·1	160	32,314	1,857	17·4
1971	1,234	343,313	15,278	22·4	67	15,203	965	15·7	164	37,119	2,023	18·3
1972	1,209	399,722	15,822	25·2	62	15,935	1,032	15·4	150	40,112	1,915	20·9
1973	1,234	448,904	17,215	26·1	70	21,515	1,111	19·4	159	42,771	2,122	20·2
1973/4	1,337	498,744	19,409	25·7	66	22,117	1,120	19·7	151	49,216	2,360	20·8
1974/5	919	606,752	21,771	27·8	62	24,647	1,139	21·6	201	78,377	3,209	24·4

Notes: The school year was January–December up to 1972, January–June in 1973. Thereafter, the school year has run from September to June. No figures for 1967 available, due to Civil War.

Source: Federal Ministry of Education, Statistics of Education in Nigeria (various years).

school population rose from 135,364 in 1960 to 448,904 in 1973. This represents a 232 per cent increase in thirteen years. This increase in secondary school enrolment was partly the result of the UPE scheme introduced in the old Western Region and in parts of the Eastern. A sharp increase in primary school enrolment usually has a corresponding impact on secondary school enrolment. An acute bottleneck situation is usually created at the secondary school level when primary school enrolment far exceeds available secondary education facilities. This appears to be the case in the Nigerian education system. In 1971, for example, there were altogether 15,324 primary schools in the country compared to 1,234 secondary schools that same year. The 15,324 primary schools had an enrolment of 3,894,539 pupils while the 1,234 secondary schools enrolled some 343,313 students – a primary/secondary school enrolment difference of 3,551,226.

Table 10.3   *Recent Trend in Primary School Out-Turn and Secondary School In-Take, 1975/6 to 1977/8*

States[1]	Primary School Out-Turn			Secondary School In-Take		
	1975/6	*1976/7*	*1977/8*	*1975/6*	*1976/7*	*1977/8*
Anambra	77,801	93,517	100,500	17,377	22,246	16,372
Bendel	45,242	90,788	90,788	23,072	26,275	27,151
Benue	17,632	—	—	4,014	8,424	—
Cross River	63,092	72,449	85,145	15,562	15,236	—
Imo	—	127,706	135,000	21,243	29,624	30,600
Kaduna	25,515	28,086	30,634	5,811	7,807	6,770
Kano	9,503	—	—	1,991	2,689	—
Kwara	—	19,555	23,158	7,400	7,928	8,661
Lagos	—	37,743	—	17,861	21,839	—
Niger	—	6,982	—	—	1,868	1,828
Ondo	37,833	45,238	48,732	10,065	14,264	20,179
Oyo	52,986	60,181	76,515	—	24,890	—
Plateau	10,127	12,144	14,669	2,536	3,021	4,594
Sokoto	11,093	15,274	22,310	1,778	1,722	2,550

Note:
1 States which did not furnish any data on either the primary school out-turn or the secondary school in-take are left out of this table.
Source: Background paper for the National Conference on Manpower Constraints to Nigeria's Economic Development, National Manpower Secretariat, September 1978.

Table 10.3 seems to confirm this unsatisfactory trend in the primary to secondary school transition rate. Anambra State, for example, had a total primary school out-turn of 77,801 in 1975/6 while only 22,246 were actually enrolled in secondary year 1 for the following school year 1976/7. This means that less than a third of those who left primary school in 1975/6 got places in Anambra State secondary schools the following year – representing about 28·57 per cent primary to secondary school transition rate for the period 1975/6 to 1976/7. Plateau State recorded about 30 per cent primary to secondary school transition rate during the same period.

The country needs to expand its secondary education at least threefold to meet the projected 70 per cent primary to secondary school transition rate in 1980. Lagos State has adopted the shift system of morning and afternoon secondary school sections to increase in-take. This device is only temporary; even then, it does not offer any satisfactory alternative to expanding the country's secondary school system. Apparently in recognition of this fact, the federal government declared in 1975 its intention to expand rapidly facilities for secondary education in order to permit 'fullest possible enrolment of primary school leavers as well as to ensure adequate input for expanded tertiary and higher education levels'. As stated in the Third National Development Plan, 'expansion with equity consideration in view will be guided by the need for even distribution of facilities on a geographical and population basis'. The planned expansion of secondary education is not simply in terms of number but also in terms of structure. In pursuance of this, the federal military government has accepted the proposal for a six-year comprehensive secondary education system comprising three years junior and three years senior secondary. This new secondary education structure is expected to come into effect in 1982. One of the merits of the proposed system is the inevitable elimination of the sixth form which is a most unnecessary bottleneck in the Nigerian education system. It is also hoped that the proposed system will ensure regular and relevant guidance and counselling services for proper chanelling of students to appropriate areas of specialisation during the senior secondary stage.

It was estimated that secondary school population would rise to about 1,500,000 by 1980. Assuming a transition rate from primary to secondary education of 50 per cent, this figure should rise to about 4,000,000 by 1988 when the first cycle of the admission of UPE leavers will have been completed. The federal government has allocated the sum of ₦996·741 million for the necessary capital expenditure in secondary education during this Plan period. Part of this money is being used for providing in each state of the federation two federal secondary schools: one for boys and girls and the other for girls only.

IV   TECHNICAL EDUCATION

There was also some modest development during the period under review in regard to technical education. By 1960 there were altogether twenty-nine technical institutions in the country enrolling 5,037 students. By 1973 the number of secondary technical institutions had increased to eighty-four and the enrolment stood at 22,588 students. This represents an increase of 248 per cent in enrolment between 1960 and 1973. By 1973 there were also eight post-secondary or tertiary technical educational institutions in the country such as colleges of technology and polytechnics enrolling altogether some 8,856 students.

The Third National Plan for the period 1975–80 made provision for a system of technical education designed to offer more areas of specialisation and to ensure a more comprehensive training programme for the various categories of technical manpower needs of the country. It was projected that enrolment in technical secondary schools would rise from 22,588 in 1973 to 117,686 in 1980. To encourage expansion of technical education a matching grant of 50 per cent was earmarked for each state with any approved technical education project. In order to make technical education more practical, an attempt will be made through a tripartite arrangement including the Manpower Board, the Industrial Training Fund and the private sector to expose students to practical work in the field.

V TEACHER EDUCATION

There have been many forms of teacher education in the country. The most common were the grade III, the grade II and the grade I systems for primary schoolteachers. To earn the grade III status, teachers received two years' training after full primary education, while grade II teachers were expected to receive training in one of the following ways:

(1) two years training after the grade III;
(2) four years' training after full primary education and some prior teaching experience; or three years' training for holders of secondary modern III certificate;
(3) two years' training after full secondary education.

The grade I status is attained after fulfilling the following conditions:

(1) passing two relevant papers at GCE A Level;
(2) at least five years' post-grade II teaching experience;
(3) passing a practical teaching test.

There were, in addition, grade I institutions that produce grade I teachers after two years and, in some cases, a one-year course of studies.

The grade III system has been phased out and the grade II certificate is now the main qualification for teaching in primary schools.

Those who successfully complete full secondary education (i.e.

holders of the West African School Certificate) now go in for only one year's training under the crash programme of teacher production. Those who did only four years of secondary education go in for two years and way down the line are those who completed primary education and who are required to do five years. The Third National Development Plan has indicated that this last system will cease after the implementation of the UPE scheme.

The number of grade II or grade III teacher training institutions, which are secondary level institutions, declined from 315 in 1960 to 157 in 1973. The decline was partly due to the continuing attempts of the governments of the federation to consolidate and standardise teacher education with a view to improving the quality of teachers. This resulted in the phasing out of grade III teacher training and the consequent closure of such colleges as well as some of the grade II institutions. Despite this, total teacher training enrolment increased from 27,908 in 1960 to 46,951 in 1973, representing a 70 per cent increase within this period.

Post-secondary but non-graduate training for teachers in secondary schools was begun by the Nigerian College of Arts, Science and Technology in 1952 but was greatly expanded as a result of the report of the Ashby Commission in 1960. It is designed for the production of well-qualified non-graduate teachers for lower secondary classes and upper primary classes. Advanced teachers' colleges, or colleges of education, as some are now called, give a three-year course leading to the award of the Nigeria Certificate in Education. Admission requirements into these institutions vary from school certificate with only three credits and a pass in English language, to school certificate with a minimum of five credits including credit in English language; the latter is the same as the entry qualification into the four year degree course. By 1973 there were thirteen colleges. Three more were proposed for the 1975–80 National Development Plan period which would have brough the total NCE-awarding institutions to sixteen. However, there were in the 1978/9 school year thirty-five such institutions and with the proposed programme by the Ibadan Polytechnic commencing in the 1979/80 school year, the country will have a total of thirty-six NCE-awarding institutions; thirty-two arts and science and four technical.

The National Development Plan upheld the view that 'the quality of the teaching staff is probably the most important determinant of educational standards at all levels'. Hence during the Plan period priority would be given to the production of trained teachers at all levels and to the upgrading of in-service training programmes. The federal military government assumed full financial responsibility for the training of teachers for the UPE scheme. The emergency training programme which started in 1973–5 is expected to continue throughout the UPE implementation period and may be absorbed into the regular training programme thereafter.

VI HIGHER EDUCATION

The introduction of higher education into Nigeria was initiated by E. R. J. Hussey. In 1930 Hussey in the Nigerian Legislature Council, introduced a three-tier system of education to be made up of an elementary level, a middle level and a third or higher level which he called 'vocational training' for the production of qualified assistants in medicine and engineering and teachers for the higher middle schools. The first institution of the higher level, called the Higher College, was sited at Yaba near Lagos, and admitted its first students in 1932.

It was hoped that the college would develop to a level at which its students would obtain at Yaba external degrees of British universities; and that it would eventually develop into a university college. This goal was realised in 1948 when the students of Yaba moved to Ibadan to form the beginning of the University College, Ibadan.

Initially the Yaba college had the following departments: medicine, agriculture, engineering, surveying and teacher training. Some of the courses lasted for upwards of five years but all led to intermediate manpower qualifications for assistant positions in their various professions.

The Higher College was controlled by the Director of Education. The college was extremely restrictive in both its entrance and graduating requirements. Only a few students, mainly from the government colleges at Ibadan and Umuahia, gained admission, and fewer still managed to go through successfully. For instance, of the 365 students admitted to the college between 1932 and 1944 only 181 managed to scrape through; the remaining 184 failed.

Partly because of the unsatisfactory progress of higher education in West Africa with its production of frustrated middle-level manpower after years of arduous labour, and partly because of the Second World War, the Colonial Office in 1943 appointed a Commission on Higher Education in West Africa under the leadership of the Rt Hon. Walter Elliot with the following terms of reference:

> To report on the organization and facilities of the existing centres of higher education in British West Africa, and to make recommendations regarding future university development in the area.

The commission submitted two reports to the Secretary of State for the Colonies in 1944. The majority report of nine members, including the chairman and the three African members, recommended as follows:

(1) There should be a university college in Nigeria, a university college in the Gold Coast, and certain reorganisation of higher education and new developments should be carried out in Sierra Leone in close connection with Fourah Bay College.

(2)   The university college in Nigeria should include arts and science courses; and professional schools of medicine, agriculture, forestry and veterinary science and teacher training.

(3)   The university college in the Gold Coast should include arts and science courses and an institute of education to specialise in educational research and teacher training.

(4)   The university college in Sierra Leone should include arts and science up to intermediate level and teacher training. Along with these would be associated an arts degree course for theological students to be financed by the Church Missionary Society, the proprietors of the college.

(5)   The university colleges should be centres of research in West Africa and the colleges should provide facilities for visiting research workers.

The commission also recommended that the university college for Nigeria should be sited at Ibadan.

The minority report was presented by five of the fourteen members. This group was headed by Arthur Creech Jones and recommended the immediate establishment of only one institution of university rank, as against four by the majority report, to serve the whole of British West Africa. This should be called the West African University College and should be sited at Ibadan in Nigeria. Each of the dependencies – Nigeria, Gold Coast and Sierra Leone – in addition was to have a territorial college to be concerned with:

(1)   provision of courses of intermediate level,
(2)   training of teachers and social welfare workers,
(3)   organisation of adult education and extra-mural activities.

After completing a two-year course at the intermediate institutions, students were to proceed to the West African University College at Ibadan for the completion of the degree course.

The report of the Elliot Commission was first accepted by the Conservative government in Britain in June 1945. The following Labour government, in which Mr Creech Jones was Colonial Secretary, preferred the minority report, but the demand for each colony to have its own university college was so strong, particularly from the Gold Coast, that the government was forced to adopt the main report.

University College, Ibadan

The university college for Nigeria came into being in January 1948 when the students of Yaba Higher College were transferred to become the foundation students of the University College, Ibadan. The group was made up of 104 students and 13 teachers.

The college started its second year in October 1948 with a total of 210 students. The curriculum was patterned on that of the University of London and the students were to sit for London degrees as external students. Admission into the college was very competitive and restrictive, hence the student population grew from 104 in January 1948 to only 367 in the 1952/3 session.

Initially the college was very limited in scope, having only three Faculties: Arts, Science and Medicine. The Faculty of Agriculture opened in the 1950/1 session with only one student. The Institute of Education started in 1956. Greek, Latin, ancient history and religious studies were all started from the beginning and fully developed before any attempt was made to begin courses in such relevant subjects as economics, political science and sociology.

The enrolment was also very limited from the outset and was only liberalised with the founding of the University of Nigeria and other universities in the 1960s. The student population rose from 104 to 1948 to only 1,250 in 1960-1. Apparently in response to the challenge posed by the new universities, the University of Ibadan added the Faculties of Education and Social Sciences. Postgraduate programmes were developed, and in January 1972 the university took an unprecedented step in Nigerian higher education by establishing a branch at Jos some 1,100 kilometres away from the main campus at Ibadan. The Jos branch is now an independent university with full degree-awarding rights.

The Nigerian College of Arts, Science and Technology

As will be recalled, the minority report of the Commission on Higher Education in West Africa appointed by the Colonial Office in 1944 recommended the establishment of an intermediate educational institution for each of the three territories as well as a university college to be sited in Ibadan. In addition to this recommendation, a delegation of the Inter-University Council for Higher Education in the Colonies, led by Sir William Hamilton-Fyfe, visited West Africa in 1947 and recommended that polytechnics instead of 'regional colleges' should be established in West Africa.

The Nigerian government in 1949 set up a commission to conduct a feasibility survey of the polytechnic idea in terms of Nigerian needs. The two-man commission, F. J. Harlow, Principal of Chelsea Polytechnic, London, and W. H. Thorp, Deputy Director of Education (Nigeria), made a strong case for technical education in order to meet the requirements of industry, commerce and society as well as to adjust to the changing needs of the environment. Thus the commission recommended the establishment of a Nigerian College of Arts, Science and Technology with branches in each of the three regions into which the country was then divided. The college was to engage in professional and sub-professional training in the following areas:

(1) secondary and primary school teachers for trade schools and junior technical institutes;
(2) building, civil engineering, surveying, mechanical and electrical engineering, mining, geology and telecommunications;
(3) agriculture, forestry and veterinary sciences;
(4) medical auxiliary services;
(5) extra-mural or adult education.

A Bill for the founding of the college was introduced into the Nigerian legislature in April 1952. The first branch of the college had already opened in Zaria in January 1952, with thirty-one students registered for the only course available in the branch – teacher training. The Ibadan branch opened in February 1954, and was to offer courses in agriculture and forestry, book-keeping and accountancy, education, arts, science and engineering. The Enugu branch opened in 1955 and was to offer courses in mining, surveying, science and arts.

The three branches of the Nigerian College of Arts, Science and Technology were closed in 1962 and absorbed into the three new universities: the Enugu brach became part of the University of Nigeria, Nsukka, the University of Ife absorbed the Ibadan branch, while Ahmadu Bello University absorbed the Zaria branch. These universities, with the exception of the University of Nigera, Nsukka were founded on the recommendation of a nine-man commission appointed in April 1959 by the federal Ministry of Education to 'conduct an investigation into Nigeria's needs in the field of post-school certificate and Higher Education over the next twenty years'.

The 1959 commission was headed by Sir Eric Ashby, a Briton. Three Nigerians served on the commission: Professor K. O. Dike, formerly Vice-Chancellor of the University of Ibadan, Sir Shettima Kashin, then the Waziri of Bornu, and Dr S. D. Onabamiro, then Minister for Education, Western Nigeria. In 1960 Sir Eric Ashby produced the report of his commission *Investment in Education*. One of the recommendations of the commission was the integration of the Nigerian College of Arts, Science and Technology into the university system to permit the concentration of university resources around existing centres of academic activities in the country. Consequently, in addition to the University College, Ibadan, and the University of Nigeria, Nsukka, two additional universities, one in Lagos and the other in the north were recommended. The two universities were subsequently sited at Yaba and Zaria and called the University of Lagos and Ahmadu Bello University respectively. The University of Nigeria, Nsukka and the Universities of Benin and Ife have peculiar histories behind their establishment.

The University of Nigeria, Nsukka

The University of Nigeria owes its creation to the initiative of Dr Nnamdi Azikiwe, who as premier of the former Eastern Nigeria prompted the regional government to enact the University of Nigeria Law 1955 which set in motion the necessary machinery for the establishment of the proposed university. Some financial and technical assistance for the university was obtained, mainly from the United States of America. Michigan State University offered advisory assistance to the new university.

The university was formally opened on 7 October 1960 with the following six faculties: arts, science, law, theology, engineering and medicine.

Classes started on 17 October 1960 with 220 students and 13 lecturers and professors. The student population rose to 2,500 as against 1,250 for Ibadan University after twelve years of existence.

The uniqueness of Nsukka lies in its being the only university in Black Africa to start, as the result of wholly African initiative, as an autonomous degree-awarding institution with a broadly-based curriculum including certain subjects which were not usually provided at degree level, for example, music, journalism and physical education.

The Nigerian Civil War of 1967–70 affected the University of Nigeria adversely.

The University of Ife

A minority report by Dr Onabamiro, a member of the Ashby Commission, recommended the creation of a regional university in each region in addition to the four universities (Ibadan, Nsukka, Lagos and Zaria) approved by the majority report.

The Western Region government under the leadership of Chief Obafemi Awolowo capitalised on this and accordingly founded the University of Ife. The university was formally opened in October 1962 on the site of the Ibadan branch of the Nigerian College of Arts, Science and Technology, with 244 students and an academic staff of 51. In 1967 the university moved to a new and permanent site of 5,260 hectares (13,000 acres) in the town of Ile-Ife. Ife has the distinction of having been the only Nigerian university which has been organised and administered by Nigerian leadership from the beginning and it has been remarkable for its course offerings and the rapid expansion of buildings and student population which rose from 1,200 in 1967 to 6,232 in 1976.

It is also the first university to start the semester system by dividing its academic year into the Harmattan and Rain semesters. With the federalisation of university education in the country in September 1975, Ife University ceased to be a regional or state university.

The University of Benin

An edict promulgated by the Mid-West government in 1970 created what was known as the Mid-West Institute of Technology, Benin City. In July 1971 the National Universities Commission recognised the institute as part of the country's university system. The Mid-West government immediately capitalised on this and converted the institution to a university, which thenceforth became known as the University of Benin.

The original aim of the 1970 edict was to create a technologically oriented institution – a higher education institution that would not follow the conventional pattern of the five older universities in the country. Hence as an institute of technology, the institution started with the faculties of science, engineering, medicine and pharmacy, but since its conversion to a university such liberal arts faculties as education and social sciences have been added.

The institute opened with 108 students in November 1970; the population rose to 1,349 in the 1975/6 school year.

Thus with the conversion of the Mid-West Institute of Technology to a full university in 1971, the number of universities in the country was raised to six. At that time, only two of these were fully federal – Ibadan and Lagos. Ahmadu Bello, Zaria, was partly federal, while Nsukka, Ife and Benin were esentially regional, though each received federal government financial support to the tune of 30 per cent. Ahmadu Bello University received 75 per cent financial support. In 1973 the University of Nigeria, Nsukka, at the request of the governments of the former East-Central and South-Eastern States – the two states then responsible for 70 per cent of the financing of the university – became a federal institution like Ibadan and Lagos.

The National Universities Commission

The National Universities Commission was established on the recommendation of the 1959 Ashby Commission. It was vested with the powers to control the affairs of the universities, particularly in terms of finance, staffing, conditions of service, programmes and postgraduate studies. Part of the function of the commission was to advise the head of the federal military government on the creation of new universities and other degree-granting institutions in Nigeria. In effect, the commission became the sole controlling body of all universities in Nigeria thus paving the way for the federal government announcement in September 1975 federalising all Nigerian universities.

Third National Development Plan (1975–80):
Impact on Higher Education

In the Third National Development Plan, the federal government spelt out its policy on higher education, part of which was the consolidation and expansion of the six existing universities to permit maximum utilisation of facilities. In addition, four new universities were to be established during the Plan period, but in fact seven were founded. These are the Univerities of Jos, Calabar, Maiduguri and Sokoto, formally opened in October 1975; and the Universities of Ilorin and Port Harcourt, and Bayero University, Kano, established in October 1977. Jos and Calabar, prior to 1975, existed as campuses of Ibadan University and the University of Nigeria, Nsukka, respectively, while Ilorin, Port Harcourt and Bayero started in 1975 as university colleges and became full universities in 1977.

The higher education policy in the Plan also provided for increased student population in Nigerian universities. Student enrolment was projected from 23,000 in 1973 to 53,000 in 1980. The Plan envisaged the distribution of students into the major disciplines so as to give greater emphasis to the study of medicine, pure science and technology. A science: humanities ratio of 60:40 was anticipated in the plan period.

The Plan also proposed that the admission policy of the university system be overhauled to make it more responsive to the great need for expanded student in-take in the interest of manpower requirements of the country. Adequate care would, however, be taken in the process to strike the right balance between this expansion need and the equally important goal of maintaining high quality in the system. In effect, the new policy aimed at liberalising the admission system of the universities and aligning it with a course system that allowed both qualified and inadequately prepared students to enter the universities. The new system would offer remedial courses to the latter to enable them to proceed with their chosen fields of study.

A high-powered committee was set up by the federal government under the direction of the National Universities Commission to look into the problem of university admissions. The committee was charged with the following terms of reference.

(1) To study the problems of admission into the universities in Nigeria with a view to removing all bottlenecks limiting entry into these institutions so that the increased opportunities for university education in all parts of the country are enhanced, and to make appropriate recommendations.

(2) To study and make appropriate recommendations on the steps to be taken both within and outside the university system, to ensure that liberalisation of admission into the universities is balanced against the need to maintain quality in the graduate output by means of appropriate course system.

(3) To review the performance of the various pre-university examining bodies in Nigeria (including WAEC) in terms of how much they constitute a bottleneck to entry into universities, and if necessary to make recommendations on appropriate alternatives such as a Joint Matriculation Board.

(4) To review the entry requirements of the various univerisites in Nigeria with a view to making them not only realistic and responsive to national needs and aspirations, but also uniform in the whole university system, if necessary, through a Common Entrance Board.

(5) To make such other recommendations as will help the Federal Military Government achieve its objectives on university entrance as enumerated in the Third National Development Plan.

One of the upshots of the committee's recommendations was the establishment of a body to handle all admission and matriculation matters for all Nigerian universities. The body, known as the Joint Admissions and Matriculation Board (JAMB), took off in 1977; and in October 1978, Nigeria universities registered the first JAMB admitted students for the three- and four-year degree programmes.

Thus far, we have shown the great advance in university education particularly since 1975. Today the university system seems to be facing a crisis of loss of autonomy brought about by the harmonisation scheme which attempts to relate the university administration and conditions of service to those of the civil service. Administrative centralisation under the National Univerities Commission and the increased federal government's involvement in university affairs such as the appointment, transfer and dismissal of vice-chancellors do not augur well for the traditional rights and academic freedom of the universities. The universities also have to grapple with the government's directives for increased graduate out-turn in face of decreasing yearly government subvention. Internally, some reorganisation has been taking place, particularly in the academic calandar and examination system. The trend now is for a two-semester system started by Ife University, and the course unit, credit system in place of the trimester and sessional examination system respectively.

Student population in Nigerian universities has shown a remarkable increase particularly since 1975 (see Table 10.4). Enrolment rose from 26,448 in 1974/5 to 32,286 in 1975/6, and from 41,499 in 1976/7 to 47,670 in 1977/8. Graduate out-turn (see Table 10.5) has shown a similar rise.

University Teaching Staff
Nigerian universities have also recorded substantial growth in the area of teaching staff, particularly in terms of 'Nigerianisation'. In 1948, when the University College, Ibadan was founded, the college had forty-four expatriate staff and only six Africans. While the expatriate staff increased to eighty-one by 1951, the African staff remained six in number.

By April 1977 non-Nigerian staff constituted only about 26 per cent

Table 10.4 Enrolment Figures in Nigerian Universities, 1964/5 to 1978/9

	Ibadan	Lagos	Nsukka	Zaria	Ife	Benin	Jos	Calabar	Kano	Maidu Guri	Sokoto	Ilorin	Port Harcourt	Total
1964/5	2,284	563	2,482	719	659									6,707
1965/6	2,687	773	2,579	957	713									7,709
1966/7	2,729	1,116	3,125	973	945									8,888
1967/8	2,593	1,859		1,352	1,254									7,058
1968/9	3,118	2,062		1,745	1,663									8,588
1969/70	3,146	2,395		2,351	1,803									9,695
1970/1	3,639	2,535	2,931	2,844	2,411	108								14,468
1971/2	3,742	2,918	3,363	3,835	2,985	250								17,093
1972/3	3,783	3,053	3,891	5,177	4,568	417								20,889
1973/4	4,618	3,400	4,677	5,828	4,005	700								23,228
1974/5	5,304	3,639	5,800	6,257	4,400	1,048								26,448
1975/6	6,961	4,416	6,059	7,299	5,671	1,365		515						32,286
1976/7	8,586	5,982	6,661	7,321	7,249	1,871	579	952	1,158	743		397		41,499
1977/8	8,865	7,447	6,727	7,477	8,322	2,257	1,339	1,209	1,796	1,396	194	327	314	47,670
1978/9	7,781	7,743	7,009	8,010	7,234	2,611	1,971	1,675	2,390	1,462	455	912	650	49,903

Source: Lagos National Universities Commission, 1980.

Table 10.5 *Recent Trend in Graduate Out-Turn from the Universities, 1974/5 to 1976/7*

Discipline	Graduate Out-turn			% Increase	
	1974/5	*1975/6*	*1976/7*	*1974/5 to 1975/6*	*1975/6 to 1976/7*
Arts	561	692	746	23·3	7·2
Sciences	592	735	1,043	24·1	41·9
Medicine and Related Disciplines	440	494	570	12·3	15·4
Agriculture	301	365	605	21·3	65·7
Veterinary Medicine	40	54	900[1]	35·0	—
Engineering	305	431	559	41·3	29·7
Environmental Studies	162	166	137	2·5	-17·4
Administration	186	242	677	30·6	64·1
Education	675	854	1,756	26·5	105·6
Social Sciences	562	727	1,149	29·3	58·0
Mass Communication, Law and Others	180	237	452	31·7	90·7
All Disciplines	4,004	4,998	8,594	24·8	71·9

Note:
1 The figure for veterinary medicine in 1976/7 seems unlikely but the total adds up correctly. However, there is no percentage increase given. It would be 1,008% which strains credulity and would make the overall figure, given as 71·9%, very large.
Source: National Universities Commission.

of the total teaching staff in Nigerian universities. This achievement was due largely to the staff development programmes initiated by the universities in the early 1970s.

Financing of the Universities
One of the greatest problems currently facing Nigerian universities is inadequate finance. It has become increasingly clear over the last two years that the universities cannot continue to rely on the government for all their financial needs.

In the 1978/9 school year the NUC recommended total recurrent grant expenditure to all the universities was N208,738,000. The actual government grant to the universities was N148,900,000 for the NUC summary sheet calculation of recommended recurrent expenditure 1975/6 to 1984/5.

VII ADMINISTRATION OF THE EDUCATIONAL SYSTEM

During the colonial era, in order to control the educational expansion, maintain standards and have a system for the determination of eligibility for grants-in-aid, the colonial government created an educational department with only two divisions – Administrative and

Inspectorate. Educational policies and decision-making processes were highly centralised.

With the 1951 constitution by which Nigeria became a federation of three regions, education became a regional function and regional departments of education were created. Education was placed on the concurrent lists of both the federal and the regional legislatures. Educational decisions were shared accordingly. Since then the federal authorities in Lagos have performed supervisory, advisory, or consultative functions with the view to maintaining standards. The federal Ministry of Education formulates education policy within the framework of the prevailing education ordinance.

With regard to primary, secondary, teacher training, adult and technical education, the advisory functions are channelled through the Joint Consultative Committee on Education set up in 1955. The committee has succeeded in being not only a consultative body but also a co-ordinating and rationalising agency. The Inspectorate Division of the federal Ministry of Education is also helping in the general advisory and supervisory functions, particularly with regard to secondary schools.

With the new structure of the National Universities Commission (NUC) and the consequent takeover of university education by the federal government, the NUC now performs more than advisory functions. It is, in fact, today the main policy formulation body in regard to university education in the country. It determines the creation of new universities; it makes plans for balanced development, including the determination of the programme and the establishment of new faculties or postgraduate institutions; it advises the federal government on the financial needs of each university; and it undertakes periodic reviews of the conditions of service of personnel in order to make recommendations to the federal government.

The present trend is towards more and more direct involvement of the federal government in education. This is being justified on the grounds that education is an instrument for national unity and as a means of rectifying the imbalance in educational opportunities among the states. However, the states are in charge of education below the university level. For example, the polytechnics and the advanced teachers' colleges are under both state and federal control.

Each state of the federation has a ministry of education headed by a commissioner. Common divisions of the ministries include: administration, inspectorate, scholarship, standards or examinations, research and planning, and finance. Each state also has a state school management board. There are also divisional school boards or local education authorities. Most of the states have taken over the ownership and management of all primary and secondary schools from the voluntary agencies. Thus, the management of primary and secondary schools is largely in the hands of the state school boards and divisional school boards or local education authorities.

In general, the state school boards formulate policies with regard to the management and administration of post-primary schools, including secondary schools and teacher training colleges. The state ministries of education, through their inspectorate divisions, see to the maintenance of educational standards. They control examinations and the curriculum. In other words, the state ministries of education and the state school boards own and operate the schools, formulate educational policies, and perform leadership, regulatory and co-ordinating functions with regard to primary schools, secondary schools, teacher training colleges and technical institutes.

The divisonal school boards or local education authorities formulate policies with regard to the administration of primary schools.

The divisional school boards or the local education authorities are supposed to handle all the administrative functions of the primary schools apart from routine day-to-day administration. In some states, there is for each school a school committee which sees to the general welfare of the school. Parent–teachers' associations are also being created in many parts of the country, and these again perform vital functions with regard to the welfare of the schools. Headmasters of schools take charge of the day-to-day administration but, in general, principals of secondary schools and headmasters of primary schools have very few statutory powers in regard to the schools they administer. Consequently, in some states, they have to run to the headquarters for every little administrative decision. Since the government takeover, schools are unfortunately being run like civil service departments with all the red tape and administrative bureaucracy. The principals and headmasters are invariably rendered ineffective in day-to-day administration and so useful time is often unnecessarily spent at headquarters for mere routine matters. Lack of adequate tele-communication and road communication have increased difficulties considerably in some parts of the country. Some principals are known to spend upwards of five days out of twenty-five working days each month at headquarters.

VII THE SCHOOL CURRICULUM

The Nigerian education system is largely examination-oriented. This conclusion seems warranted considering the fact that the requirements of the various examinations to which pupils and students are exposed at every level of the system largely determine the curriculum at that level.

With regard to primary education, the initial objectives of colonial education affected the curriculum tremendously. These objectives were:

(1) to supply the European traders with native assistants who could read, write and talk a little English;
(2) to prepare pupils for entrance into an English type of grammar school; thus the curriculum of the primary school has remained largely literary and academic.

The report of the 1969 National Curriculum Conference was the first national effort to change the colonial orientation of the Nigerian educational system. The report states that the primary schools must fulfil two basic functions:

(1) prepare children for life,
(2) give those with the necessary background the opportunity to proceed to secondary school.

The primary school curriculum is to reflect these functions, and through the school curriculum education should serve to:

(1) help the child to realise himself;
(2) help the child to relate to others in an atmosphere of mutual understanding;
(3) promote self and national economic efficiency;
(4) promote effective citizenship through civic responsibility;
(5) facilitate national consciousness in the area of national unity and survival;
(6) promote social and political awakening;
(7) create scientific and technological awareness.

These views are gradually permeating the primary school curriculum, thereby making it more realistic and functional. The problem is still with the actual practices in the schools. Classroom instruction is largely still in the form of rote learning. The teachers are not sufficiently prepared to make the teaching-learning experience a process of exploration and discovery. The system is also still burdened with examination requirements. Primary school leaving certificates should no longer be dependent on the result of an external examination, although an examination may be necessary for those wishing to continue up the educational ladder.

The lack of sufficient relevance in the school curriculum is more apparent in the secondary schools. The requirements of the West African School Certificate Examination largely control the secondary school curriculum. In the past few years the council has been trying through its subject panels to modify its inheritance from the Cambridge Examination Syndicate but these attempts have not been fully successful. Secondary schools have remained essentially academic and cater effectively only for less than 5 per cent of their population: those who proceed to further education. The present system is completely unsuitable for the remaining 95 per cent of the secondary school population. Those for whom secondary education is terminal need saleable skills for vocational efficiency and a considerable amount of guidance in order to be able to make wise choices with regard to their life vocation. For instance, a large percentage of secondary school leavers end up seeking civil service employment requiring typing skills and knowledge of office practice and these are hardly subjects for the secondary grammar schools.

Thus, the secondary school curriculum needs more diversification than at present. Courses such as typing, shorthand, office practice, sociology, Nigerian languages, music, fine and applied arts, bicycle repairing, woodwork, metalwork and elementary electronics should be available in all secondary schools. We hope that the proposed 3-3 comprehensive secondary school system will take care of this diversification of subject offerings.

Another problem still exists – that of the supreme importance of paper qualifications – which emanates from the disproportionate emphasis on examinations. This situation also enthrones the West African Examinations Council in a position of pre-eminence in the secondary school system. To correct this situation there should be two forms of certificates at the end of secondary education. One certificate, which should be nationally recognised, would be issued by the schools to their pupils. This certificate should help pupils obtain employment within the civil service and business firms. Another certificate should be in the form of a matriculation certificate for those wishing to enter higher educational institutions.

The curricula of the universities and other higher educational institutions suffer from the same extreme academic orientation, lack of relevance to the needs of the learners or of the society, and narrowness. The present trend in higher education is for a broad-based first degree course followed by narrower specialisation for the higher degrees, but most Nigerian universities still operate the single honours degree programmes. This has tended to reduce the number of eligible post-graduate students. A broad-based first degree followed by a year or two of in-depth study preparatory to specialisation before thesis research tends to produce a more balanced academic.

The offerings in the universities also need to be liberalised. Thus, the universities should participate actively in the production of vocational manpower wherever it is needed; not only doctors and lawyers, but also accountants, business managers, surveyors, architects, musicians, artists, entertainers, etc. It is encouraging to note that the universities, especially in the past three years, have expanded their offerings to meet these national needs.

VIII   FINANCING

Education is never free; it has to be paid for either directly by the individuals or by the government and other bodies. Historically, the financing of education in Nigeria has been accomplished through three main sources:

(1) grants-in-aid from the various governments;
(2) collection of fees,
(3) levies by cultural unions or voluntary contributions by parents and guardians.

In the case of mission and community schools, buildings and other facilities were largely provided through community contributions. Some communities provided free labour for the construction of school buildings.

Since 1955, when the Western Nigeria regional government introduced a system of universal primary education, the various governments in Nigeria have consistently spent a large percentage of their annual recurrent budget on education. The bulk of the government expenditure on education was in the form of grants-in-aid to the

Table 10.6   *Expenditure on Education as a Percentage of Total Expenditure, 1955–62*

Region	1955	1956	1957	1958	1959	1960	1961	1962
Recurrent Expenditure								
Northern	20·1	25·4	24·0	24·5	24·4	23·0	22·4	23·3
Eastern	37·6	42·5	49·0	43·4	45·2	44·9	41·5	38·2
Western	40·7	36·5	42·8	41·3	40·8	43·9	44·6	47·3
Federation	16·0	18·7	22·0	21·2	21·4	22·6	21·3	—
Capital Expenditure								
Northern	21·1	10·0	12·5	11·7	13·6	22·2	25·9	17·3
Eastern	6·6	40·9	10·9	5·7	4·6	6·9	3·4	6·5
Western	34·2	40·9	41·9	17·1	9·7	10·1	5·6	4·1
Federation	12·1	13·5	11·7	10·2	5·5	5·8	5·8	—
Recurrent and Capital Expenditure								
Northern	20·5	19·5	19·5	19·7	20·7	23·9	23·6	21·5
Eastern	28·4	42·3	43·0	34·0	34·8	36·7	28·2	26·9
Western	38·7	37·5	42·6	33·7	28·1	30·5	29·1	29·5
Federation	18·7	17·3	18·7	17·0	15·2	16·1	15·5	—

Source: A. Gallaway and A. Musone, *Financing of Education in Nigeria,* African Research Monograph 15 (Paris: Unesco International Institute for Educational Planning, 1968), p. 24.

voluntary agencies. In the Western and Eastern Regions, this source alone accounted for 82·2 per cent and 78·7 per cent respectively of their total expenditure on education between the years 1955 and 1962.

The government expenditure on education has continued to be on the upward trend since 1955 (Table 10.6). It went from £6·2 million in 1952/3 to £31·1 million in 1962/3. The figure for capital expenditure alone rose to a phenomenal figure of N367,886,000 in 1975/6 and this is expected to rise to N556,051,000 by 1979/80. The budget for education alone in one of the nineteen states for the 1976/7 year was N82,262,880 or 54·8 per cent of the total recurrent expenditure for the year. This represents more than all the governments of the federation spent in the year 1962/3.

With the takeover of schools by the state governments, financial responsibilities have completely shifted to the governments. With the introduction in September 1976 of the scheme of UPE, the federal government now assumes full financial responsibility for primary education throughout the country. During the Plan period 1975–80 the federal government set aside the sum of N300 million to cover capital expenditure on primary education.

With regard to secondary education, provision was made for capital expenditure of N966·741 million for some additional 800 secondary schools in the 1975/80 Plan period.

In the past, the financing of teacher training institutions was largely the responsibility of the missions which owned most of these institutions. They, however, received grants-in-aid from the various governments. With the takeover of schools, this responsibility has shifted completely to the state governments, but because of the UPE scheme the federal government has accepted full financial responsibility for teacher training institutions throughout the country.

Before the federal government takeover of higher education the regional universities were financed on the basis of 30 per cent federal and 70 per cent state governments in regard to the Universities of Nigeria, Ife and Benin. The federal government paid up to 75 per cent of the annual expenditures of Ahmadu Bello University. The federal government, of course, took complete financial responsibility in regard to the then two federal universities – Ibadan and Lagos. But with the takeover of all the universities in the country, the federal government now finances all the universities through the National Universities Commission, which acts as a universities grants commission. Experience since the federal takeover does not indicate much financial health for the universities. It has been observed, for example, that the University of Ife, as a state university, made the greatest capital expansion of all Nigieran universities from its inception until the federal takeover.

IX NON-FORMAL EDUCATION

Non-formal education generally was usually in the form of a programme for the attainment of literacy and numeracy by adults who had missed the opportunity of formal education at the appropriate time. It could also take the form of further education outside the formal school system for adults who were already literate. The concept of non-formal education now includes all forms of training outside the formal school system, such as the apprenticeship system in mechanics, bicycle repairing and carpentry.

The further education of the already literate adult has received most attention in Nigeria through the activities of university extra-mural departments. Such programmes are largely directed towards helping adults acquire more paper qualifications. But what seems to be needed more in Nigeria today is a development-oriented non-formal education such as special training for farmers, craftsmen, artisans and industrial workers and in-service training for teachers and civil servants.

The problem of organising and administering non-formal education is perhaps more complicated than that of formal education. This is because the organisation of the latter is concentrated with the ministries of education while that of the former normally involves many different bodies – the ministries, universities, industries and private agencies.

However, in the Third National Development Plan, 1975–80, provision was made for the establishment of a Centre for Adult Education by the federal government at a cost of N1 million. The centre, when fully developed, would, apart from running correspondence and adult education courses, be expected to conduct research into various aspects of adult and non-formal education. It is hoped that the centre becomes a reality for a more effective attention to this apparently much neglected aspect of educational activities.

NOTES: CHAPTER 10

1   A. B. Fafunwa, *History of Education in Nigeria* (London: Allen & Unwin, 1974).
2   ibid., pp. 463–70.
3   *Third National Government Development Plan: 1975–1980* (Lagos: Government Printer, 1975), p. 246.

Chapter 11

Education in Tanzania

JULIUS NYERERE

EDUCATION FOR SELF-RELIANCE

In March 1967 President Nyerere issued the first of his 'post-Arusha' policy directives, on education. It analysed the system and attitudes of education as they had evolved in Tanganyika, and then went on to demand an educational revolution – a recasting of the system in the light of Tanzania's needs and social objectives.

After this paper was issued a whole series of working parties – involving teachers and educational administrators – was set up to examine the means of implementing the new ideas. At the same time, many schools in the country – and particularly the secondary schools – began the work of opening farms, establishing workshops and undertaking 'nation-building tasks'.

Since long before independence the people of this country, under the leadership of TANU, have been demanding more education for their children. But we have never really stopped to consider why we want education – what its purpose is. Therefore, although over time there have been various criticisms about the details of curricula provided in schools, we have not until now questioned the basic system of education which we took over at the time of independence. We have never done that because we have never thought about education except in terms of obtaining teachers, engineers, administrators, etc. Individually and collectively we have in practice thought of education as a training for the skills required to earn high salaries in the modern sector of our economy.

It is now time that we looked again at the justification for a poor society like ours spending almost 20 per cent of its government revenues on providing education for its children and young people, and began to consider what that education should be doing. For in our circumstances it is impossible to devote Shs 147,330,000 every year to education for some of our children (while others go without) unless its results have a proportionate relevance to the society we are trying to create.

The educational systems in different kinds of societies in the world have been, and are, very different in organisation and in content. They are different because the societies providing the education are different, and because education, whether it be formal or informal, has a purpose. That purpose is to transmit from one generation to the next the accumulated wisdom and knowledge of the society, and to prepare the young people for their future membership of the society and their active participation in its maintenance or development.

This is true, explicitly or implicitly, for all societies – the capitalist societies of the West, the communist societies of the East, and the pre-colonial African societies too.

The fact that pre-colonial Africa did not have 'schools' – except for short periods of initiation in some tribes – did not mean that the children were not educated. They learned by living and doing. In the homes and on the farms they were taught the skills of the society and the behaviour expected of its members. They learned the kind of grasses which were suitable for which purposes, the work which had to be done on the crops, or the care which had to be given to animals, by joining with their elders in this work. They learned the tribal history, and the tribe's relationship with other tribes and with the spirits, by listening to the stories of their elders. Through these means, and by the custom of sharing to which young people were taught to conform, the values of the society were transmitted. Education was thus 'informal'; every adult was a teacher to a greater or lesser degree. But this lack of formality did not mean that there was no education, nor did it affect its importance to the society. Indeed, it may have made the education more directly relevant to the society in which the child was growing up.

In Europe education has been formalised for a very long time. An examination of its development will show, however, that it has always had similar objectives to those implicit in the traditional African system of education. That is to say, formal education in Europe was intended to reinforce the social ethics existing in the particular country, and to prepare the children and young people for the place they will have in that society. The same thing is true of communist countries now. The content of education is somewhat different from that of Western countries, but the purpose is the same – to prepare young people to live in and to serve the society, and to transmit the knowledge, skills, and values and attitudes of the society. Wherever education fails in any of these fields, then the society falters in its progress, or there is social unrest as people find that their education has prepared them for a future which is not open to them.

COLONIAL EDUCATION IN TANZANIA AND THE INHERITANCE OF THE NEW STATE

The education provided by the colonial government in the two countries which now form Tanzania had a different purpose. It was not designed to prepare young people for the service of their own country; instead it was motivated by a desire to inculcate the values of the colonial society and to train individuals for the service of the colonial state. In these countries the state interest in education therefore stemmed from the need for local clerks and junior officials; on top of that, various religious groups were interested in spreading literacy and other education as part of their evangelical work.

This statement of fact is not given as a criticism of the many individuals who worked hard, often under difficult conditions, in teaching and in organising educational work. Nor does it imply that all the values these people transmitted in the schools were wrong or inappropriate. What it does mean, however, is that the educational system introduced into Tanzania by the colonialists was modelled on the British system, but with even heavier emphasis on subservient attitudes and on white-collar skills. Inevitably, too, it was based on the assumptions of a colonialist and capitalist society. It emphasised and encouraged the individualistic instincts of man, instead of his co-operative instincts. It led to the possession of individual material wealth being the major criterion of social merit and worth.

This meant that colonial education induced attitudes of human inequality, and in practice underpinned the domination of the weak by the strong, especially in the economic field. Colonial education in this country was therefore not transmitting the values and knowledge of Tanzanian society from one generation to the next: it was a deliberate attempt to change those values and to replace traditional knowledge by the knowledge from a different society. It was thus a part of a deliberate attempt to effect a revolution in the society; to make it into a colonial society which accepted its status and which was an efficient adjunct to the governing power. Its failure to achieve these ends does not mean that it was without influence on the attitudes, ideas and knowledge of the people who experienced it. Nor does that failure imply that the education provided in colonial days is automatically relevant for the purposes of a free people committed to the principle of equality.

The independent state of Tanzania in fact inherited a system of education which was in many respects both inadequate and inappropriate for the new state. It was, however, its inadequacy which was most immediately obvious. So little education had been provided that in December 1961, we had too few people with the necessary educational qualifications even to man the administration of government as it was then, much less undertake the big economic and social development work which was essential. Neither was the school population in 1961 large enough to allow for any expectation that this situation would be speedily corrected. On top of that, education was based upon race, whereas the whole moral case of the independence movement had been based upon a rejection of racial distinctions.

ACTION SINCE INDEPENDENCE

The three most glaring faults of the educational inheritance have already been tackled. First, the racial distinctions within education were abolished. Complete integration of the separate racial systems was introduced very soon after independence, and discrimination on grounds of religion was also brought to an end. A child in Tanzania can now secure admittance to any government or government-aided school in this country without regard to his race or religion and without fear that he will be subject to religious indoctrination at the price of learning.

Secondly, there has been a very big expansion of educational facilities available, especially at the secondary school and post-secondary school levels. In 1961 there were 490,000 children attending primary schools in Tanganyika, the majority of them only going up to standard 4. In 1967 there were 825,000 children attending such schools and increasingly these will be full seven-year primary schools. In 1961, too, there were 11,832 children in secondary schools, only 176 of whom were in form 6. This year there are 25,000 and 830. This is certainly something for our young state to be proud of. It is worth reminding ourselves that our present problems (especially the so-called problem of the primary school leavers) are revealing themselves largely because of these successes.

The third action we have taken is to make the education provided in all schools much more Tanzanian in content. No longer do our children simply learn British and European history. Faster than would have been though possible, our University College and other institutions are providing materials on the history of Africa and making these available to our teachers. Our national songs and dances are once again being learned by our children; our national language has been given the importance in our curriculum which it needs and deserves. Also, civics classes taken by Tanzanian are beginning to give the secondary school pupils an understanding of the organisation and aims of our young state. In these and other ways changes have been introduced to make our educational system more relevant to our needs. At this time, when there is so much general and justified questioning of what is being done, it is appropriate that we should pay tribute to the work of our teachers and those who support their work in the Ministry, in the Institute of Education, the University college and the district councils.

Yet all these things I have mentioned are modifications of the system we have inheritied. Their results have not yet been seen; it takes years for a change in education to have its effect. The events of 1966 do suggest, however, that a more thorough examination of the education we are providing must be made. It is now clearly time for us to think seriously about this question: 'What is the educational system in Tanzania intended to do – what is its purpose?' Having decided that, we have to look at the relevance of the existing structure and content of Tanzanian education for the task it has to do. In the light of that examination we can consider whether, in our present circumstances, further modifications are required or whether we need a change in the whole approach.

WHAT KIND OF SOCIETY ARE WE TRYING TO BUILD?

Only when we are clear about the kind of society we are trying to build can we design our educational service to serve our goals. But this is not now a problem in Tanzania. Although we do not claim to have drawn up a blueprint of the future, the values and objectives of our society have been stated many times. We have said that we want to create a socialist society which is based on three principals: equality and respect for human dignity; sharing of the resources which are produced by our efforts; work by everyone and exploitation by none. We have set out these ideas clearly in the National Ethic; and in the Arusha Declaration and earlier documents we have outlined the principles and policies we intend to follow. We have also said on many occasions that our objective is greater African unity, and that we shall work for this objective while in the meantime defending the absolute integrity and sovereignty of the United Republic. Most often of all, our government and people have stressed the equality of all citizens, and our determination that economic, political, and social policies shall be deliberately designed to make a reality of that equality in all spheres of life. We are, in other words, committed to a socialist future and one in which the people will themselves determine the policies pursued by a government which is responsible to them.

It is obvious, however, that if we are to make progress towards these goals, we in Tanzania must accept the realities of our present position, internally and externally, and then work to change these realities into something more in accord with our desires. And the truth is that our United Republic has at present a poor, undeveloped and agricultural economy. We have very little capital to invest in big factories or modern machines; we are short of people with skill and experience. What we do have is land in abundance and people who are willing to work hard for their own improvement. It is the use of these latter resources which will decide whether we reach our total goals or not. If we use these resources in a spirit of self-reliance as the basis for development, then we shall make progress slowly but surely. And it will then be real progress, affecting the lives of the masses, not just having spectacular show-pieces in the towns while the rest of the people of Tanzania live in their present poverty.

Pursuing this path means that Tanzania will continue to have a predominantly rural economy for a long time to come. And as it is in the rural areas that people live and work, so it is in the rural areas that life must be improved. This is not to say that we shall have no industries and factories in the near future. We have some now and they will continue to expand. But it would be grossly unrealistic to imagine that in the near future more than a small proportion of our people will live in towns and work in modern industrial enterprises. It is therefore the villages which must be made into places where people live a good life; it is in the rural areas that people must be able to find their material well-being and their satisfactions.

This improvement in village life will not, however, come automatically. It will come only if we pursue a deliberate policy of using the resources we have – our manpower and our land – to the best advantage. This means people working hard, intelligently and together; in other words, working in co-operation. Our people in the rural areas, as well as their government, must organise themselves co-operatively and work for themselves through working for the community of which they are members. Our village life, as well as our state organisation, must be based on the principles of socialism and that equality in work and return which is part of it.

This is what our educational system has to encourage. It has to foster the social goals of living together, and working together, for the common good. It has to prepare our young people to play a dynamic and constructive part in the development of a society in which all members share fairly in the good or bad fortune of the group, and in which progress is measured in terms of human well–being, not prestige buildings, cars, or other such things, whether privately or publicly owned. Our education must therefore inculcate a sense of commitment to the total community, and help the pupils to accept the values appropriate to our kind of future, not those appropriate to our colonial past.

This means that the educational system of Tanzania must emphasise co-operative endeavour, not individual advancement; it must stress concepts of equality and the responsibility to give service which goes with any special ability, whether to be in carpentry, in animal husbandry, or in academic pursuits. And, in particular, our education must counteract the temptation to intellectual arrogance; for this leads to the well-educated despising those whose abilities are non-academic or who have no special abilities but are just human beings. Such arrogance has no place in a society of equal citizens.

It is, however, not only in relation to social values that our educational system has a task to do. It must also prepare young people for the work they will be called upon to do in the society which exists in Tanzania – a rural society where improvement will depend largely upon the efforts of the people in agriculture and in village development. This does not mean that education in Tanzania should be designed just to produce passive agricultural workers of different levels of skill who simply carry out plans or directions received from above. It must produce good farmers; it has also to prepare people for their responsibilities as free workers and citizens in a free and democratic society, albeit a largely rural society. They have to be able to think for themselves, to make judgements on all the issues affecting them; they have to be able to interpret the decisions made through the democratic institutions of our society, and to implement them in the light of the peculiar local circumstances where they happen to live.

It would thus be a gross misinterpretation of our needs to suggest that the educational system should be designed to produce robots, who work hard but never question what the leaders in government or TANU are doing and saying. For the people are, and must be, government and TANU. Our government and our party must always be responsible to the people, and must always consist of representatives – spokesmen and servants of the people. The education provided must therefore encourage the development in each citizen of three things; an inquiring mind; an ability to learn from what others do, and reject or adapt it to his own needs; and a basic confidence in his own position as a free and equal member of the society, who values others and is valued by them for what he does and not for what he obtains.

These things are important for both the vocational and the social aspects of education. However much agriculture a young person learns, he will not find a book which will give him all the answers to all the detailed problems he will come across in his own farm. He will have to learn the basic principles of modern knowledge in agriculture and then adapt them to solve his own problems. Similarly, the free citizens of Tanzania will have to judge social issues for themselves; there neither is, nor will be, a political 'holy book' which purports to give all the answers to all the social, political and economic problems which will face our country in the future. There will be philosophies and policies approved by our society which citizens should consider and apply in the light of their own thinking and experience. But the educational system of Tanzania would not be serving the interests of a democratic socialist society if it tried to stop people from thinking about the teachings, policies, or the beliefs of leaders, either past or present. Only free people conscious of their worth and their equality can build a free society.

SOME SALIENT FEATURES OF THE EXISTING EDUCATIONAL SYSTEM

These are very different purposes from those which are promoted by our existing educational arrangements. For there are four basic elements in the present system which prevent, or at least discourage, the integration of the pupils into the society they will enter, and which do encourage attitudes of inequality, intellectual arrogance and intense individualism among the young people who go through our schools.

First, the most central thing about the education we are at present providing is that it is basically an elitist education designed to meet the interests and needs of a very small proportion of those who enter the school system.

Although only about 13 per cent of our primary schoolchildren will get a place in a secondary school, the basis of our primary school education is the preparation of pupils for secondary schools. Thus 87 per cent of the children who finished primary school last year – and a similar proportion of those who will finish this year – do so with a sense of failure, of a legitimate aspiration having been denied them. Indeed we all speak in these terms by referring to them as those who failed to enter secondary schools, instead of simply as those who have finished their primary education. On the other hand, the other 13 per cent have a feeling of having deserved a prize – and the prize they and their parents now expect is high wages, comfortable employment in towns and personal status in the society. The same process operates again at the next highest level, when entrance to university is the question at issue.

In other words, the education now provided is designed for the few who are intellectually stronger than their fellows; it induces among those who succeed a feeling of superiority, and leaves the majority of the others hankering after something they will never obtain. It induces a feeling of inferiority among the majority, and can thus not produce either the egalitarian society we should build, or the attitudes of mind which are conducive to an egalitarian society. On the contrary, it induces the growth of a class structure in our country.

Equally important is the second point; the fact that Tanzania's education is such as to divorce its participants from the society it is supposed to be preparing them for. This is particularly true of secondary schools, which are inevitably almost entirely boarding schools; but to some extent, and despite recent modifications in the curriculum, it is true of primary schools too. We take children from their parents at the age of 7 years, and for up to seven and a half hours a day we teach them certain basic academic skills. In recent years we have tried to relate these skills, at least in theory, to the life which the children see around them. But the school is always separate; it is not part of the society. It is a place children go to and which they and their parents hope will make it unnecessary for them to become farmers and continue living in the villages.

The few who go to secondary schools are taken many miles away from their homes; they live in an enclave, having permission to go into the town for recreation, but not relating the work of either town or country to their real life – which is lived in the school compound. Later a few people go to university. If they are lucky enough to enter Dar es Salaam University College they live in comfortable quarters, feed well and study hard for their degree. When they have been successful in obtaining it, they know immediately that they will receive a salary of something like £660 per annum. That is what they have been aiming for; it is what they have been encouraged to aim for. They may also have the desire to serve the community, but their idea of service is related to status and the salary which a university education is expected to confer upon its recipient. The salary and the status have become a right automatically conferred by the degree.

It is wrong of us to criticise the young people for these attitudes. The new university graduate has spent the larger part of his life separated and apart from the masses of Tanzania; his parents may be poor, but he has never fully shared that poverty. He does not really know what it is like to live as a poor peasant. He will be more at home in the world of the educated than he is among his own parents. Only during vacations has he spent time at home, and even then he will often find that his parents and relatives support his own conception of his difference, and regard it as wrong that he should live and work as the ordinary person he really is. For the truth is that many of the people in Tanzania have come to regard education as meaning that a man is too precious for the rough and hard life which the masses of our people still live.

The third point is that our present system encourages school pupils in the idea that all knowledge which is worthwhile is acquired from books or from 'educated people' – meaning those who have been through a formal education. The knowledge and wisdom of other old people is despised, and they themselves are regarded as being ignorant and of no account. Indeed, it is not only the education system which at present has this effect. Government and party themselves tend to judge people according to whether they have 'passed school certificate', 'have a degree', etc. If a man has these qualifications we assume he can fill a post; we do not wait to find out about his attitudes, his character, or any other ability except the ability to pass examinations. If a man does not have these qualifications we assume he cannot do a job; we ignore his knowledge and experience. For example, I recently visited a very good tobacco-producing peasant. But if I tried to take him into government as a tobacco extension officer, I would run up against the system because he has no formal education. Everything we do stresses book learning, and underestimates the value to our society of traditional knowledge and the wisdom which is often acquired by intelligent men and women as they experience life, even without their being able to read at all.

This does not mean that any person can do any job simply because he is old and wise, nor that educational qualifications are not necessary. Our farmers have been on the land for a long time. The methods they use are the result of long experience in the struggle with nature; even the rules and taboos they honour have a basis in reason. It is not enough to abuse a traditional farmer as old-fashioned; we must try to understand why he is doing certain things, and not just assume he is stupid. But this does not mean that his methods are sufficient for the future. The traditional systems may have been appropriate for the economy which existed when they were worked out and for the technical knowledge then available. But different tools and different land tenure systems are being used now. Again, therefore, our young people have to learn both a practical respect for the knowledge of the old 'uneducated' farmer and an understanding of new methods and the reason for them.

Yet at present our pupils learn to despise even their own parents because they are old-fashioned and ignorant; there is nothing in our existing educational system which suggests to the pupil that he can learn important things about farming from his elders. The result is that he absorbs beliefs about witchcraft before he goes to school, but does not learn the properties of local grasses; he absorbs the taboos from his family but does not learn the methods of making nutritious traditional foods. And from school he acquires knowledge unrelated to agricultural life. He gets the worst of both systems!

Finally, and in some ways most important, our young and poor nation is taking out of productive work some of its healthiest and strongest young men and women. Not only do they fail to contribute to that increase in output which is so urgent for our nation; they themselves consume the output of the older and often weaker people.

How many of our students spend their vacations doing a job which could improve people's lives but for which there is no money – jobs like digging an irrigation channel or a drainage ditch for a village, or demonstrating the construction and explaining the benefits of deep-pit latrines, and so on? A small number have done such work in the National Youth Camps or through school-organised, nation-building schemes, but they are the exception rather than the rule. The vast majority do not think of their knowledge or their strength as being related to the needs of the village community.

CAN THESE FAULTS BE CORRECTED?

There are three major aspects which require attention if this situation is to change: the content of the curriculum itself, the organisation of the schools and the entry age into primary schools. But although these aspects are in some ways separate, they are also interlocked. We cannot integrate the pupils and students into the future society simply by theoretical teaching, however well designed it is. Neither can the society fully benefit from an education system which is thoroughly integrated into local life but does not teach people the basic skills – for example, of literacy and arithmetic – or which fails to excite in them a curiosity about ideas. Nor can we expect those finishing primary schools to be useful young citizens if they are still only 12 or 13 years of age.

In considering changes in the present structure it is also essential that we face the facts of our present economic situation. Every penny spent on education is money taken away from some other needed activity – whether it is an investment in the future, better medical services, or just more food, clothing and comfort for our citizens at present. And the truth is that there is no possibility of Tanzania being able to increase the proportion of the national income which is spent on education; it ought to be decreased. Therefore we cannot solve our present problems by any solution which costs more than is at present spent; in particular we cannot solve the 'problem of primary school leavers' by increasing the number of secondary school places.

This 'problem of primary school leavers' is in fact a product of the present system. Increasingly children are starting school at 6 or even 5 years of age, so that they finish primary school when they are still too young to become responsible young workers and citizens. On top of that is the fact that the society and the type of education they have received both led them to expect wage employment – probably in an office. In other words, their education was not sufficiently related to the tasks which have to be done in our society. This problem therefore calls for a major change in the content of our primary education and for the raising of the primary school entry age so that the child is older when he leaves, and also able to learn more quickly while he is at school.

There is no other way in which this problem of primary school leavers can be solved. Unpleasant though it may be, the fact is that it is going to be a long time before we can provide universal primary education in Tanzania; for the vast majority of those who do get this opportunity, it will be only the equivalent of the present seven years' education. It is only a few who will have the chance of going on to secondary schools, and quite soon only a proportion of these who will have an opportunity of going on to university, even if they can benefit from doing so. These are the economic facts of life for our country. They are the practical meaning of our poverty. The only choice before us is how we allocate the educational opportunities, and whether we emphasise the individual interests of the few or whether we design our educational system to serve the community as a whole. And for a socialist state only the latter is really possible.

The implication of this is that the education given in our primary schools must be a complete education in itself. It must not continue to be simply a preparation for secondary school. Instead of the primary school activities being geared to the competitive examination which will select the few who go on to secondary school, they must be a preparation for the life which the majority of the children will lead. Similarly, secondary schools must not be simply a selection process for the university, teacher's colleges, and so on. They must prepare people for life and service in the villages and rural areas of this country. For in Tanzania the only true justification for secondary education is that it is needed by the few for service to the many. There can be no other justification for taxing the many to give education to only a few.

Yet it is easy to say that our primary and secondary schools must prepare young people for the realities and needs of Tanzania; to do it requires a radical change, not only in the education system but also in many existing community attitudes. In particular, it requires that examinations should be downgraded in government and public esteem. We have to recognise that although they have certain advantages – for example, in reducing the dangers of nepotism and tribalism in a selection process – they also have severe disadvantages too. As a general rule they assess a person's ability to learn facts and present them on demand within a time period. They do not always succeed in assessing a power to reason, and they certainly do not assess character or willingness to serve.

What we need to do now is think first about the education we want to provide, and when that thinking is completed think about whether some form of examination is an appropriate way of closing an education phase. Then such an examination should be designed to fit the education which has been provided.

Most important of all is that we should change the things we demand of our schools. We should not determine the type of things children are taught in primary schools by the things a doctor, engineer, teacher, economist, or administrator needs to know. Most of our pupils will never be any of these things. We should determine the types of things taught in the primary schools by the things which the boy or girl ought to know – that is, the skills he ought to acquire and the values he ought to cherish if he, or she, is to live happily and well in a socialist and predominantly rural society, and contribute to the improvement of life there. Our sights must be on the majority; it is they we must be aiming at in determining the curriculum and syllabus. Those most suitable for further education will still become obvious and they will not suffer. For the purpose is not to provide an inferior education to that given at present. The purpose is to provide a different education – one realistically designed to fulfil the common purpose of education in the particular society of Tanzania. The same thing must be true at post-primary schools. The object of the teaching must be the provision of knowledge, skills and attitudes which will serve the student when he or she lives and works in a developing and changing socialist state; it must not be aimed at university entrance.

Alongside this change in the approach to the curriculum there must be a parallel and integrated change in the way our schools are run, so as to make them and their inhabitants a real part of our society and our economy. Schools must, in fact, become communities – and communities which practise the precept of self-reliance. The teachers, workers and pupils together must be the members of a social unit in the same way as parents, relatives and children are the family social unit. There must be the same kind of relationship between pupils and teachers within the school community as there is between children and parents in the village. And the former community must realise, just as the latter do, that their life and well-being depend upon the production of wealth – by farming or other activities. This means that all schools, but especially secondary schools and other forms of higher education, must contribute to their own upkeep; they must be economic communities as well as social and educational communities. Each school should have, as an integral part of it, a farm or workshop which provides the food eaten by the community, and makes some contribution to the total national income.

This is not a suggestion that a school farm or workshop should be attached to every school for training purposes. It is a suggestion that every school should also be a farm; that the school community should consist of people who are both teachers and farmers, and pupils and farmers. Obviously if there is a school farm, the pupils working on it should be learning the techniques and tasks of farming. But the farm would be an integral part of the school – and the welfare of the pupils would depend on its output, just as the welfare of a farmer depends on the output of his land.

This is a break with our educational tradition, and unless its purpose and its possibilities are fully understood by teachers and parents, it may be resented at the beginning. But the truth is that it is not a regressive measure, nor a punishment either for teachers or pupils. It is a recognition that we in Tanzania have to work our way out of poverty, and that we are all members of the one society, depending upon each other. There will be difficulties of implementation, especially at first. For example, we do not now have a host of experienced farm managers who could be used as planners and teachers on the new school farm. But this is not an insuperable difficulty; and certainly life will not halt in Tanzania until we get experienced farm managers. Life and farming will go on as we train. Indeed, by using good local farmers as supervisors and teachers of particular aspects of the work, and using the services of the agricultural officers and assistants, we shall be helping to break down the notion that only book learning is worthy of respect. This is an important element in our socialist development.

Neither does this concept of schools contributing to their own upkeep simply mean using our children as labourers who follow traditional methods. On the contrary, on a school farm pupils can learn by doing.

The important place of the hoe and of other simple tools can be demonstrated; the advantages of improved seeds, of simple ox-ploughs and of proper methods of animal husbandry can become obvious; and the pupils can learn by practice how to use these things to the best advantage.

But the school farms must not be, and indeed could not be, highly mechanised demonstration farms. We do not have the capital which would be necessary for this to happen, and neither would it teach the pupils anything about the life they will be leading. The school farms must be created by the school community clearing their own bush, and so on – but doing it together. They must be used with no more capital assistance than is available to an ordinary, established co-operative farm where the work can be supervised. By such means the students can learn the advantages of co-operative endeavour, even when outside capital is not available in any significant quantities. Again, the advantages of co-operation could be studied in the classroom, as well as being demonstrated on the farm.

The most important thing is that the school members should learn that it is their farm, and that their living standards depend on it. Pupils should be given an opportunity to make many of the decisions necessary – for example, whether to spend money they have earned on hiring a tractor to get land ready for planting, or whether to use that money for other purposes on the farm or in the school, and doing the hard work themselves by sheer physical labour. By this sort of practice and by this combination of classroom work and farm work, our educated young people will learn to realise that if they farm well they can eat well and have better facilities in the dormitories, recreation rooms, and so on. If they work badly, then they themselves will suffer. In this process government should avoid laying down detailed and rigid rules; each school must have considerably flexibility. Only then can the potential of that particular area be utilised; and only then can the participants practise – and learn to value – direct democracy.

By such means our students will relate work to comfort. They will learn the meaning of living together and working together for the good of all, and also the value of working together with the local non-school community. For they will learn that many things require more than school effort – that irrigation may be possible if they work with neighbouring farmers, that development requires a choice between present and future satisfaction, both for themselves and their village.

At the beginning it is probable that a good number of mistakes will be made, and it would certainly be wrong to give complete untrammelled choice to young pupils right from the start. But although guidance must be given by the school authorities and a certain amount of discipline exerted, the pupils must be able to participate in decisions and learn by mistakes. For example, they can learn to keep a school farm log in which proper records are kept of the work done, the fertilisers applied, or food given to the animals, etc., and the results from different parts of the farm. Then they can be helped to see where changes are required, and why. For it is also important that the idea of planning be taught in the classroom and related to the farm; the whole school should join in the programming of a year's work, and the breakdown of responsibility and timing within that overall programme. Extra benefits to particular groups within the school might then well be related to the proper fulfilment of the tasks set, once all the members of the school have received the necessary minimum for healthy development. Again, this sort of planning can be part of the teaching of socialism.

Many other activities now undertaken for pupils, especially in secondary schools, should be undertaken by the pupils themselves. After all, a child who starts school at 7 years of age is already 14 before he enters secondary school, and may be 20 or 21 when he leaves. Yet in many of our schools now we employ cleaners and gardeners, not just to supervise and teach but to do all that work. The pupils get used to the idea of having their food prepared by servants, their plates washed up for them, their rooms cleaned and the school garden kept attractive. If they are asked to participate in these tasks, they even feel aggrieved and do as little as possible, depending on the strictness of the teacher's supervision. This is because they have not learned to take a pride in having clean rooms and nice gardens, in the way that they have learned to take a pride in a good essay or a good mathematics paper. Can none of these things be incorporated into classroom teaching so that pupils learn how to do these things for themselves by doing them? Is it impossible, in other words, for secondary schools at least to become reasonably self-sufficient communities, where the teaching and supervisory skills are imported from outside, but where other tasks are either done by the community or paid for by its productive efforts?

Obviously such a position could not be reached overnight. It requires a basic change in both organisation and teaching, and will therefore have to be introduced gradually, with the schools taking an increasing responsibility for their own well-being as the months pass. Neither would primary schools be able to do so much for themselves – although it should be remembered that the older pupils will be 13 or 14 years of age, at which time children in many European countries are already at work.

But, although primary schools cannot accept the same responsibility for their own well-being as secondary schools, it is absolutely vital that they, and their pupils, should be thoroughly integrated into the village life. The pupils must remain an integral part of the family (or community) economic unit. The children must be made part of the community by having responsibilities to the community, and having the community involved in school activities. The school work – terms, times, and so on – must be so arranged that the children can participate, as members of the family, in the family farms, or as junior members of the community on community farms. At present children who do not go to school work on the family or community farm, or look after cattle, as a matter of course. It must be equally a matter of course that the children who do attend school should participate in the family work – not as a favour when they feel like it, but as a normal part of their upbringing. The present attitudes whereby the school is regarded as something separate, and the pupils as people who do not have to contribute to the work, must be abandoned. In this, of course, parents have a special duty; but the schools can contribute a great deal to the development of this attitude.

There are many different ways in which this integration can be achieved. But it will have to be done deliberately, and with the conscious intention of making the children realise that they are being educated by the community in order that they shall become intelligent and active members of the community. One possible way of achieving this would be to give to primary school pupils the same advantages of learning by doing as the secondary school pupils will have. If the primary schoolchildren work on a village communal farm – perhaps having special responsibility for a given number of acres – they can learn new techniques and take a pride in a school community achievement. If there is no communal farm, then the school can start a small one of its own by appealing to the older members to help in the bush-clearing in return for a school contribution in labour to some existing community project.

Again, if development work – new buildings or other things – are needed in the school, then the children and the local villagers should work on it together, allocating responsibility according to comparative health and strength. The children should certainly do their own cleaning (boys as well as girls should be involved in this), and should learn the value of working together and of planning for the future. Thus, for example, if they have their own *shamba* the children should be involved not only in the work, but also in the allocation of any food or cash crop produced. They should participate in the choice between benefit to the school directly, or to the village as a whole, and between present or future benefit. By these and other appropriate means the children must learn from the beginning to the end of their school life that education does not set them apart, but is designed to help them be effective members of the community – for their own benefit as well as that of their country and their neighbours.

One difficulty in the way of this kind of reorganisation is the present examination system; if pupils spend more of their time on learning to do practical work, and on contributing to their own upkeep and the development of the community, they will not be able to take the present kind of examinations – at least within the same time-period. It is, however, difficult to see why the present examination system should be regarded as sacrosanct. Other countries are moving away from this method of selection, and either abandoning examinations altogether at the lowest levels, or combining them with other assessments. There is no reason why Tanzania should not combine an examination, which is based on the things we teach, with a teacher and pupil assessment of work done for the school and community. This would be a more appropriate method of selecting entrants for secondary schools and for university, teacher training colleges, and so on, than the present purely academic procedure. Once a more detailed outline of this new approach to education is worked out, the question of selection procedure should be looked at again.

This new form of working in our schools will require some considerable organisational change. It may be also that the present division of the school year into rigid terms with long holidays would have to be re-examined; animals cannot be left alone for part of the year, nor can a school farm support the students if everyone is on holiday when the crops need planting, weeding, or harvesting. But it should not be impossible for school holidays to be staggered so that different forms go at different periods or, in double-stream secondary schools, for part of a form to go at one time and the rest at another. It would take a considerable amount of organisation and administration, but there is no reason why it could not be done if we once make up our minds to it.

It will probably be suggested that if the children are working as well as learning they will therefore be able to learn less academically, and that this will affect standards of administration, in the professions and so on, throughout our nation in time to come. In fact it is doubtful whether this is necessarily so; the recent tendency to admit children to primary schools at ages of 5 and 6 years has almost certainly meant that less can be taught at the early stages. The reversion to 7 or 8 years for entrance will allow the pace to be increased somewhat; the older children inevitably learn a little faster. A child is unlikely to learn less academically if the studies are related to the life he sees around him.

But even if this suggestion were based on provable fact, it could not be allowed to over-ride the need for change in the direction of educational integration with our national life. For the majority of our people the thing which matters is that they should be able to read and write fluently in Swahili, that they should have an ability to do arithemtic, that they should know something of the history, values, and workings of their country and their government, and that they should acquire the skills necessary to earn their living. (It is important to stress that in Tanzania most people will earn their living by working on their own or on a communal *shamba*, and only a few will do so by working for wages which they have to spend on buying things the farmer produces for himself.) Things like health science, geography and the beginning of

English are also important, especially so that people who wish may be able to learn more by themselves in later life. But most important of all is that our primary school graduates should be able to fit into, and to serve, the communities from which they come.

The same principles of integration into the community, and applicability to its needs, must also be followed at post-secondary level, but young people who have been through such an integrated system of education as that outlined are unlikely to forget their debt to the community by an intense period of study at the end of their formal educational life. Yet even at university, medical school, or other post-secondary levels, there is no reason why students should continue to have all their washing-up and cleaning done for them. Nor is there any reason why students at such institutions should not be required as part of their degree or professional training to spend at least part of their vacations contributing to the society in a manner related to their studies. At present some undergraduates spend their vacations working in government offices – getting paid at normal employee rates for doing so. It would be more appropriate (once the organisation has been set up efficiently) for them to undertake projects needed by the community, even if there is insufficient money for them to constitute paid employment. For example, the collection of local history, work on the census, participation in adult education activities, work in dispensaries, etc., would give the students practical experience in their own fields. For this they could receive the equivalent of the minimum wage, and any balance of money due for work which would otherwise have been done for higher wages could be paid to the college or institution and go towards welfare or sports equipment. Such work should earn credits for the student which count towards his examination result; a student who shirks such work – or fails to do it properly – would then find that two things follow. First, his fellow students might be blaming him for shortfalls in proposed welfare or other improvements; and secondly, his degree would be downgraded accordingly.

CONCLUSION

The education provided by Tanzania for the students of Tanzania must serve the purposes of Tanzania. It must encourage the growth of the socialist values we aspire to. It must encourage the development of a proud, independent and free citizenry which relies upon itself for its own development, and which knows the advantages and the problems of co-operation. It must ensure that the educated know themselves to be an integral part of the nation and recognise the responsibility to give greater service the greater the opportunities they have had.

This is not only a matter of school organisation and curriculum.

Social values are formed by family, school and society – by the total environment in which a child develops. But it is no use our educational system stressing values and knowledge appropriate to the past or to the citizens in other countries; it is wrong if it even contributes to the continuation of those inequalities and privileges which still exist in our society because of our inheritance. Let our students be educated to be members and servants of the kind of just and egalitarian future to which this country aspires.

NOTE: CHAPTER 11

These extracts are taken from President Julius K. Nyerere's post-Arusha policy directives on education issued in March 1967 and first published in *Freedom and Socialism* (Dar es Salaam: Oxford University Press, 1968), pp. 267-90.

Chapter 12

Education in Africa: Progress and Prospect

A. BABS FAFUNWA AND J. U. AISIKU

Irrespective of the philosophical positions of each country covered in this survey, there is a very clear indication that each country has had phenomenal growth in educational development, and consequently in the financing of education as compared with their respective colonial eras. Countries such as Egypt, Liberia and Ethiopia which have been independent from the colonial rule for many decades have also registered unprecedented growth in their educational programmes. Indeed, all over Africa education has been emancipated from the strictures of service to the few to freedom of educational opportunity for the many.

Increased primary school enrolment was one of the direct results of a significant development in post-independence Africa, namely, the introduction of universal primary education. Evidence of this development abounds all over Africa. For example, the first constitution of Egypt on the attainment of independence in 1923 made primary education free and compulsory. By the education Act of 1961 in Ghana primary education became free and compulsory. Kenya introduced partial free primary education in 1971 when a presidental decree abolished tuition fees in some parts of that country considered educationally backward, and in 1974 free primary education was extended to all parts of Kenya. Similarly, primary education became free in all parts of Nigeria in 1976.

The introduction of universal primary education and the resultant increase in primary school enrolment had a tremendous impact on secondary education. First, more secondary schools had to be opened while the existing ones were expanded to offer more places to the increasing number of primary school leavers aspiring to secondary education. Secondly, the boarding system of secondary education received less emphasis in preference to the day system. In places like Tanzania, for example, the boarding system was abolished. Given the explosive bottleneck situation at the secondary level of education all over Africa and the acute accommodation problems in the universities, we predict an entirely day system not only for the secondary schools but also for the universities post-1980.

Another mark of progress in African education is in the area of increased facilities for higher education. Prior to independence most African countries had no universities of their own; instead there were, as in British East Africa, territorial universities serving a number of countries. Today every country represented in this work has at least one university. For example, Ghana has three universities, Kenya and Ethiopia have two universities each; Sierra Leone has one university and an affiliate institution of university status, while Nigeria has as many as thirteen universities. Indeed, Africa has recorded phenomenal progresss in the provision of more education for more people. But what seems lacking in most African countries is enough concern for the quality and relevance of the education provided.

It should be emphasised that with the expansion of educational facilities at all levels and the corresponding financial commitment the African countries must, of necessity, re-examine the goals of education in relation to their people's needs and aspirations. The traditional system which Africa tends to cling to almost religiously should be jettisoned to intensify the search for newer and more relevant systems, because not only the volume of education but also its very nature demands change to meet the challenge of a rapidly expanding economy, population and the attendant rising expectations of youth and adults alike. As Paul Longrand has rightly observed:

> Whatever the speed and scale of achievement of traditional structures might be, schools, universities and institutions can no longer meet the strain . . . The work of education will have to be pursued well beyond the school-leaving age to ensure the spread of knowledge and the types of training that individuals and societies will increasingly require. Such action can indeed only be envisaged through large-scale recourse, beyond the traditional functions of education, to all the vast modern media for spreading knowledge and providing training.[1]

As we know too well, there are three major ways of acquiring knowledge or training:

(1) through the formal 'school' system – nursery, primary, secondary, and post-secondary or higher education;
(2) non-formal system – apprenticeship, on-the-job-training (learning by doing), etc;
(3) informal system – learning through various experiences and exposures otherwise known as incidental education.

Most developing countries have placed undue emphasis on formal education which in turn has resulted in the 'craze for paper qualification' in terms of diplomas, certificates and university degrees of all types.

Consequently we have erroneously assumed that only those who go to school and receive paper qualifications are 'educated' and those who do not go to school or who went and failed to receive paper qualifications are 'not educated', nor are they intelligent enough to do the work of those with certificates. It is clear that under the present traditional systems of education training and employment it is generally graduates with first or second class honours who are required to fill vacancies in the administrative cadre, while graduates with 'pass' in any field may be recruited for the executive officer cadre. As for technicians, fitter mechanics and masons, only those with 'recognised certificates' need apply. This excludes the well-trained or partially trained 'road-side' mechanics, masons and fitters principally because they are not 'schooled' or 'certificated'. It will be generally admitted that most of them are not only as good as but in some cases better than their well-schooled counterparts both in ability and productivity. Yet this sizeable sector of the economy is not only ignored but snubbed. Indeed, excellence in plumbing or carpentry is discounted while a poor degree or diploma in engineering, classics, law, or social sciences is exalted, glorified and overpriced.

We have to assume at this point in the history of Africa that education is expected to be geared to the needs of the individual and the nation. Consequently education must be 'development-oriented'. That being the case, manpower training must of necessity be so oriented. But alas, we cannot use yesterday's tools for today's business and still expect to be in business tomorrow. The traditional approach to manpower training and procurement will certainly keep Africa abnormally short of manpower for ever unless Africans change their attitudes to the Western traditional concept of education and training.

African countries need to re-examine their curriculum and training programmes at all levels of education. They need to satisfy themselves that each level is interrelated and that they all relate to the world of work, whether in the private or public sector. There is no other appropriate way to conclude this survey than to refer to a portion of the United Nations Economic Commission for Africa's memorandum of January 1966. The statement contained in the memorandum is as true today as it was in 1966.

MANPOWER REQUIREMENTS FOR AFRICAN DEVELOPMENT[2]

1. The present economic development in the African Region compares very unfavourably with levels already attained by the developed countries as well as by a number of developing countries in other regions. In terms of the need for accelerated economic and

social development in the region and of the potential resources available for exploitation, present development efforts in African countries are relatively modest.

2. But even this modest effort to accelerate the tempo of development and raise the level of national income is continually being hampered in virtually all countries of the region by lack of adequate numbers and quality of technical, scientific, professional and managerial personnel for implementing development programmes. There is acute shortage of trained indigenous personnel to undertake feasibility studies, evaluate development projects, determine what projects would best further their country's development, formulate viable development programmes, and manage and supervise the implementation of projects. In a number of professional and technical occupations Africans are poorly represented to the extent that their countries rely heavily on external sources of recruitment in order to carry out even modest activities in important sectors . . .

Deficiences in African Educational System

5. African countries experience trained manpower shortages because their educational systems have not yet been devised to meet the challenge of rapid transition from a traditional economy to an industrial one. Educational programmes in both objective and course substance are lacking in those elements that most rapidly foster innovation and economic growth. Even though in recent years there has been a marked increase in student enrolment at all levels of the educational ladder, the patterns of departmental and subject structure, educational type, and the relative expenditures by levels have not markedly changed from what prevailed over the last two decades.

6. Recent ECA evaluations of the potentiality of existing educational institutions, particularly at the university level, to supply the trained manpower of varied occupational skills needed for economic modernization, have shown that our educational systems suffer from inadequacies and gaps in course content and objectives, from under-utilized available resources, and from insufficient co-operation in our human resource development efforts.

7. An examination of the content of higher educational curricula in most African countries will show a prevailing tendency for higher educational institutions to be conventional in outlook and largely satisfied with conditions and facilities which are increasingly proving unsatisfactory in meeting the challenge of rapid economic development and the application of modern technology. A number of specialised training courses in the professional and technological fields are generally either absent or inadequately developed. In terms

of student enrolment, liberal arts and the humanities predominate while insufficient numbers are enrolled in agricultural, scientific, engineering and technological fields and in specialized professional fields where acute shortages of trained indigenous personnel are known to exist. Training in the natural sciences has received more attention in recent years; but courses in this field lack sufficient emphasis on applied sciences and technology, and laboratory work is too often divorced from the needs of local industries and agriculture.

8.   A comparison of the departmental and subject structure of African universities with those of the rapidly developing countries such as are operative in a number of universities in India, Australia, Canada and Japan, for example, will show that African institutions of higher education, with a few exceptions, are not yet fully awake to the necessity to provide training courses in the newer study subjects aimed at equipping indigenous personnel with new techniques for solving development problems, particularly problems peculiar to local socio-economic conditions.

9.   The extensive and intensive application of modern technology has enabled many newly industrialized countries to achieve rapid economic and social advancement. In this development, universities have played a primary leadership role both in the development of new technology and its application to facilitate the process of economic growth. Under African conditions this leadership role is an inevitable task for universities. But not sufficient is being done at present to develop both technological faculties and a cadre of indigenous technological research personnel as well as to adapt known technology to African development needs. As it were, African institutions of higher learning are still largely celebrated seats of literary academic activities, fighting shy of applied science and technology, and have yet to develop technical workshops and laboratories for the region's technological revolution and for facilitating the transfer of scientific and technical knowledge to business enterprises which could apply them to revolutionize African economies.

10.   Quantitative increase in student enrolment and graduate output in every institution of higher education in the region, have, under the pressure to produce more trained men, ensured more economical utilization of expensive institutional facilities. But there are still substantial under-utilized resources in the form of faculty staff and facilities. More use could be made of these facilities to provide training courses tailored to the special needs of African personnel required in specific fields of development. In this regard, universities could contribute immensely in solving African manpower problems through the provision of more diploma courses, vacation courses and

correspondence courses directed to meet the training requirements of essential categories of skilled manpower requirements . . .

11.   An important factor that has accentuated the deficiencies in the capacity of existing African educational institutions to cope with manpower requirements, in both quantity, quality and skill variety, is the limitation of human material resources at the disposal of these institutions. But in utilizing available scarce resources, maximum benefits could be derived only when efforts are concentrated through specialization and co-operation, with resources being deployed into developing priority needs, which in the context of education and training, means producing the critical skills that are assessed to have the most profound impact on the development process. In this regard, the tendency for higher educational institutions to proliferate as under-developed sources of high-level manpower supply and the want of sufficient co-operation among African universities in developing complementary, non-competitive academic and technical courses are obvious constraints on the capacity of these institutions to produce the essential skills required for development.

Education for Development

12.   While not detracting from the cultural value of education, increasing emphasis is being placed on the value of education in imparting knowledge and techniques necessary for development. It is fully recognized that education with training in skills develops human talents, creates dissatisfaction with the social milieu, fosters the acceptance of innovation and a willingness for change. These attributes of education are essential ingredients for technological, economic and social progress in any society.

13.   Thus in order to alleviate the shortage of essential skills and hence an elimination of one of the major bottlenecks in national development efforts, developing countries are increasingly placing emphasis on 'education for development', particularly at the secondary and post-secondary school levels. This implies the orientation of the content and objective of education and training towards realizing the goal of economic and social advancement. In this connection, for example, the current Tanzanian five-year development plan has rightly considered the need to ensure that the national education system provides the essential trained personnel for implementing the plan. Accordingly, the country's educational policy has been geared to educating the group that would have immediate impact on production during the life of the plan.[3]

14.   With the present low level of economic and social development in the region, with the eagerness of the masses and their political leaders for substantial increases in standards of living and with

present shortages of highly skilled technical, scientific and professional personnel in virtually every sector of development, education for development must of necessity require an orientation of the scope and purpose of educational curricula to development needs. Such an orientation calls for:

- changes in student and staff attitudes towards certain 'hard' and the so-called low prestige courses which are vital to economic progress;
- an evaluation of the adequacy of existing courses and of the media for the transfer of knowledge and techniques to those in a position to apply them;
- the adoption of new courses essential to development;
- a re-allocation of educational resources for the development of different occupational skills in relative importance to their impact on the development process;
- maximum utilization of available institutional facilities in developing essential skills required for national development;
- the adoption of novel methods and techniques for imparting knowledge;
- and for marked expansion in the output of technical and science teachers.

15.   If African institutions of higher education are to adequately face the task of producing the required number and skill variety of high-level manpower for development, without allowing the shortage of indigenous skilled personnel to retard economic progress, full consideration would have to be given to widening the present departmental and subject structure of the curricula of these institutions to include . . . newer subjects that actively promote economic development, but in which training facilities in the African Region are at present either unavailable or inadequately developed.

Finally, it must be emphasised that the political, social and economic conditions differ from country to country; however, African aspirations are basically the same – to evolve a socio-political system that will eliminate disease, ignorance and poverty; and at the same time to evolve a truly egalitarian society.

It is hoped that through shared experience with fellow Africans the various African states will find answers to many of their problems.

NOTES: CHAPTER 12

1   Paul Longrand, *An Introduction to Lifelong Education* (Paris: Unesco, 1975), p. 27.

2 See Memorandum of the United Nations Economic Commission for Africa, January 1966.
3 *Tanganyika's Five-Year Plan for Economic and Social Development, 1st July 1964 – 30th June 1969,* Vol. I, preliminary edition (an address by President Mwalimu Julius K. Nyerere to Parliament, 12 May, 1964), Ministry of Information and Tourism (PRO/21), April 1964.

Index